Alcohol in the Movies, 1898–1962

Alcohol in the Movies, 1898–1962

A Critical History

JUDY CORNES

McFarland & Company, Inc., Publishers
Jefferson, North Carolina, and London

Frontispiece: The quintessential alcoholic in the movies: Ray Milland as Don Birnam in *The Lost Weekend* (Paramount, 1945).

LIBRARY OF CONGRESS CATALOGUING-IN-PUBLICATION DATA

Cornes, Judy, 1945–
    Alcohol in the movies, 1898–1962 : a critical history / Judy Cornes.
        p.   cm.
    Includes bibliographical references and index.

    ISBN 978-0-7864-2633-1
    ISBN 0-7864-2633-0
    (softcover : 50# alkaline paper) ∞

    1. Alcoholism in motion pictures.   2. Drinking of alcoholic beverages in motion pictures.   I. Title.
PN1995.9.A45C67   2006
791.43'655 — dc22   2006018555

British Library cataloguing data are available

Cover images ©2006 PhotoSpin

Manufactured in the United States of America

McFarland & Company, Inc., Publishers
  Box 611, Jefferson, North Carolina 28640
  www.mcfarlandpub.com

For Bonnie, Lillian, and Jeanine

Table of Contents

Preface

It was a cold night in January 1963, and the Loew's Midland Theatre in Kansas City, Missouri, was preparing for a special showing of the recently released *Days of Wine and Roses*. One of its stars, Jack Lemmon, was scheduled to speak on stage before the screening, an appearance that had been highly publicized in *The Kansas City Star*. A girlfriend and I had looked forward to this event for days. We were both seventeen and fancied ourselves madly in love with the popular star. So we bundled ourselves in layers of warm clothing and eagerly set out for the theater. As we did so, we checked under our coats to make sure we still had the books we were bringing along in the hope that we could get Lemmon to autograph them. Not wanting to miss seeing our idol, we arrived about one hour early and found a seat close to the stage. And our wait was rewarded, for there he was— on time, in person — Jack Lemmon himself, introducing the movie. But then he left, having spoken for only three minutes or so. We were immensely disappointed that we had missed the chance to introduce ourselves and to get his autograph.

What I remember, then, about my first viewing of *Days of Wine and Roses* is closely entwined with my memory of actually seeing Jack Lemmon — a real movie star — on stage. Nevertheless, what I do recall about the movie itself is still vivid; I had never before seen a film that showed people with a serious drinking problem. The only other movie drunks I had ever seen were funny drunks; they fell down, mixed up their words, embarrassed their friends— but in a humorous way. Only a few years earlier, I had laughed at Rosalind Russell with all of her madcap, inebriated, party-going friends in *Auntie Mame* (1958). I thought that it would be great fun to live with Rosalind Russell: a rich, witty, stylishly attired woman who gave cocktail parties every night, slept until two in the afternoon, and never thought of unpleasant consequences.

Like many other adolescents of my generation, I lived a rather sheltered existence, my world circumscribed by school, summer vacations, outings with friends, and car trips with my parents. I knew little about alcoholism, except for a few tedious paragraphs that I had been required to read in health textbooks. But *Days of Wine and Roses* revealed some truths about alcohol addiction that the textbooks never discussed. The movie expanded my narrow adolescent boundaries.

Many early motion pictures also had a limited, naïve point of view in their attitude toward alcohol; after all, the movies were coming of age at the beginning of the twentieth century. We might even say that, in their approach toward the subject, the movies passed through a relatively trouble-free childhood and adolescence for approximately the first twenty years of their existence. From 1896, when the first motion picture was projected onto a screen, until 1919, when D. W. Griffith finally depicted the brutality of an alcoholic in *Broken Blossoms*, most movies presented alcohol as a source of humor and a sign of good fellowship and good times. The first silent movies featured comedians who used drunkenness to highlight their broad, humorous movements and to heighten their sense of camaraderie with their fellow drunks.

However, by the 1920s, Prohibition-era movies began to treat alcohol and its effects much more seriously. Then, in the 1930s, with the repeal of Prohibition and the subsequent finish of the gangsters' bootlegging rackets, movies depicted some ambivalence toward alcohol. Some satirized the lives of the rich and the plastered, while others took a more serious approach. On the other hand, the brilliant comic actor and auteur W. C. Fields occupied a special place in movies of the 1930s, for he capitalized on his reputation as the quintessential inebriate: here was a man drunkenly grasping at a bourgeois life in the midst of an absurd world. Finally, with the release of *The Lost Weekend* in 1945, the motion picture portrayal of alcoholism reached a maturity that has lasted to this day.

The first three chapters of this book are organized chronologically, as I examine alcohol and its appearance in movies during the years between 1903 and 1939. Subsequent chapters do not adhere to a strict chronology but instead follow the growing complexity of the movies, beginning in the early 1930s and ending in December 1962 with the release of *Days of Wine and Roses*. Throughout the study, I have classified the treatment of alcohol in various ways, specifically exploring subjects, genres, and motifs. This investigation has led me to conclude that the subject of alcohol is a pervasive one in film history. Furthermore, it is a subject that transcends traditional boundaries. Whether treated seriously or humorously in motion pictures, it is a topic that affects all social classes, that strikes at people of many occupations. Nor does it discriminate on the basis of sex: both men and women feel its consequences. In short, an examination of alcohol as it is depicted in the first sixty-five years of motion picture history offers some insights of universal significance. Such a study not only reveals much about the history of twentieth century western culture but also illuminates the growth and development of the motion picture itself. And perhaps it tells us something about ourselves as well, for most of us have been touched in one way or another by the use and abuse of alcohol.

Introduction

Fear of death makes for life. But the curse of the White Logic is
that it does not make one afraid. The world-sickness of the White
Logic makes one grin jocosely into the face of the Noseless One
and to sneer at all the phantasmagoria of living.... "Drink" says
the White Logic. "The Greeks believed that the gods gave them
wine so that they might forget the miserableness of existence."

— Jack London, *John Barleycorn,* 1913

Alcohol at the Turn of the Twentieth Century

In April 1896, Koster & Bial's Music Hall, located in New York City's
Herald Square, advertised an exciting coming attraction: "Thomas A. Edison's latest marvel, the Vitascope." On the night of April 23, 1896, theater-
goers were able to see just what the Vitascope could do: for the first time,
they watched a motion picture projected onto a screen, which was a breath-
taking twenty feet wide and surrounded by a gilt frame.[1] Yet many of these
first patrons were frightened by the images springing from this screen, for
they assumed that the waves of water and the jerky figures moving about
were closing in on their heretofore secure seats: that these images would
somehow jump their gilt-framed track and leap off the screen in order to
attack. Audiences, of course, would soon lose their apprehension and
become accustomed to this new form of entertainment. Moreover, in keeping with the long-standing American entrepreneurial spirit, advertisers
wasted no time in taking advantage of this new medium, for they soon recognized its potential as a means of marketing their products. And the product that they thought would be worth their while to advertise was liquor.

1

Consequently, the first known appearance of alcohol on the screen occurred a brief two years later in 1898 when the Edison Manufacturing Company released what is believed to be the first advertising film: the product being peddled is whiskey. Entitled *DeWar's — It's Scotch*, the movie runs approximately thirty seconds. In addition, in some ways, it looks quite modern in its soft-sell approach to the whiskey. Featured are four anonymous gentlemen in Scottish kilts. They are doing a sort of lumbering dance, which consists of their waving their arms about while they jump around and exhibit their legs to the accompaniment of an unheard melody. Their enthusiastic bouncing and benign smiles indicate that they are having fun, doubtless because they have just sampled some DeWar's Scotch. Yet the understated selling technique is evident in two ways. First, we never see them actually drinking the whiskey. Second, we are never shown the brand name. Rather, in the background, dimly seen above the heads of the cavorting four, are the words *Scotch Whiskey*. The name *DeWar's* is not evident, at least not in the print that survives today.

That the first advertising film should be one devoted to the promotion of alcohol is a significant cultural statement. Alcohol consumption in the United States at the turn of the twentieth century was widespread and, as a consequence, generated a decided problem for social reformers. A search of library catalogs under the general subject of *alcoholism* for the years between 1890–1920 turns up 1,418 books in English alone. A review of the titles of these studies reveals the concern of experts on the social ills resulting from alcohol and drug addiction: *Inebriety: Its Source, Prevention, and Cure* (1907); *Habits that Handicap: the Menace of Opium, Alcohol* (1916); *Fifty Doctors against Alcohol. A Call to National Defence* (1912); *Substitutes for the Saloon* (1901); *The Federal Government and the Liquor Traffic* (1917); *The Mortality from Alcohol in the United States* (1912); *Socialism and the Drink Question* (1908); *The Psychology of Alcoholism* (1907). And there is even a book with the oxymoronic title of *Drink and Be Sober* (1915). Without a doubt, social reformers of the early twentieth century had good reason to be worried about alcohol consumption. Even before the passage of the Prohibition amendment to the U.S. Constitution in 1920, homemade concoctions presented an added threat to the health of consumers. For instance, many drinkers at the turn of the twentieth century were known to mix their liquor with benzine, a volatile, flammable petroleum distillate that can be used as a solvent or as a motor fuel. Such a mixture apparently gave the alcohol an added "kick," but the cost in permanent brain damage must have been quite high.

Fictional accounts of alcoholism and such subsequent brain damage were popular with turn-of-the-century readers and illustrate the popularity of alcohol as the drink of choice throughout the United States. Perhaps the best known of these narratives is Stephen Crane's naturalistic novel, *Maggie: A Girl of the Streets*, first published in 1893 and revised by Crane himself in 1896. In this graphic study of the sordidness of late nineteenth century tenement life in New York City, Crane depicts in all its squalid detail the mind-numbing effects of liquor on families such as Maggie Johnson's. In fact, Maggie's mother is so constantly smashed that her complexion as described throughout the novel resembles that of a yellowing piece of parchment, though she is probably not more than thirty-five. When Mrs. Johnson is not breaking up furniture and tearing down curtains in the family's small apartment or sleeping off another binge, she spends a few days every month at Blackwell's Island asylum, temporarily drying out. Furthermore, Crane depicts immigrant life in 1890s New York as holding out no hope, no escape from a life of everyday drudgery or an existence filled with exploitation from and outright danger in the workplace.

At the time that Crane was chronicling the desperate lives of crowded urban dwellers in New York, some of the city's more prosperous uptown inhabitants were at Koster & Bial's Music Hall being introduced to the projected motion picture. However, initially, the middle and upper classes saw this technological innovation as a third-rate amusement for the poor, whose other favorite pastime was drinking. Indeed, this new entertainment form would soon offer to the slum inhabitants, particularly immigrants with limited knowledge of English, a brief diversion from their bleak existence.

In short, the history of alcohol and its relationship to the movies stretches back over one hundred years. Both forms of escape were cheap and were readily available to the "huddled masses"—many of them immigrants who were targets of social commentators of the day. One such social critic expressed his disgust by condemning this ominously increasing mixture of foreigners, booze, and politics: "The influx of foreigners into our urban centers, many of whom have liquor habits, is a menace to good government."[2]

It is doubtful, however, if these newly arrived inhabitants were especially concerned with either local or national government, whether good or bad. What they were concerned with was a way to make their life more tolerable. And liquor seemed to hold out an answer, some promise of temporary relief. Consequently, just as appealing as this new moving picture toy to the immigrants was the alcohol that could be purchased cheaply at their neighborhood taverns or at the multitude of noisy, smoke-filled halls where the poor spent what leisure time they had when they were not laboring in factories, saloons, sweatshops, or whorehouses. These entertainment halls featured fifth-rate acts and equally bad, but cheap and liberal, amounts of beer, wine, and whiskey. At this time, for instance, one could buy a glass of rye whiskey for ten cents and a pitcher of beer for five cents. People drank before work, during work, and after work. "Factory workers sent 'pail boys' to nearby taverns to bring back buckets filled with beer."[3] Small wonder, then, that the first advertising film was a promotion for whiskey, featuring four performers who would have felt right at home in a beer hall, doing their dance for inhabitants of New York's Lower East Side.

Yet excessive alcohol consumption at the turn of the twentieth century was not limited to people living in large cities nor was it the exclusive habit of the lower class. In 1896, a government report revealed that there were 161,483 separate establishments throughout the country dedicated in some way to the distribution and sales of liquor. By 1900, the manufacture of alcohol in the United States constituted one of the largest and most important industries in the country. For instance, in 1900 there were 2,850 enterprises producing whiskey, beer, and wine. Their capital investment was estimated at $457,674,087, a sum that went into buildings, land, machinery, and hardware. Not included in this total was the capital stock of the many public corporations, whose total worth ran into the hundreds of millions. Moreover, by 1903, the government estimated that liquor was being sold in a total of 254,498 places. And these estimates included only those firms that had responded to the government's 1903 census; the actual total was probably much higher.[4] The per capita alcohol consumption in the United States in 1903 reflects these large numbers. That year, each person consumed about 19.90 gallons.[5] By 1911, the numbers had considerably increased; in that year, per capita consumption of alcohol was 22.79 gallons.[6]

Despite the immense amount of alcohol consumed throughout the country and in spite of the obvious concern on the part of abstinence advocates, early filmmakers of the first decade of the twentieth century showed little alarm over the realities of alcohol addiction. In fact, *movement* of any kind was the most important aspect of these earliest attempts at filmmaking. Possibly the second known motion picture to show alcohol was *Let Me Dream Again* (1900). It was made by George Albert Smith (1864–1959) for the Warwick Trading Company.[7] The brief but fairly clever scenario shows a man in a restaurant drinking with a young woman. He has clearly spent some money on her, for both have their own liquor bottle from which to pour their separate drinks. Both are fancily dressed, he in a ruffled dress shirt and suit jacket and she in a bizarre outfit including a pointed cap and a ruffled blouse. The cap and blouse are decorated here and there with small fluffy round balls, some of which are located in provocative places on her breasts. She looks like a circus clown. When the gentleman leans over to kiss her, there is a dissolve, after which he is magically transported back to his own bed and to his wife. Both he and she are cozily tucked away in nightshirts and nightcaps. His spouse bears an odd resemblance to Shemp Howard, later of the Three Stooges. Perhaps there is a moral to the story, but the object lesson for 1900 audiences had nothing to do with alcohol.

Likewise, in the second decade — the years between 1910 and 1920 — the majority of motion pictures, although they were developing more coherent storylines, focused on the comic possibilities inherent in inebriation. Silent clowns such as Max Linder, Charlie Chaplin, and Fatty Arbuckle fought among themselves and against various implacable objects while remaining pleasantly plastered.

Prohibition

By the 1920s, with the onset of Prohibition in the United States, the number of books dedicated to the alcohol problem had declined dramatically. From 1920 to 1930, only 242 books in English are listed in catalogs worldwide. The titles that *are* available, however, demonstrate the concern of the writers with the passage of the Eighteenth Amendment to the U. S. Constitution, the Noble Experiment that forbade the manufacture, sale or transportation of alcohol: *Prohibition and Public Health* (1928); *Temperance Education in American Public Schools* (1930); *Alcoholic Psychoses Before and After Prohibition* (1922). Also to be found is a series of books by Irving Fisher, a professor of economics at Yale, who was obviously determined to deal in depth and in sequential afterthoughts with the Prohibition issue: *Prohibition at Its Worst* (1926); *Prohibition at Its Worst, Revised Edition (1926–1927)*; *Prohibition Still at Its Worst* (1928); and, in a startling change of pace, *The "Noble Experiment"* (1930). The repetitious, negative titles of these first three books are misleading. In reality, Fisher was a firm supporter of Prohibition and consequently provides a massive amount of statistics to counter the arguments of the "moderates," who argued that Prohibition was unsuccessful because the law was ignored. Rather, writing in the mid–1920s, Fisher argues that alcohol use had declined since the passing of the Prohibition amendment. Clearly, Fisher does not want a return to the bad old days of legal alcohol consumption because, under Prohibition, liquor is no longer such a great social problem.

On the other hand, there were many who disagreed with Fisher. A great number of book titles from the 1920s demonstrate their authors' ongoing concern with alcohol's continuing menace to American society, in spite of Prohibition: *Scourges of To-day (Venereal Disease, Cancer, Tuberculosis,*

Alcoholism) (1926); *Prohibition and Public Health* (1928); *Alcohol, Tobacco, and Drug Habit Cures* (1922); *The Effect of Alcohol on Longevity; a Study in Life Insurance Statistics* (1922); *What of the Drink Cures?* (1922); *The Action of Alcohol on Man* (1923); *The Social Diseases: Tuberculosis, Syphilis, Alcoholism, Sterility* (1920); and *Health Education: a Suggested Procedure for Teaching Alcoholism and Narcotism, 1930* (1929).

Prohibition and the Movies

Many movies of the Jazz Age reflect the same dual concern evidenced by the titles of these books published in the 1920s. Such films of the decade deal both with alcohol abuse and with the effects of Prohibition on the manners and morals of the nation. These pictures include *The Mad Whirl* (1925), *After Midnight* (1927), *Our Dancing Daughters* (1928), *Our Modern Maidens* (1929) and *The Docks of New York* (1929). Many use speakeasies as the setting for conflict, whether of a serious or comic nature. Bootlegging gangsters were popular subjects for movies in the late 1920s and early 1930s. Even following the repeal of the Eighteenth Amendment in 1933, a few motion pictures continued to use Prohibition as a backdrop, notably *The Roaring Twenties* (1939).

After Prohibition

In 1935, two years after the Eighteenth Amendment's repeal, two alcoholics founded Alcoholics Anonymous. Their recognition that others with the same addiction could benefit through mutual understanding and support represented a new, serious direction in the treatment of alcoholism. Yet many motion pictures made between 1933 and 1941 still treated drunkenness as a subject for humor and satire.

With the coming of World War II, alcohol consumption as a central focus of movies, whether comedy or drama, took a backseat to patriotic stories about the Allies and their noble sacrifices to preserve freedom. Nonetheless, by late 1944, the landmark film *The Lost Weekend* was already in production; it would provide one of the most clinically accurate representations of the alcoholic's dilemma ever put on screen.

Following World War II, Hollywood made an effort to produce more socially conscious movies, notably films dealing with such serious issues as anti–Semitism —*Gentlemen's Agreement* (1947) and *Crossfire* (1947); racism —*Home of the Brave* (1949) and *Pinky* (1949); and war veterans' readjustment to civilian life —*The Best Years of Our Lives* (1946) and *The Men*

(1950). And Victor Mature, Anne Baxter, and Claire Trevor gave superb performances as doomed alcoholics in *My Darling Clementine* (1946), *The Razor's Edge* (1947) and *Key Largo* (1948), respectively. By the 1950s, there continued to be many realistic treatments of the alcoholic personality in films such as *Come Fill the Cup* (1951), *Come Back, Little Sheba* (1952), *The Country Girl* (1954), *I'll Cry Tomorrow* (1955), *Written on the Wind* (1956), and *The Bottom of the Bottle* (1956). One exception to this serious examination of alcohol in motion pictures of the 1950s is *Auntie Mame* (1958). In this movie adaptation of the Broadway hit, Rosalind Russell successfully repeats her stage role as the fun-loving Mame Dennis. Significantly, a good portion of *Auntie Mame* is set during the Roaring Twenties, so bootleg booze is evident throughout. The setting naturally encourages numerous jokes to be made about the illegal but festive, drunken antics of Mame and her followers in fun. Mame's mantra—"Live! Live! Life is a banquet and most poor suckers are starving to death!"—testifies to her hedonism, with all of its attendant pursuit of the pleasures of drink during Prohibition.

The Scope of This Book

My analysis of alcohol and the movies encompasses the first six decades of the twentieth century. I decided to narrow my focus to a number of representative films made between 1898 and 1962—from the DeWar's advertising movie to the impressive *Days of Wine and Roses*. In selecting these films, I used a number of criteria. First, all have some artistic or historical value—some obviously more than others. Next, I have chosen films from each decade since 1900. Likewise, I have attempted to examine pictures from a number of different genres, including various subcategories of comedy, drama, and the musical. Finally, I have selected both well-known pictures (*The Lost Weekend, A Star Is Born,* and *Days of Wine and Roses*) and some that are largely forgotten today but that I believe nonetheless contain significant statements about alcohol (*The Last Flight, After Office Hours,* and *Three Blind Mice*). The sixty-four years covered in this study represent not only the coming-of-age and subsequent maturity of the motion picture industry itself but also the maturing of the film presentation of alcohol and alcohol addiction. Although movies such as D. W. Griffith's *Broken Blossoms* (1919) and King Vidor's *The Crowd* (1928) show some somber scenes depicting the consequences of too much alcohol, it was not until the World War II era that pictures began to reveal as the centerpiece of their narratives a serious portrayal of the alcoholic. Two significant pacesetters are *The Lost Weekend* (1945) and *Days of Wine and Roses* (1962). Furthermore, although movies have presented variations on these last two pictures in the years since 1962, there have been no significant modifications of the themes that prevailed in these earlier movies. Both *The Lost Weekend* and *Days of Wine and Roses* continue to be touchstone films in the long tradition of alcohol and the movies.

White Logic

A major motif that recurs throughout this book comes from a phrase used by Jack London in his 1913 memoir, *John Barleycorn*. In my epigraph to this introduction, I have cited one of London's many descriptions of White Logic, which he refers to as a world-weary sickness that accompanies the contemptuous awareness of the ills everyday life: a disillusionment brought on by and exacerbated by alcohol. London makes this White Logic a character, an omnipresent companion with whom he converses. White Logic is forever tormenting London, reminding him of "the face of the Noseless One." What London confronts in this White Logic is his own mortality, for the Noseless One is the skull of death, the memento mori, the reminder that we all become bone and ash and all of our petty, earthly desires come to naught. White Logic taunts the drunk into drinking even more because this world is only an illusion anyway. Never mind the reformers, argues White Logic as he speaks to London, but listen instead to my irrefutable logic:

> "Let the doctors of all the schools condemn me," White Logic whispers as I ride along. "What of it? I am truth. You know it. You cannot combat me. They say I make for death. What of it? It is truth. Life lies in order to live. Life is a perpetual lie-telling process. Life is a mad dance in the domain of flux, wherein appearances in mighty tides ebb and flow, chained to the wheels of moons beyond our ken. Appearances are ghosts. Life is ghost land, where appearances change, transfuse, permeate each the other and all the others, that are, that are not, that always flicker, fade, and pass, only to come again as new appearances, as other appearances.... Life is apparitional, and passes. You are an apparition. Through all the apparitions that proceded [sic] you and that compose the parts of you, you rose gibbering from the evolutionary mire, and gibbering you will pass on, interfusing, permeating the procession of apparitions that will succeed you."[8]

Embedded in these overlong, Darwinian-inspired, naturalistic sentences is London's theory of alcohol dependence, which he sees as both the effect of and the cure for a person's cynicism and despair. A man listens to the wisdom of White Logic and decides to drink because the White Logic reminds him that we all eventually become that skull's head. On the other hand, after a man becomes so drunk that he cannot stand, he is convinced that he has the strength to combat anything the world throws at him. In *John Barleycorn*, London describes the way alcohol helped him get through one of his many spirit-numbing and backbreaking adventures: "I remember passing coal on an ocean steamer through eight days of hell, during which time we coal-passers were kept to the job by being fed whisky. We toiled half drunk all the time. And without the whisky we could not have passed the coal."⁹ Indeed, Jack London's world is filled with peer pressure, uncertainty, constant hard work, battles with nature, and drinking bouts with other men. It is a chaotic world that can be forgotten only when a man is drunk. And always the White Logic is present: the noseless memento mori, a grinning talisman representing the omnipresence of futility and death.

When we closely examine the meaning of the two words in the phrase *white logic*, we can more fully understand just how appropriate this definition is to our understanding of alcohol and its presentation throughout movie history. The words themselves seem contradictory, with *white* suggestive of emptiness, blankness, barren frigidity. Yet *logic* denotes rationality, enlightenment, order, tidiness, and balance. Nevertheless, when the words are juxtaposed, we can see how appropriate such seemingly contradictory meanings are when applied to liquor's effects. Most drunks as they are depicted in films persuade themselves that their worlds make sense: that, when they are drunk, they have managed to overcome chaos by carefully controlling and mapping their own destinies. Yet the lines they have drawn across their personal maps are crooked and haphazard, their rationality only an illusion; as barren and cold and lifeless as the color *white* would indicate. What is more, even when drunkenness is played for laughs, the laughter typically comes from the comic actor's awareness of the empty chaos in our lives—a chaos symptomatic of the impermanence of reality. For instance, the comic personas adopted by Chaplin and W. C. Fields are as aware of the illogic of the White Logic as are those individuals portrayed by such serious actors as Gladys George, Ray Milland, James Cagney, and Burt Lancaster. Fields *knows* that those lines he is drawing are squiggly ones, and he perversely delights in this knowledge. Finally, even among those Prohibition-era gangsters who only exploit the public that still craves alcohol — those lawbreakers who do not themselves succumb to the enticements of liquor — there is still that world-weary cynicism that accompanies the White Logic.

In short, because there are so many implications behind the phrase *White Logic*, and because these implications are so relevant to the ways in which alcohol has been fashioned into onscreen motifs, I refer many times throughout this book to the white logic that underscores the actions of various characters. It is, after all, the white logic of alcohol that affects their behavior and sometimes, ultimately, their lives.

1

Comic Situations

"Will you walk into my playhouse?"
　　Said a manager to me;
　　"'Tis the prettiest little playhouse
　　That ever you did see!"
I accepted his kind offer
　　And saw the picture play:
And I liked it all so very much,
　　I now go every day!

— *Motion Picture Magazine*, September 1914

Comic Beginnings

A well-dressed man, clad in top hat and formal attire, is seated by himself in a fancy restaurant. He is frantically eating and drinking in a fashion that belies his elegant apparel. His only companions are the numerous half-empty liquor bottles scattered about the table. It is possibly a good thing that he is eating alone, as his table manners would doubtless kill the appetite of even the least fastidious of dinner companions. After stuffing his mouth for a moment or two, he pauses briefly to take a gulp from one of the glasses he has set down before him. And he is ever ready to refill these glasses from one of his haphazardly arranged bottles. At one point, he pauses and, in an unappetizing gesture, spits out the alcohol that he has just tossed down. Finished at last, he emerges from this posh eating and drinking establishment and weaves down a city street, staggering noiselessly from side to side, doing an awkward waltz minus a partner, and bumping into a few inconvenient objects as he tries to find his way home.

But the trip is not a pleasant one. He floats across the sky, clinging to a pillar as it waves him back and forth as though he were a mouse caught on some gigantic metronome. Once he has landed back home, he discovers that he has entered a surreal environment, complete with disappearing furniture and Lilliputian devils who visit him in bed and pound on the top of his skull with pitchforks. He experiences a nightmare calculated to make anyone think twice about overindulgence in food and drink, for his bed levitates, whirls him around like a manic dervish, and flies out the window, carrying its clinging passenger over the city rooftops and spires, an aerial performer without a net.

The name of the man portraying this unfortunate, hallucinatory gentleman is Jack Brawn, a long-forgotten movie actor; the motion picture is *The Dream of a Rarebit Fiend*, which was photographed and directed in 1906 by Edwin S. Porter for Edison. In this early film, which Porter shot in nine days for $350.00, the director makes effective use of double exposure photography, panning shots, and montage to create a spooky atmosphere for audiences who were gradually becoming accustomed to seeing such onscreen magic. In fact, the picture was so successful that it was reissued seven times.[1] No longer were moviegoers frightened at seeing such strange apparitions darting across the screen. Nor were they likely to be concerned about the hero's battle with time and space. The movie was simply entertaining, so much so that it is doubtful that any parents who saw it would have used it to teach their children about the evils of drinking. In fact, until the time of World War I, onscreen drinking was ordinarily treated as a subject for comedy and ridicule. Moreover, as we will see, alcohol was a favorite comic subject in Britain and France as well.

For instance, in Britain, Robert W. Paul (1870–1943) directed a number of films that were relatively innovative in their cinematography and editing. Paul was especially adept in his ability to hint at off screen action for comic effect. In *A Chess Dispute* (1903), two men are seated in a fancy restaurant playing chess. One is smoking a pipe and drinking. Next to these two on the table is a mixer, probably a bottle of seltzer water. They get into a dispute over their game; one takes the seltzer and sprays it in the face of the drinker. Their ensuing fight takes place out of the frame; the only actions that the audience can see involve legs flailing in air, clothes being tossed about, and one arm clutching a bottle and striking downward on an unseen opponent. In another Robert W. Paul film, *Buy Your Own Cherries* (1904), two men — one well dressed and the other scruffy looking — are positioned at opposite ends of a bar behind which we can see a sign advertising brandy. Four spigots are also prominently displayed behind the bar; one assumes that they all dispense brandy. The scruffy man tries to sample some cher-

Here is what happens when you have too much to drink before you retire for the night. Jack Brawn is the man clinging to his bed as it flies over the city in *The Dream of a Rarebit Fiend* (Edison Manufacturing Company, 1906). The spooky effect is created through double exposure photography (Photofest).

ries that are in a dish on the bar; at this, the barmaid becomes angry, so the scruffy man also gets mad and leaves in a huff, minus the cherries.

While these early efforts at mixing comedy and alcohol are somewhat entertaining, they cannot match *Rescued by Rover* (1905) for sophisticated storytelling. In this British film, an uncouth gypsy (Lindsay Gray) in ragged clothes kidnaps an infant (played by director Cecil Hepworth's own child, billed simply as "Baby Hepworth") and takes the child to her hole-in-the-wall dwelling, which subsequently becomes a makeshift hideout. The unkempt kidnapper's hideaway looks like a medieval dungeon lacking in any of the amenities necessary for comfort, such as a bed, chair, sink, stove, or toilet. When the shifty thief is not waving the baby in the air — much as someone would display an enemy flag captured by a conquering army — or removing the infant's clothing, she demonstrates what a disreputable character she is by eagerly taking a swig out of the bottle of spirits that she has stashed in her hovel. After fortifying herself, she gently places the bottle down and lies next to the captured baby. But Rover, the clever Hepworth dog that looks like a mixture of Rin-Tin-Tin and Lassie, leads his master —

the distraught father of the missing infant — into the gypsy's quaint home. Father, played naturally enough by Cecil Hepworth (1873–1953), wastes no time in reclaiming the baby and hastening out of the squalid surroundings, whereupon the gypsy grudgingly accepts her temporary setback by having another swig and settling back down for an afternoon nap. We may assume that she will sleep until her alcoholic stupor wears off, at which time she will soon venture out again in search of another infant to grab.

Audiences in 1905 would have laughed at the character of the gypsy, the stereotypical, nomadic derelict. Moreover, while the movie is suspenseful and sophisticated for its era, effectively using jump cuts, simultaneous time, and scene repetition to show the loss and recovery of the baby, *Rescued by Rover* has an overall light touch, treating the gypsy as a comic recluse and the baby as a cherubic, cheerful little infant whose safety is no more in doubt than that of the drunken diner in *Dream of a Rarebit Fiend*. By the same token, in France, Ferdinand Zecca (1863–1947) made a film that *Rarebit Fiend* somewhat resembles in its light tone. In this earlier French movie, *Rêve à la Lune* (1905), a drunk has visions of dancing champagne bottles.[2]

Even D. W. Griffith (1875–1948) succumbed in an early film to the temptation presented by the humorous possibilities attendant upon drunkenness. In *The Curtain Pole* (1908), an effeminate man in a top hat enters a drawing room where an attractive girl is trying to hang a drape. The man is played by Mack Sennett (1880–1960), who is here trying to imitate Max Linder. In an effort to impress the girl, Sennett's officious snob instead breaks the pole on which the drape should rest. He quickly reassures all that he will fetch a new pole, but on his way to the draper's, he passes a saloon and enters for some refreshment and fortification. However, rather than following this fellow into the saloon, the camera keeps the viewer waiting outside. We watch the building's façade for what seems like a fairly long time. Finally, this hiatus in the action becomes funny: "After this entirely static shot, the fop reappears, drunk. The camera has fantasized time by telescoping it outrageously; and it has made comedy of its own altogether deadpan behavior."[3]

Mack Sennett, in his first and only leading film role, does a splendid job as a soused roué, especially as he totes the pole back to his girl. Griffith filmed Sennett tottering along the streets of Fort Lee, New Jersey, trying to maneuver both himself and the unwieldy pole. Richard Schickel has described the result of the Griffith/Sennett collaboration: "It remains one of Griffith's few ventures into pure farce and for an essentially humorless man, it is a rather surprisingly successful one, very possibly because Griffith allowed Sennett a full, free rein."[4]

By the 1910s, comic actors such as Charles Chaplin — who began his career under the direction of Sennett — Max Linder, Ben Turpin, and Roscoe "Fatty" Arbuckle were portraying excessive drinking as a physically humorous phenomenon. In these pre–Prohibition days, silent clowns treated drunkenness as a subject for slapstick, in spite of the fact that reformers and critics were deploring the horrible social consequences of alcoholism. However, these comics combined their adroit physical skills with their inebriated efforts to battle seemingly obstinate objects; these slippery substances forever appeared to slide just out of range of their fuzzy vision. For a closer look at these comic efforts, we first return to France.

Max Linder

The great French comedian Max Linder (1883–1925) made his first film in 1906. He had been a well-known stage performer when he began making one-reel situation comedies in France. In most of these comedies he played a dapper bon vivant. Linder has been called the first actor to develop a distinct motion picture acting style.[5] So too, he was a skilled comic actor and director, with a technique that influenced Chaplin. In fact, Linder came to America in 1917 to replace Chaplin at Essanay; at that time, Chaplin, feeling badly treated by Essanay's ferocious boss George K. Spoor, left the studio to go to Mutual.[6] Before Linder began his brief — and tragically unsuccessful — stay in America, however, he had been an extremely popular star at a time when French films were dominant; Linder was consequently known throughout the world.[7]

One of the best of Linder's French movies is *Max, victime du quinquina* (1911) in which he does some funny bits as a drunk. First, he visits his doctor and complains of fatigue. The obliging physician writes him a prescription for a mixture guaranteed to fortify him and to restore his flagging energy. And indeed it does. Linder's antics upon obeying doctor's orders to take his medication are immediate and revitalizing, for his medicine consists of a 120 proof, two-quart bottle of alcohol. Following doctor's orders, Linder pours the entire liquid contents into what looks like a beaker, the kind used by chemists. Then he takes a straw, places it into the beaker, and amuses himself for about thirty seconds by drinking the contents of whole bottle. All the while, Linder is immensely enjoying himself, looking for all the world as though he were just sipping a soda fountain drink.

Yet the effects of this cure are scarcely what one would expect from drinking a soda. In fact, the results are quick: Linder jumps up, flapping his arms and then awkwardly removing his jacket. Somehow he winds up in a nightclub where he sits between two tables and pesters the customers at both. Eventually, he stumbles back onto the street and gets his dinner jacket caught on a lamppost. In his efforts to extricate himself from his physically awkward position, he looks like an intoxicated scarecrow. A bemused cop finally frees him and carries him up stairs to an apartment, where he gets thrown out by the person living there.

On the street once again, he is picked up by a different cop, who carries him to another apartment, where he is again ejected. Each time that he lands on the street, he shows a different identity card to the cop who happens to be watching, so each time, he is toted upstairs to a different apartment, until he finally lands in a bed, top hat and all, with a strange woman. When the woman's husband notes with chagrin an oddly dressed man in bed with his wife, he tosses Linder out. The movie ends with the three cops on the street comparing the three different names that Linder has given them and retaliating for this deception by tossing the hapless inebriate into the air. *Max,victime du quinquina* is a fast paced, funny movie, with a good performance by Linder and some effective support from the other actors.[8] Critic Walter Kerr has astutely observed of Linder: "[He] was essentially an indoor man ... insisting on restraint in his gagging, thoroughly disliking chases, refusing or failing to drain from his initial extravagances the vast logical absurdity that was in them. Thrown into a physical situation, he seems to have found his comedy in evading it."[9]

Another Linder comedy touting the funny side of inebriation is one that also supports Kerr's opinion of Linder as a restrained comic actor: *Max et la Statue* (1912). In this one, Max goes to a costume ball dressed in a suit of armor. He amuses himself by drinking all night, then totters onto the street at dawn and passes out on the sidewalk. Meanwhile, two thieves have entered the Louvre and stolen a suit of armor. The police find Max's prone figure and assume that this is the missing museum piece. Accordingly, they restore the costumed Max to the museum pedestal and drape him in preparation for a grand unveiling, which soon takes place. Throughout this ceremony, Max simply looks dazed, while the museum patrons fail to notice that there is something odd about the statue. The movie ends with the thieves recapturing Max, taking him to their hideout where Max fights them off after they have tried to pry open his armor with some tools. The movie ends with a shot of Max still clad in armor and strumming a guitar.[10]

Charlie Chaplin

When Charlie Chaplin (1889–1977) worked at Keystone for Mack Sennett, he portrayed a series of drunks, all of whom got entangled with objects, women, and gigantic men. These short Keystone films, among them *Tango Tangles* (1914), *His Favorite Pastime* (1914), and *The Rounders* (1914), demonstrate Chaplin's agility in gleefully extricating himself from oddly precarious situations. In *Tango Tangles*, Chaplin gets potted in a restaurant/dance hall and fights in the cloakroom with Fatty Arbuckle, where they destroy every coat awaiting its owner's return.

His Favorite Pastime refers, of course, to the Chaplin character's love of drinking. The incoherent plot contains some excessively violent, dark comedy with racially insensitive overtones, with two of the secondary characters appearing in blackface. Here, Chaplin is first viewed in a bar where he is imbibing a large glass of ale, which he shares with a feeble-looking fellow drunk, a bearded man who looks like a dissipated gold prospector. Chaplin gets into a number of fights at the bar, including one with a looming lout played by Edgar Kennedy who, like Chaplin, made his first film appearances for Mack Sennett. As Chaplin's assailant, Kennedy is made up to look like a dockworker or a nightclub bouncer, or perhaps a menacing masseur. Even in this routine short comedy, Chaplin shows his penchant for using everyday household items for comic effect. In one brief scene, fully clothed and dry, he nonetheless uses a washroom towel to dry his back. Then he turns the towel into a shoeshine rag and draws it across his shoe, blackening the towel with shoe polish.

The Rounders has a more complex and logical plot than Chaplin's previous Sennett pictures, perhaps because Chaplin had more artistic control over this film. In this movie, Chaplin and Roscoe "Fatty" Arbuckle have a rollicking time as two supremely happy drunks who try to outwit their not-so-happy wives. A major source of amusement in the film, aside from the drunken antics of Chaplin and Arbuckle, is the contrast between the actors' sizes: Chaplin, small and wiry; Arbuckle, large and ungainly. And the contrast is not only between the two men but also between their wives, played by Phyllis Allen and Minta Durfee as Chaplin's wife and Arbuckle's wife, respectively. Allen offers a contrast to Chaplin in her imposing, buxom appearance; alternatively, Durfee is in decided contrast to Arbuckle. She is short, slender, and fragile in appearance. But neither lady will take anything from her husband. In the course of this short picture, both husbands are knocked down, beaten about the head, and tossed around. Both, however, are so blissfully soused that they scarcely notice the indignities being foisted upon their bodies by their irate wives.

Once again, Chaplin demonstrates in *The Rounders* his ingenious ability to put objects to good use. In one scene, Arbuckle drags the nearly comatose Chaplin into a place called Smith's Café, which, despite its name, looks like a fairly posh eating establishment. Here these two adept silent clowns do some bits of business that both were especially good at carrying out; they take ordinary objects and transform them into something else — something not intended for the use to which these pals put them. For instance, Arbuckle sits on a convenient chair, pulls up what looks like an upright ashtray holder, and turns the object into a footstool by propping his feet on the holder. Now the portly actor precariously balances himself, trying to settle in for a nice snooze. But he needs a blanket, so he grabs a tablecloth from off the table and wraps himself in it. He looks like a very large mummy. Chaplin joins his companion by yanking a tablecloth from an angry diner's table. Soon both are on the floor, cozily tucked in for the evening: mummified.

Chaplin soon tired of the assembly-line products that he was turning out for Sennett and, in 1915, he moved on to Essanay. His second film for that studio was *A Night Out* (1915). Here Chaplin and Ben Turpin, appearing in their first film together, indulge in a woozy night on the town. Audiences undoubtedly found much amusement in watching the toll that booze is taking on the constitutions of these two drunken fellows, who pass the evening insulting and assaulting unfortunate people on whom they stumble in the course of their night out. In one incident, Chaplin is seated in a restaurant where he rests, spread-eagled on the seat of his chair, and proceeds to harass a gentleman at the next table by gracefully placing his foot on the man's leg and then knocking the man's hat off with his cane. Then, he compounds the insult by taking a drink from a nearby glass and spitting alcohol on the neighboring diner. His uncouth spraying is reminiscent of the careless drinker in *The Dream of a Rarebit Fiend*, but this time, the tippler has a target.

In this slapstick comedy, both Chaplin and Turpin demonstrate their athletic style and balletic grace. Shortly after Chaplin's impolite behavior toward his fellow diner, a bouncer appears and ejects Turpin, whose body movements in this scene suggest a certain gymnastic ability. In fact, the bouncer handles Turpin as though he were an inflatable doll and casually tosses him out the restaurant door. Meanwhile, Chaplin's insouciant air as he watches Turpin's abrupt exit suggests that he his bored by the whole proceeding.

But he is not bored for long. The jokes concerning inebriation continue when a hefty lady seats herself alongside the unfortunate gentleman at the next table. She will become Chaplin's next target, and a risqué one at that. Engrossed in conversation with her escort, she swings the strap of her purse. Then, while she is still holding onto the strap, the purse itself hurtles between Chaplin's legs. Seemingly oblivious to her proximity to Chaplin's anatomy, she next gestures wildly while she talks to her dinner companion. Some of her enthusiastic hand movements culminate on Chaplin's thigh and groin. The humor arises from the fact that she remains pleasantly unaware of the consequences of her frenetic motions, and from the equally obvious fact that Chaplin has arrived at a supremely relaxed state of intoxication and is vastly amused by his surroundings.

By 1916, Chaplin was exerting more tight control over action and setting. Nowhere is this fact more evident than in *One A.M.* (1916). Gerald Mast has said that Chaplin's *The Pawnshop* and *One A.M.* "are perhaps the two best films with and about objects ever made."[11] Another film historian has argued that in *One A.M.* Chaplin comes the closest to demonstrating the debt he owed to Max Linder.[12] As with earlier films in which Chaplin plays an amusing drunk, *One A.M.* (1916), which he made for Mutual, traces the humorous trials of a formally attired gentleman suffering from excessive alcohol consumption: in this case, Chaplin devotes the entire film to show us a man's efforts to get upstairs to bed following a riotous night on the town. Further, with the exception of a taxi driver (Albert Austin), seen very briefly at the beginning of the movie, Chaplin is the only performer in the film, a fact that contributes to its being one of the most inventive of the early Chaplin pictures.

The first object that presents Chaplin with a formidable obstacle is the cab itself. As the picture opens, the cab is parked in front of Chaplin's house, with the driver waiting for Chaplin to alight. But Chaplin cannot find the way out; the door presents some difficulties. Looking for the handle is especially troublesome. Since he cannot locate it inside the cab, Chaplin tries reaching through the window and feels around on the outside of the door. The title card records Chaplin's fuzzy thought here: "They should build these handles nearer the door." Once he manages to open the recalcitrant door, Chaplin faces another hurdle: he drops his handkerchief and cannot reach the pavement to retrieve it because the open door is now in his way. But even this challenge is not too much for the circuitous determination of the intoxicated. With the cab door still open, he reaches from the inside through the window and picks up the handkerchief. Now it's time to pay the driver, who has been sitting stoically all the while Chaplin has been performing acrobatic feats. But the driver is about to get his revenge for the wait; while Chaplin searches his pockets for coins, the driver decides to play with the meter. An uncomprehending Chaplin watches as the meter turns over and over, like some out-of-whack slot machine.

Having paid the driver a doubtlessly excessive sum, Chaplin faces his house at last, but he cannot find the key. After looking in all the usual places outside, he gives up and climbs through the window. A medium shot of the interior shows an orderly, balanced room, one of almost perfect symmetry. Chaplin will effectively use this balance as an antithetical point of departure for his attempts to recover his own equilibrium and climb the stairs to bed. On either side are two identical staircases that form a semicircle, meeting on a landing at the top. At the central point of the landing, equidistant from each staircase, is an enormous clock with an equally gigantic swinging pendulum. Just below the staircases is a table with liquor bottles on top. The setting is done so expertly and the pendulum is so obvious that we know danger lies ahead for anyone getting in the way of that clock. But Chaplin has just gotten inside, so this threat lies in the future. Once inside, he naturally finds his key, so, in a maneuver that would be echoed a number of times by Laurel and Hardy, he goes back outside through the same window, unlocks the front door, and enters.

On his way to grab the bottles upon the table, he is spooked by two stuffed wild animals on the floor. Alternately kicking and patting them, he makes his way to the real object of his affection: those bottles. And what a problem those bottles present, largely because the table is a revolving one, so what Chaplin is faced with here is a large Lazy Susan. The more he chases the bottles, the faster he revolves the table. Holding a glass in his hand, he observes, with pun intended: "That's the fastest round of drinks I ever saw." At last, table and bottles and Chaplin's head are lined up evenly, with Chaplin once again seated on the floor. Although he appears for the time being to have won this game of liquor roulette, Chaplin still lacks the eye-hand coordination necessary to perform even the simplest tasks. For instance, in one hand he holds a spray bottle containing a chaser; in the other, a glass to receive the chaser. Knowing somehow that the chaser should go into the glass, he pushes the nozzle on the bottle and sprays its contents in a direction opposite to the empty glass. He never notices anything out of the ordinary. Assuming that the mixer is ready, he next adds the liquor to the glass. This time he pours the booze onto his legs and shoes, and this time he does notice.

Resolving to climb the stairs to bed, Chaplin discovers that the stairs prove to be nearly insurmountable. He begins with those on the left side and carries on his ascent with a nimble two-step movement; that is, two steps forward and two steps backward. Chaplin accomplishes this motion with such ease that he makes it look as though the steps are moving: an in-home escalator. Meanwhile, the clock on the landing at the top of the stairs continues its precise, rhythmic swaying: an appropriate counterpoint to Chaplin's uneasy weaving. Here, Chaplin prepares us for a collision between man and pendulum, but he surprises us this time. He falls back down the stairs of his own accord. There is no surprise the second time, however. As Chaplin's ever-resourceful drunk clings to the banister to aid his efforts and does indeed almost reach his goal at the top of the stairs, he receives the inevitable sock on the chin from the reliable pendulum, and he again tumbles back to the first floor. Then he attempts the identical stairs on the right side, but has no luck with them either.

So he momentarily gives up on attaining that second floor. Nonetheless, Chaplin is never one to relax, never one to bore his audience. He climbs onto the table; after all, this is an easier climb than those obstinate stairs. This time he dances upon the constantly moving table, a revolving treadmill that finally revolves him right off of it. Blessed with seemingly inexhaustible energy, Chaplin again tries the stairs on the left, only to tumble down once more, this time bringing the stair carpeting with him. By the time he reaches the bottom, he resembles a large roll of paper towels. Encased in carpeting, but unfazed by his current awkward position, he pauses to take another drink.

Now to tackle the right staircase again. On this try, he uses a hat stand to vault over the railing and, with one motion, reach the top landing. But the pendulum has its own motion to be conquered. Chaplin is repeatedly hit until he finally gets to his bedroom door by dint of dodging this pesky machine. The remainder of the film involves Chaplin's fight with his Murphy bed, a piece of recalcitrant furniture that literally twists him around and catches him like a revolving door. He finally conquers the bed but retreats to the bathtub to spend the remainder of the night.

Another Chaplin movie that features drunkenness is *Easy Street*. One of his most famous short films, it was released in January 1917. It contains more social criticism and commentary than many of the other early Chaplin pictures. Indeed, the title itself has a triple significance. First, the phrase "easy street" alludes to a condition of wealth and the leisure associated with such an excess of money. Next, the term "easy" is often used to describe someone whose morals are suspect, as in a woman of "easy virtue." Finally, "easy" suggests something that is readily obtainable or readily learned. All three readings here are apt, for the first meaning is fraught with bitter irony when it is applied to the urban skid row conditions depicted in the film; specifically, Chaplin shows us this horrible poverty in scenes where dozens of children are packed into a one-room tenement and a woman steals bread because she is starving. The second meaning also applies because the various thugs and addicts that people this movie are in fact individuals of questionable moral virtue. Likewise, the third meaning is equally applicable, for the movie does indeed portray a world in which alcohol, drugs, and violence abound on a street where it is "easy" to get mugged or addicted or both.

Parts of this picture are humorous, but what little comedy can be found in this movie results from the conflict between Chaplin and the formidable Eric Campbell, who acted as Chaplin's foil in many of these early comedies before his untimely death in an auto accident in December 1917. In this movie, Campbell is a hulking roughneck with large, dark, threatening eyebrows that look as though they have been painted on with a thick brush; these curve upward and resemble old-fashioned typewriter ribbons that have not yet been stretched taut. Hanging out with drunks and drug addicts, Campbell is impervious to the blows that the diminutive Chaplin levels with his policeman's nightstick on Campbell's skull. Yet, despite the occasional comic bits provided by these two adversaries, the picture's tone is bittersweet. In short, the comedy in *Easy Street* is offset by the dark undercurrent of social criticism, the squalid setting reminiscent of Chaplin's own hardscrabble childhood environment in the London slums.

Another short Chaplin movie, one that features alcohol as its centerpiece and has a lighter tone than *Easy Street*, is *The Cure* (1917). Here, Chaplin dispenses with his Little Tramp clothing and shows his indebtedness to Max Linder by dressing as an inebriated bon vivant who is visiting a fancy health spa where the restorative waters purport to make him a new man. But this transformation will not be easy, for Chaplin's character is a sublimely contented drunk, happy to be at this posh health establishment.

This elegance is established in the movie's opening scene where we see some formally dressed ladies, obviously wealthy and obviously elderly, but very proper; these ladies are enjoying themselves as they dip their cups into a small pool of water the circumference of a shower stall. While they are scooping and sipping, Chaplin staggers in, but keeps getting ejected by the hotel's staff, who let The Inebriate know that his presence is not welcome. However, one whose presence is desirable is the character played by Eric Campbell, he of the inky, menacing, quizzical eyebrows. We know that Campbell is rich and therefore a desirable guest at the spa because an enormous bandage on his foot proves that he has the gout. At one time, gout was considered a disease suffered solely by rich males. Furthermore, Campbell's gouty foot becomes a source of slapstick humor throughout the rest of the picture when it becomes an inviting target for Chaplin to trounce upon.

The setting at this ritzy spa provides much opportunity for Chaplin, Campbell, and Edna Purviance to play with each other. Campbell, bandaged foot flailing clumsily about, lumbers along in pursuit of Edna Purviance, who is not in the least interested in his attentions, probably because he looks like a large male fiddler crab waving its claw to attract a mate. They eventually end their chase seated across from each other, daintily sipping coffee. Into this tête-à-tête lurches Chaplin, while Campbell warily watches his foot, lest Chaplin trounce it again. With the relaxed benignity typical of those who remain perpetually inebriated and just a little off balance, Chaplin sits between Campbell and Purviance and watches with amusement as Campbell throws longing glances in the lady's direction. But Chaplin's drunken state remains a danger to all around him. He upends Campbell by moving the loveseat on which the generously proportioned comedian had been intending to sit. Then, blissfully unaware of the havoc he is creating, he bows gallantly to Edna, and subsequently topples over and onto Campbell's preciously guarded foot.

All of these early Chaplin movies feature Chaplin the drunk at his athletic best. Furthermore, each one reveals Chaplin's uncanny gift for transforming inanimate obstacles into conquerable objects. In addition, with the exception of *One A.M.,* all demonstrate Chaplin's ability to play off against other talented players. He works exceedingly skillfully in tandem with such well-known silent players as Fatty Arbuckle, Eric Campbell, Ben Turpin, and Edgar Kennedy.

Yet, as film historian and critic Anthony Slide has observed of Chaplin: "He is singularly out of favor with modern audiences. His films generate little response and few, if any, laughs.... his films are too quietly measured, too carefully planned and executed to appeal to audiences that find the Three Stooges or any of the MTV-generated comedians funny."[13] Even in these early movies, Chaplin's gift for pulling together such disparate elements involving both plot and characterization is clearly evident. In addition, as Slide suggests, there is a subtlety to all of Chaplin's silent film work. In fact, much of what he does appears deceptively simple. A close study of his depiction of the Little Fellow in various stages of inebriation demonstrates how gracefully Chaplin could play individuals whose physical dexterity was compromised through an excess of alcohol. It is a pity that such adroitness has all but vanished from modern comedy.

2

No Way Out

The popular idea is that a man is not drunk if he does not stagger and is reasonably clear in his speech and senses. But intoxication is not a matter of mere muscle control. The average regular drinker is always drunk.

— Harry S. Warner, *Social Welfare and the Liquor Problem*, 1913

A Girl, a Little Unconventional, and a Little too Sincere, Almost Loses Her Chance for Love and Happiness

— Fan Magazine Promotion for *Our Dancing Daughters*,
Screen Book Magazine, March 1929

Naturalism in Fiction and Film

Naturalism is a literary theory that emphasizes the role of heredity and environment upon human life and character development. This theory was the basis of a late nineteenth and early twentieth century aesthetic movement that, in literature, extended the tradition of realism, aiming at an even more faithful, unselective representation of reality. The world of the naturalists was one that passed no moral judgment. Naturalism in fiction differed from realism in its assumption of scientific determinism, which led naturalistic authors to emphasize the accidental, physiological nature of their characters rather than their moral or rational qualities.

This determinism was in part an outgrowth of social Darwinism. Individuals who advocated adopting Darwin's theories did so by distorting one of Darwin's basic tenets: that those species who are able to adapt genetically to changes in environment will be more likely to survive than those who do not. Rather, the social Darwinists maintained that those who are naturally the *fittest* to survive by virtue of heredity and social class will live. Consequently, individual characters who are born into poverty are seen as unfit, helpless products of heredity and environment, motivated by strong instinctual drives from within, and harassed by social and economic pressures from without. Furthermore, traditional havens of safety associated with security and tradition — such as the church, the family, and the school — offer no protection against the malevolent universe bent on destroying the strivings of puny humans. For a large number of unfortunate literary characters, such as those in Stephen Crane's *Maggie: A Girl of the Streets* (1896), Frank Norris's *McTeague* (1899), and Theodore Dreiser's *An American Tragedy* (1925), there is no way out.

By the late 1910s and early 1920s, naturalism had become an important element in American film as well as in American literature. The 1920s and 1930s saw a movement away from the clever pratfalls of the comics in the short films of the previous decade toward a gloomier, more complex view of reality. What is more, naturalism in American film extended its deterministic tenets to include individuals from all classes. Whether these onscreen characters are poor, middle class, or wealthy, they are doomed by an existence that offers no hope — by the world-weary sickness of Jack London's White Logic. This chapter will explore the depiction of alcohol as a background to the lives of those caught in a futile world that is, at best, indifferent and, at worst, malevolent.

D. W. Griffith, Lillian Gish, and the Terrors of the Slums

As we have seen, by the late 1910s, a more serious picture of alcohol abuse began to emerge in the increasingly sophisticated, naturalistic movies of the middle silent period. One of the best examples of this growing maturity is found in the loutish character of Battling Burrows (Donald Crisp) in D. W. Griffith's impressive *Broken Blossoms* (1919). Burrows is a brutal drunk who terrorizes his adolescent daughter Lucy, played by Lillian Gish, who was appearing in her sixty-fourth motion picture.[1]

Early in the narrative, the audience is told how, fifteen years earlier, the unfortunate baby Lucy had been left by her mother with Battling Burrows; through title cards, we also learn that the child is the consequence of Battling Burrows's visit to one of the many prostitutes available in the foul and decaying neighborhood. Though the original story, called "The Chink and the Child," from Thomas Burke's short story collection, *Limehouse Blues,* depicted Lucy as only twelve, the title writers doubtless added three years to her age in order to approximate the actual age of Lillian Gish, who was twenty-five at the time of filming. In fact, in her memoir of her long and memorable association with Griffith, Gish claims that she protested against playing a twelve-year-old, maintaining that she was "too tall."[2] (Interestingly, she did not assert that she was "too old.") Mary Pickford had urged director D. W. Griffith to read "The Chink and the Child," and Griffith had been fascinated by the story's depiction of a fragile, innocent child woman.[3] Such a character had become a stock one in many Griffith films.

Though Gish probably could not have passed for twelve, the petite actress is nonetheless believable as a fifteen-year-old; her youth adds pathos to her characterization and emphasizes her vulnerability to the brutal father. That the dissipated Burrows wants Lucy only as his slave is one of the least offensive characteristics associated with his ugly personality. And what a despicable character he is, as expertly played by Donald Crisp, a director as well as an actor. Crisp would easily make the transition to sound and would subsequently be known for playing kindly fathers, uncles, and other older mentors. But here he is ruthless, overbearing, animalistic in his primal passions, and totally, frighteningly convincing. The distinguished critic and film historian Richard Schickel finds that Crisp overplays his part, that he is out of control as Battling Burrows, his performance filled with "eye-rolling ... grimacing ... monstrousness."[4] Yet Crisp's depiction is in keeping with what is known today about the nearly superhuman, extremely violent propensities of the serious alcohol/drug addict.

Our first glimpse of Burrows reveals his thoroughgoing relish for alcohol. We see him sitting alone in his dismal dwelling, contentedly pouring liquor from his bottle into a glass, looking smug and happy and clearly enjoying his company of one. Yet the alcohol ultimately fails to give him a warm and fuzzy feeling; rather it serves only to enrage him whenever he feels that he has been crossed, which occurs quite often. For example, Burrows's fight manager is constantly berating him for his frequent visits to the local bar. However, such chastising only sends Burrows into a frenzy, which he then takes out on Lucy. In one such instance, he menacingly circles the sticks of wood that pass for their dining table, stalking her as they revolve around this decrepit piece of furniture, on the top of which is a liquor bottle that serves as an ominous centerpiece to their conflict. All the while that she is being threatened, Lucy cowers, arms folded inward, both in anticipation of and fearful of the beatings that always accompany his drunkenness. Only after Burrows leaves is she able to eat her own supper: she gathers together from his plate the scraps that he has left behind in his haste to return to the tavern.

And the tavern scene that follows depicts once more Burrows at odds with his manager, for this man intrudes on Burrows's fun, interrupting Burrows's flirtation with one of the female patrons as well as his drinking. Directly confronting Burrows, the manager reminds the fighter that his alcoholic bouts are getting tiresome. So Battling Burrows, afraid of standing up to his manager, goes home in another murderous rage to vent his frustration on the girl. Griffith superbly utilizes both of his actors in the subsequent scene, with Burrows terrorizing Lucy with a whip, while she desperately, frantically tries to distract him by kneeling at his feet and dusting his boots. But her servile submissiveness fails, as he yanks her up and whips her till she collapses on the floor. Their actions foreshadow the grim, naturalistic climax of the movie; in fact, though Lillian Gish had by this time already made several dozen pictures for Griffith, who always emphasized her naïve, gentle beauty, she rarely appeared as vulnerable as she does in this movie. Her fragility here was doubtless accentuated by the fact that she had barely recovered from influenza at the start of the filming, and that her illness had been serious enough to leave her quite weak. It will be remembered that this particular strain of influenza was the one that wreaked havoc throughout the world, spreading and becoming a dreaded worldwide epidemic by 1918, the year *Broken Blossoms* was filmed.[5]

Gish's weakness and her vulnerability are no more evident than in one of the final scenes, which reveals Battling Burrows, his courage fortified by another trip to the tavern, dragging her from the home of The Yellow Man (Richard Barthelmess), where she has gone for shelter following Burrows's earlier beating. Not only is Burrows a drunken brute, but he is also a drunken brute of a racist; angered beyond any semblance of sanity by the fact that his daughter has been keeping house with a "Chink," Burrows suddenly has some perverse spasms of fatherly duty as he moves in on his prey for the last time. Through close-ups and crosscutting, Griffith creates one of the most suspenseful, visceral scenes of the silent era. Dragged back to their hovel by the infuriated Burrows and pitifully clutching a little doll given to her by the Yellow Man, Gish's Lucy breaks away from her father long enough to lock herself in a closet. But the door is flimsy and Burrows the prizefighter is strong; thus Lucy knows a fact that she deftly communicates to the audience: that there is no way out, save death; and so she helplessly waves her head from side to side, her eyes wide with terror, her hands grasping the doll, her silent screams puncturing the foul air within her prison. Kevin Brownlow has called this scene "the screen's highest example of emotional hysteria."[6]

What is more, adding to the realism of the episode were the corresponding shouts of D. W. Griffith, who was noted for giving just such

A wild-eyed Donald Crisp portrays a perpetually inebriated fighter with the appropriate name of Battling Burrows. He terrorizes his daughter Lucy, played by Lillian Gish, and finally beats her to death in *Broken Blossoms* (United Artists, 1919). Note the squalor of their living conditions, which heightens the sense of fatalistic despair that permeates this naturalistic film (Photofest).

emotional encouragement to his actors. Since his directorial contribution obviously could not be heard on film, he felt free to push his actors in the right, most heartrending direction. However, the combined hysteria of Griffith and Gish "could be heard on the streets outside. It required most of the studio staff to keep the curious from trying to invade the studio."[7] Roger Ebert adds his own oxymoronic observation: "Gish was one of the great vulnerable screamers of the silent era."[8] Edward Wagenknecht, who knew Gish personally and who had interviewed her as early as 1920, offers the following assessment of the famous scene where Burrows breaks down the closet door: "...the simulation of hysteria is not necessarily the highest form of acting, yet for all that Lillian's hysteria in the famous 'closet scene' of *Broken Blossoms* still seems to me a marvel to behold — inspired, impassioned, altogether beyond the bounds of normal experience, yet wonderfully infused with beauty."[9]

Whatever it was that kept Gish at such an exhausting emotional pitch, it worked. When Burrows grabs an ax and methodically splinters the wooden door of Lucy's refuge, leaving a hole large enough for him to enter and once more capture his doomed daughter, the audience is doubtless relieved to know that Lucy's agony is almost over. Following the last beating that he will ever give her, Burrows settles comfortably down with his liquor. Content at last with his evening's work, he now bypasses the social amenities by drinking his booze directly from the bottle.

The denouement of this otherwise well-paced movie is disappointing, like a ride down a steep hill filled with potholes, for it is melodramatic and anticlimactic. Burrows, fuzzyheaded and still charged with blood lust from the excitement of the kill and from too much alcohol, is about to throw his ax at The Yellow Man, but at that moment, he is fatally shot by the "Chink," who at least wishes to hold onto the memory of his beloved Lucy by eliminating her killer from the earth. Although the focus throughout this fine film is not necessarily the evils of alcohol addiction — the sympathetically portrayed Yellow Man is also addicted, but to opium — Griffith nonetheless does not treat alcohol abuse lightly. His narrative throughout emphasizes that liquor's effect on Battling Burrows is insidious, that alcohol causes him to lose what few vestiges of civilized inhibitions he might have possessed. Although to modern audiences *Broken Blossoms* may appear overwrought in places, the film still has the power to touch our emotions.

The Loneliness of The Crowd

One of the best movies of the 1920s is King Vidor's silent classic *The Crowd* (1928). Like *Broken Blossoms*, it is a powerful story, told in a realistic, straightforward manner, filled with tragic events yet avoiding sentimentality. Film historian Joe Franklin has called *The Crowd* "one of the most dramatic films of all time. Without a single torrid romantic exchange, it is the most poignant and moving love story I have seen."[10] Its Everyman protagonist is named John Simms (James Murray); like the later Willy Loman in Arthur Miller's *Death of a Salesman* (1949), John Simms is a little man futilely striving against an uncaring society that he doesn't understand. He works as a clerk in a high rise New York City office, filled with row upon row of desks, each one of which is occupied by a clerk identical to the one at the desk next to him. One critic has referred to John Simms as typical of "the small city frog in the high white-collar pond."[11] Like the nameless drudges in Edwin Arlington Robinson's "The Clerks," Simms will be forever stuck in a monotonous, impersonal, uncaring world. Moreover, like Arthur Miller's Willy Loman, Simms is a weak dreamer who substitutes his illusions and rationalizations for a more realistic perspective on a flawed world. Furthermore, Simms sometimes uses alcohol to soothe the wounds of his daily disappointments and frustrations.

One such occasion occurs shortly after his marriage to Mary (Eleanor Boardman): the long-suffering Everywoman, and a perfect companion to his Everyman. On this particular evening, John and Mary Simms are trying to celebrate Christmas Eve with Mary's very formidable mother and Mary's two equally fearsome brothers. John is naturally on edge about the forthcoming evening, as all three of his wife's relatives heartily disapprove of him: a man whom they see as an unambitious loser and whom they are constantly needling due to his continued lack of success in the business world. And the evening proves to be every bit as awful as John had feared. It begins badly when mother and brothers arrive with presents for Mary. The subsequent gift exchange excludes John, who disconsolately watches their happy celebration while he is standing in the bathroom doorway, where he has gone to shave in the futile hope that a neat appearance will at least somewhat appease his in-laws.

But his wife's relatives are not at all pleased to see him. When Mary asks him to give Mother a kiss, Mother frowns, tilts her cheek up, and maintains a disagreeable expression, one suggesting that she has just eaten a seven-course meal fried in lard. In an attempt to make the wheels roll more smoothly, Mary helpfully informs the company that John has just invented a new trick: he can "break" his arm. But the visitors are singularly unimpressed with John's puerile contortions as he demonstrates his trick. In fact, Mother inquires about John's financial prospects, adamantly maintaining that he should be less interested in tricks than in getting his raise. Now looking like a hurt child and remaining on the defensive, John tries to argue: "No, but everybody tells me my prospects are good."

Since the weak but well-meaning John knows that he is unwelcome at this party and that even his wife will not come to his defense against her opinionated family, he looks around for some escape, some relief from his frustrations and feelings of alienation. So he turns to the liquor supply, which is now depleted. Though we are in the Prohibition era, it is clear that alcohol is easily obtained, and John knows where to find an ample supply — from his colleague Bert (Bert Roach). Consequently, John leaves the unfriendly bunch gathered in his meager apartment, ostensibly to find liquor for this group of predators. What he is really after, however, is a place where he can have a good, uninhibited time. And friend Bert is always ready for a good time. After John crashes Bert's Christmas Eve party of four — Bert and three sexy flappers — any thought of returning to his apartment with alcohol vaporizes. John is especially flattered by the attentions of one of the stylish girls, a woman who seems to have much more flair and aggressive energy than his caring and dependable wife. He seems not at all reluctant to dance with this dame who grabs him shortly after his entrance.

Cut to Johnny and Bert stumbling down the street. Clearly, much time has passed since John left home in search of more liquor. Neither man seems fully aware of the direction he is headed or of the condition he is in. Yet Bert recognizes Johnny's place of residence, as he helpfully tries to push John up the outer steps of his apartment building; he at least gives the beleaguered husband a shove in the right direction and then points himself homeward.

When Johnny enters the darkened room, it is obvious that he has succeeded in missing the party altogether. The ever-patient Mary is in bed but is definitely awake, on edge as she waits for the return of her errant husband. The use of light and shadow in this scene by the cinematographer Henry T. Sharp is particularly effective in creating an ominous feeling. As Johnny does his best to enter the room without being noticed, he is trailed by his shadow, which hovers over the walls like a large spreading inkblot, creating the effect of a monstrous creature loose in the Simms's bedroom. Yet John doesn't feel much like a monster; in fact, he doesn't feel much at all by this point in the evening. Blissfully waving his empty bottle, he cheerfully announces that he was unable to find a shop to give him a refill. He is obviously a happy drunk.

But Mary is not particularly amused. We see a close up of her lying in bed, alert, disapproving, but resigned to John's behavior. More and more, she is beginning to see that she has married a loser. Yet she still loves him, for she finally speaks to him, "They don't understand you ... but that doesn't matter." When she adds that *she* understands him, his childish — albeit inebriated — relief is evident and he finally brings forth her presents, foolishly convinced that the two of them may now at last have a happy Christmas Eve. But that is not to be: when Mary takes the umbrella that John has just given her and opens it, the scene ends on an threatening, unhappy note, as John angrily chastises her for taking such bad luck action.

The Crowd is a stunning, remarkable film, one of the best of the silent period. In its unsparingly realistic depiction of the love between two ordinary people, their quarrels, and their ultimate tragedies, it remains as touching to audiences of the twenty-first century as it was to those who saw it for the first time in 1928. Moreover, John Simms's merry evening, including his casual encounter with booze and fast women, and his subsequently cool reception by his anxious but angry wife, contribute to our feelings of empathy with John's loneliness and frustration. Like *Broken Blossoms, The Crowd* demonstrates that alcohol slowly but inexorably destroys trust, ruins reputations, and shatters relationships. Although *The Crowd* does not show us the blatant violence that is integral to the narrative of *Broken Blossoms*, nonetheless it does reveal the psychological tensions stemming from the uncertain haze brought about by alcohol.

Even contemporary reviewers of *The Crowd* saw its maturity, its realism, its uniqueness among films of the twenties. Writing in 1928, shortly after the film opened, one anonymous critic compared it to other films of the decade:

> It is an encouraging sign when the screen, beyond its technical and artistic progress, can also show an advance in social criticism, a greater penetration into the problems of our everyday life. The fairy tale, with its quick and easy realization of our wishes for wealth and love, has been worked to death in the movies. The astonishing popularity of *The Crowd* is first rate testimony to the surfeit which the ordinary screen diet has produced among picture fans.... For *The Crowd* is a study of failure, an ever hopeful and unconscious failure, but inevitably a failure.[12]

Another film historian notes: "The film's strength lies in its naturalistic simplicity, its beauty in the truth Vidor draws from the average and the commonplace. John is everyman, and Mary is everywoman. Their clothing looks as real as their surroundings— the New York City streets and tenements where Vidor took his cast and crew to maintain an ordinary sense of actuality."[13]

A tragic sidelight of this movie may be found in the fate of James Murray, whose performance as the hapless John Simms is so moving. Murray was an unknown doing extra work when director King Vidor saw him walking through the lot and thought he had the right face and build for the part of an average guy. But Vidor was worried that, although Murray looked the part, he would not be able to act, so the director ordered an unusual screen test. He picked one scene from the picture and arranged for a real set to be used for the filming of the test. He also enlisted the female lead, Eleanor Boardman (Vidor's wife at that time), to play the scene with Murray. Murray's performance was so convincing that Vidor, according to one account, was worried that Murray would not do so well in subsequent scenes. So he asked Murray to stay for more filming; throughout the day, the actors did various bits from the picture, always following the script. Vidor, his actors, and crew worked the entire Saturday; the film was printed that night and screened on Monday morning. The next day, Murray went to the studio and was offered a contract.[14]

Yet, following his promising introduction to movie stardom, Murray was unable to find any acting work comparable to what he had done in *The Crowd*. His own private battle with the white logic of alcohol haunted him for the rest of his brief life. In a surprisingly honest interview that he gave in 1933, Murray discusses his love of drinking, even in his early years in Hollywood, before he landed the lead in *The Crowd*. His description of the camaraderie associated with binges sounds much like Jack London's picture of the male-focused drinking bouts that the hard-living novelist frequently enjoyed:

> I had come out here to Hollywood, hoping to make a name for myself. I kicked around, doing extra work for some time, and then began to get a few bits. Things came easier then and I soon found myself climbing along at a fair rate of speed. When I began to make money, I found myself surrounded by lots of friends, who gladly joined in the celebrations that followed each engagement or the completion of a picture. It was "easy come, easy go—and the elbow bent" on all occasions. Oh, it was fine for a while. I thought it was great stuff to have a gang around me who patted me on the back and celebrated with me!
>
> And then I landed the lead in "The Crowd" and thought that I had arrived. But the cup that allegedly cheers had got such a hold on me that I couldn't stop — or thought I couldn't. Soon it began to be noised about that I was indulging too much. It was true, and producers lost faith in me. I am not blaming them. I should have known better. Finally, I couldn't get a job at all. A few of my real friends tried to help me throw off the habit. They couldn't. So I wound up in the Los Angeles County Jail.[15]

After two weeks in jail, Murray was transferred to a prison camp at Big Pine. After four months at the camp, he was released on parole and married actress Marion Sayers who, he hoped, would bring love, comfort, and stability to his life. Then director William Wellman offered Murray what might have led to another chance for stardom: a part in a Warners picture. This role, in turn, enabled Murray to find other screen work. Thus, by the time of this 1933 interview, Murray had completed a number of films and was convinced that his luck had changed. Determined to turn his life around, he thought he had his alcoholism licked:

> No more of the old-time drinking friends. I learned my lesson. They are with you to help you while you have the bankroll—then they are gone, looking for another pal with a pay envelope. I have only one thought now— to make good for my own self-respect, for my wife who helped me, and for the producers who have shown faith in me and have given me another chance. My money goes into the bank now. My evenings are spent at home and quietly. They will be from now on. It took a session at Big Pine to do it, but it has been done.[16]

Yet Murray's resolution to spend those quiet evenings at home did not last long. Though he made twenty-eight movies from 1928 until his death in 1936, most were mediocre, second-half-of-a-double-bill features. At one point in 1934, Murray, desperate for a drink, was even reduced to asking King Vidor for money to buy liquor. But Vidor refused and told Murray to pull himself together, advice that Murray apparently ignored.[17] On July 11,

1936, eight years after James Murray had made such a splendid impression in *The Crowd*, he died by drowning, his body found floating in a New York City river. Whether suicide or accident would never be known.

In hindsight, then, there is something sadly ironic about the magazine interview that James Murray gave in 1927, shortly after he had completed *The Crowd*—even before the picture had premiered:

> It's the kind of part I've always wanted to do, although I certainly would not have hesitated even if it had not been. It does make it even more wonderful anyway, that I've longed to do on the screen the simple, natural, human, ordinary roles.[18]

Likewise, this 1927 interviewer offers the following commentary about the difficulty of playing such a role as Murray attempted in *The Crowd*:

> The story is rather a departure for Vidor. It is an ordinary story of ordinary American life and ordinary people, of an average American lad. If it sounds like an easy role, you don't know the show business. To act perfectly natural on either stage or screen is the sure test of genius. The greatest actors are those who don't act. But the ability to "live," instead of to act, in front of the camera, comes, as a rule, only after years and years of experience. Yet James Murray walks right into a difficult role and plays it to the utter satisfaction of the director and every other member of the cast.
>
> He was born for the screen, because he is so perfectly natural.[19]

Perhaps James Murray's very "naturalness" as the modern, luckless, weak-willed Everyman was indeed his poignant undoing.

Joan Crawford and Anita Page: The Noble Dame and the Hedonistic Flapper

Another depiction of alcohol in the 1920s is demonstrated in Jazz Age flapper novels and movies. F. Scott Fitzgerald popularized the flapper in such novels as *This Side of Paradise* (1920) and the classic study of the Roaring Twenties, *The Great Gatsby* (1925). Jay Gatsby is the quintessential boot-legger: the man who hosts lavish parties at his mansion on Long Island, complete with Prohibition booze — most of it made from wood alcohol. *The Great Gatsby* is filled with vacuous partygoers for whom time is measured out in droplets of gin. Such riotous living is also found in movies of the period. Audiences were doubtless titillated by pre-Code scenes of young men and women drinking, undressing, and obviously enjoying illicit sex. In contrast to the down-to-earth, dependable girl Mary Simms, as portrayed by Eleanor Boardman in *The Crowd*, party girls predominate in movies such as *Our Dancing Daughters* (1928), *The Docks of New York* (1928), *Our Modern Maidens* (1929), and *No Limit* (1931). Joan Crawford and Anita

Page, two eminently flamboyant actresses whom no one would mistake for ordinary, dependable housewives, starred in a number of late-silent and early-talking movies in which Prohibition liquor flowed and any thoughts of consequences were carelessly cast aside.

A late silent film, *Our Modern Maidens*, which has a pretty racy scenario by Josephine Lovett, opens with a shot of several careening autos filled with so many young revelers that it is difficult to tell who, if anyone, is driving. At the center of this wild car ride is a smiling Joan Crawford (Billie), who is gyrating wildly from a sitting position atop one of these weaving cars. All of these happy youths are enjoying an end-of-school party— though, in truth, the joy riders look decidedly too old for prom night festivities.

The party continues on a train, where Crawford and one of her school chums, the vigorous, imposing Anita Page (Kentucky), discuss the fun they will have trying to catch a man. Their serious conversation is interrupted by a porter, who carries a tray filled with drinks as he moves through the train, announcing via a title card, "Lunch is poured!" A few moments later, the revelers have been magically transported to a different setting and are dancing at a party, where Anita Page and Douglas Fairbanks Jr. (Gil) have decided to ignore for the moment the awkward fact that Fairbanks and Crawford are engaged. They start on this journey to obliviousness by drinking cocktails; Fairbanks, caught in the passion of the instant, proposes, "Let's drink— to romance!"

However, in the course of the evening, they apparently engage in other activities besides drinking, for the next day, both are filled with remorse. They feel especially guilty about betraying Crawford, though Page clearly understands the value of equivocation and moral relativism when she admonishes Fairbanks not to tell Crawford of their dreadful deed, lest Crawford be "hurt" by the news. And we are to surmise that it is *drink* that has brought them face to face with this terrible dilemma, this loss of their innocence. What's more, their physical attributes emphasize not only their wistful naïveté but also their healthy, energetic lust. Both actors are blonde, fair-skinned, and well built, with a cheerful attitude that conveys the possibility of a good deal of athletic prowess in everything they attempt, including their exercises of the previous evening.

Nonetheless, alcohol and sexual exercise lead to drastic consequences, including a self-effacing, self-destructive final gesture on the part of Crawford by the movie's end. Blissfully ignorant of the Page/Fairbanks liaison, Crawford marries Fairbanks, while Page has an emotional crack up at the wedding as she bids Fairbanks a hysterical farewell. Witnessing this odd scene, Crawford—the concerned friend—rushes to Page's side with a comforting cocktail to ease the distress. Remembering that earlier cocktail, the one that had brought about her downfall, Page bitterly lifts her glass and mockingly toasts a reprise, "To Romance." She finally hurls the glass down and collapses on a nearby settee, her sobs reiterating her dilemma. Then, in a provocative gesture, Crawford embraces her from behind and strokes her hair. Crawford's next move is inexplicable and intrusive, reflecting an odd hunch, but it furthers the plot; she goes to Page's purse, opens it, and finds a doctor's appointment card therein. She notes that the name on it is prefaced by the title *Mrs.*, so she draws the obvious conclusion: that Page is pregnant. Rather than being angry and defensive at the fact that her privacy has been so blatantly violated, Page is contrite and apologetic: "I didn't want you to know, Billie! I didn't want you ever to know!" Here Fairbanks enters. He seems to be something of a dunderhead; it is unclear from Page's next remark to him whether he had known of Page's interesting condition: "Gil, I tried to be so brave ... and now I've spoiled it all." While he stands around looking pained and indecisive, Crawford turns noble:

CRAWFORD: Kentucky, dear ... if you'd only spoken ... even an hour ago.

PAGE: I'm not going to spoil anything. You and Gil must go away ... and be happy.

At this command from his former lover, Fairbanks appears to agree, having already decided that a legal bird in the hand is worth one little fledgling who is willing to allow him to fly away. He does condescend to grab his former lover's arms and embrace her, while murmuring, "You poor little brave kid."

Ah, but here comes Crawford to the rescue. Even as the photographers are waiting to take pictures of the happy newlyweds before they leave on their honeymoon, Crawford announces to her father that she must go away without Gil. Her reason is self-annihilating and reflective of the double sexual standard pervasive even in the ostensibly liberated 1920s; she claims that Gil has just discovered something terribly disgraceful about her: so disgraceful, in fact, that he could not possibly have her as his wife now. We are left to guess the nature of this disgrace, but it clearly has nothing to do with drink, drugs, bank robbery, shoplifting, or even murder. The disgrace would naturally involve sexual misconduct outside the bounds of matrimony. Never mind that Fairbanks is hardly innocent in this realm of endeavor; it is the woman who always pays. And Crawford's father is naturally, respectably, horrified at news of this unnamed "disgrace": he informs her that she must find her own way out of the scandal.

So Crawford gets the marriage annulled, goes on a groomless honeymoon to Paris, and is reunited with an old suitor (Rod La Roque), whom we assume that she will eventually marry. Yet anyone who has bothered to follow the plot of this movie will remember that this old flame had previously tried, in an unromantic gesture, to rape Crawford, so he is hardly an ideal substitute for her previous groom. But despite the apparently upbeat ending, Crawford is the one who ultimately suffers for the sin of having an airhead girlfriend and a faithless fiancé; she will thus undoubtedly spend the rest of her days trapped in a horribly violent marriage.

Contemporary reviews of the movie were favorable. Interestingly, popular magazines downplayed the role of Prohibition liquor in the film. One reviewer called it "this vivid picture of ultra-modern youth, as the movies see our younger folk." This same writer also believed that the movie was unconventional enough to "undoubtedly create quite a stir." Crawford earns most of the reviewer's praise:

> Joan plays the role she does so well, that of a pampered play-girl bored with the world her rich father gives her to play with. The climax of the pictured is based on a thoroughly original and unique situation.[20]

At the time of the release of *Our Modern Maidens*, Joan Crawford had been a featured player at MGM for four years, and she was one of the top box office attractions of 1929. This was her last silent picture. MGM took a chance that the movie would be a hit with young people, even though 1929 was a transitional year between the silents and sound, and "most silent films were getting a quick playoff as remnants of a fast-dying breed."[21] In addition, the MGM publicity department took advantage of the fact that, off screen, Crawford and Fairbanks Jr. were an "item." In fact, they had officially announced their engagement shortly before *Our Modern Maidens* went into production. Thus, it was hoped that this real-life romance would spark added interest in the duo and encourage the public to see the film.[22] A real love match was considered a more effective sales gimmick than the movie's display of illicit sex and illegal booze.

Following the release of *Our Modern Maidens*, one fan magazine even included an advertisement for a fashion accessory known as "Priscilla Jewelry." Featured prominently in the ad is a large picture of Crawford and Fairbanks in formal wedding attire: he looking stiff and awkward and staring straight ahead; she looking demure and pleased, with one hand resting gently in his white-gloved hand. To the right of the happy newlyweds is the headline: "The Preference of 'Our Modern Maidens.'" Just beneath this is a statement signed by none other than Joan Crawford herself: "My Priscilla Wedding Ring is my most cherished possession."[23] At the bottom of the ad is a photograph of the wedding scene from *Our Modern Maidens*, which, we are reminded, was "produced by Metro-Goldwyn-Mayer Studios."[24] The studio publicists fail to mention, however, that the cinematic union of Crawford/Fairbanks is a very brief one.

By the late 1920s, Crawford's costar, Anita Page, had become almost as popular as Crawford. Another 1929 fan magazine capitalized on Page's appearance in *Our Modern Maidens* with a large photo of Page. Again, there is no mention of alcohol's part in the moral lapse Page suffers in the movie. Instead, the caption reminds the 1929 reader of Page's latest venture: "*One of Our Modern Maidens is Anita Page, wholesome and sparkling blond beauty, whose current picture is the Metro-Goldwyn-Mayer production of that name.*"[25] Like Crawford, Page was well known to audiences, largely on the strength of her appearance in a similar role the previous year. In 1928, Page, as a party girl named Ann, had portrayed another capricious flapper girlfriend to Joan Crawford's noble dame (Diana) in the silent *Our Dancing Daughters* (1928). Only in this one, Page is not at all "wholesome and sparkling." This celebration of flappers finds her more cunning, more decidedly opportunistic and decidedly evil, as she snatches another attractive bachelor Ben Blaine (John Mack Brown) out from under Crawford's gracious, decent countenance. Furthermore, although the character of Ann is still an adolescent, she is also a drunk. Some film historians have called Page's performance the best in this film. According to one critic: "Anita managed to bring a touch of pathos to the ruthless golddigger with limited moral education who is the product of an equally materialistic mother. Her sordid life ends in tragedy when she goes on a drunken spree."[26]

Indeed, liquor is more evident in this picture than in *Our Modern Maidens*. The flimsy plot of *Our Dancing Daughters* centers around partying, dancing, drinking, or the planning of the next party, dance, or round of drinks. As in *Our Modern Maidens*, Crawford here looks frantic yet controlled, completely at ease with herself and with her muscular body. In fact, in this picture, she looks more like a football player — albeit a balletic one — than does John Mack Brown, who was, in real life, an ex-football star for the University of Alabama. Moreover, as in *Our Modern Maidens*, virtue triumphs in the end for Crawford. But she has an excruciatingly painful journey before she finally gets there.

The contrast between Crawford and Page is clear from the outset. Though both are wealthy party girls who love to drink, Crawford is livelier, more openly rebellious. Page is quiet, calculating, and devious, with an air of innocent, clinging passivity that she hopes will get her a millionaire husband. Though both young women are seen in these pre-Code days in various stages of undress all the while fiddling with hosiery and undergarments, once dressed, Crawford appears more demure. Page's clothing is provocative, lower cut, looser, and looks as though it might fall off momentarily were she to make a sudden movement. Whereas Crawford is open about her drinking — in the first scene she swigs the contents of four cocktail glasses in about ten seconds— Page is a sly drinker. Upon their first meeting, when John Mack Brown offers Page a drink, she replies disingenuously, "No thanks, I *never* drink." At this remark, Page's brother — who also enjoys getting tipsy — whispers to Crawford, "She just *inhales*."

At first, John Mack Brown enjoys Crawford's healthy, spirited, unpretentious joie de vivre. As a sign that both understand there is more to life than smoking, drinking, and dancing, they engage in some out-of-doors lovemaking. Crawford is certain that Brown now belongs to her. But Brown switches allegiance quickly; his next outdoor scene is with Page, who is all wilting gentility: "You were sweet to walk with me, Ben. I was afraid to come out alone —" Just what Page has to fear in this non-threatening pastoral setting is not clear. We know that she is not agoraphobic, so perhaps she is terrified because she sees no liquor on the horizon. In his infatuation with Page, Brown seems as thickheaded as Fairbanks in *Our Modern Maidens*. But he pays for his blundering stupidity when he marries Page and too late discovers that she ignores her marriage vows, which she sees only as an inconvenient legality hampering her efforts to play and drink with other men.

One evening, not long after her wedding to the benighted Brown, she arrives drunk at a party given by one of the sophisticated crowd with whom she has always amused herself. She is escorted by Freddie (Edward Nugent), a weak-willed, callow, but handy fellow, who is as potted as she. It is in these, the last scenes of this picture, that we can see why Anita Page was such a popular actress of the time, one who was receiving hundreds of fan letters each week by 1929. Here she gives a realistic interpretation of an exceedingly intoxicated, desperately unhappy young woman who fears that she might be losing her grip on everything she has tried so hard to grab and keep for herself. Furthermore, while it might appear to a modern viewer — one unaccustomed to the broad gestures of the silent era — that Page overplays her hysterical role, it must be remembered that the character of Ann is quite young, is spoiled and selfish, and is accustomed to taking what she wants. Therefore, the fact that she acts like an overwrought teenager is very much in keeping with what we have already learned about her personality. In fact, Page was only eighteen at the time of filming; her real age and her onscreen age were probably meant to be identical.

Like a jealous adolescent, then, Page reacts with fury when she discovers Crawford and Brown sitting together at the party, having a cozy conversation. To all who will listen, she rails against her husband and the intruder Crawford, mocking Crawford as the "saintly Diana." Her clothing

Enjoying Prohibition liquor is Joan Crawford as Diana, the Jazz Age flapper in *Our Dancing Daughters* (MGM, 1928). Helping her to a cocktail is Nils Asther as Norman. Also eager to join in the party and to entertain Diana are Gordon Wescott (center) and Johnny Mack Brown, who plays Ben — a terrifically shallow fellow who eventually marries Diana (Photofest).

highlights her desire for the spotlight. She is wearing a loose-fitting, white chemise sewn from sparkling fabric; in addition, her very expensive jewelry glitters in the artificial light. Finally, her blonde hair sets off her appearance as a perverse avenging angel. Wobbling on spiked heels, arms flailing, she continues her tirade, even as Brown tries to grab her and prevent his errant wife from toppling. Freddie, who might have averted the coming tragedy, refuses to take her away, protesting that he doesn't want the scandal.

At last, the party breaks up. Only a few of the crowd remain. Among them are the recently married Bea (Dorothy Sebastian) and Norman (Nils Asther). Although these two belong to the same social set as the others present, Norman is something of a prig who has condescended to marry Bea, in spite of the fact that she has admitted to him that she is a loose woman with a "past." Bea tries to enlist Norman's help in getting Page home, but Page is now in a very precarious position. Standing at the top of a long flight of stairs, Page sways unsteadily, all the while still vainly trying to maintain an air of wounded virtue. Some terrific camera work accompanies this next scene, as we shift from a shot of Page, out of control on the landing, to a point of view shot from Page's perspective: at the bottom of the stairs are three cleaning ladies, scrubbing the floor. Perhaps they are meant to be a reminder of the Three Furies, the three avenging deities of Greek mythology: all women, all meant to punish sinners.

If they are indeed sent to earth to punish sinners, these ladies do an admirable job with Page. At first, she taunts them from her unstable spot several feet above them. A low angle shot now focuses on Page as she calls out to them: "Hey—why are you working? Haven't you any daughters—pretty daughters?" She sits unsteadily on the top stair and continues her exhortation: "Pretty daughters—doll 'em up—a rich man wants his money's worth!" Then she boasts that she was given everything, while poor little Diana had nothing. Now once again standing, Page is propped up by Norman and Bea. Truth to tell, however, they do only a halfhearted job of protecting her, as though they are tired of her self-absorbed tantrums. And, of course, the inevitable happens—something that we have been expecting since Page first appeared at the top of the stairs. When Norman and Bea look away for a moment in order to consult one another about how best to handle the obstreperous flapper, Page tumbles down the stairs. She is, of course, instantly killed: a circumstance that allows the noble, ever patient Crawford to have access to Brown, the not-so-bereaved widower. But before this happy conclusion can come about, one of the three cleaning ladies has the final word on the cosmic irony that has overtaken and defeated Page. Examining Page's lifeless arms and the glistening jewelry thereon, the charwoman sagely observes: "Them won't do her no good—now." Page's excellent acting in this climactic scene is underscored by the fact that the real-life Page was, in fact, a teetotaler who simulated intoxication throughout the movie by imagining that she was dizzy.[27]

Although hers is not a familiar name today, Anita Page was a popular actress of the mid– to late 1920s; fan magazines were filled with photographs of the blonde, attractive, vivacious young woman, who was usually fashioned as a wholesome girl-next-door type, completely devoted to her parents. In fact, Page was promoted as the antithesis of her onscreen persona as a hard-drinking, high-living flapper. Once again, in its promotion of a popular star, MGM failed to capitalize on the tantalizing aspects of bootleg liquor's destructive force. Rather, studio heads wanted to reassure movie fans that their stars were, after all, just plain folks. Perhaps such emphasis on wholesomeness was the result of the industry's efforts to clean up its image following the early 1920s drug and sex scandals, which involved such popular stars as Fatty Arbuckle and Wallace Reid. In any event, one

1929 magazine reports that Anita Page is a dutiful daughter from a respectable professional family. She keeps herself fit, gets 9 1/2 hours sleep every night, and according to her father, who is described as a successful businessman: "Every day that she doesn't work I take her golfing with me."[28] We are also informed that Anita adores being an actress. Note the reference here to *Broadway Melody*, an Academy Award winning musical in which Anita had just starred as Bessie Love's sister — and in which Anita had taken Bessie's fiancé (Charles King) away from her.

> Anita likes the movies. She's seen "Broadway Melody" eight times. She never goes out alone. Her father is always with her. Not even her cousin may take her unchaperoned. It's all a business proposition. It's to make a success in pictures. And Anita is satisfied. She knows they are right.[29]

Unlike her sometime costar Joan Crawford, Page would ultimately embody this wholesome image by choosing a private life over a public one; she retired from movies, married only once: a Naval officer — Rear Admiral Herschel A. House — had two daughters, and presumably settled into a quiet, domestic lifestyle.[30] As of this writing (2005), Page is still alive. Crawford, who died in 1977 at the age of 73, would eventually have five husbands; Douglas Fairbanks Jr. was her second, a fact not mentioned in the gushing 1929 publicity for *Our Modern Maidens*. In real life, then, the Noble Dame and the Hedonistic Flapper appear to have been the opposites of their 1920s onscreen personas.

"No Profession. No Belief. No Limit."

One of the most darkly cynical films of the early 1930s is Frank Capra's *The Miracle Woman* (1931). As with *Our Modern Maidens* and *Our Dancing Daughters*, its major characters appear trapped in an absurdly nihilistic world not of their own making. When Bob Hornsby (the appropriately-named, devilish Sam Hardy) encourages Florence Fallon (Barbara Stanwyck) to take advantage of her knowledge of the Bible and go into business with him so that they might bilk thousands out of their cash by selling religion, she quickly agrees. He tells her that their private motto should be: "No Profession. No Belief. No Limit." And so, broadcasting her uplifting message on radio station GOD, Florence becomes a national star.

In Hornsby, we see most clearly the nihilism that underlies much of the film. He is a crass exploiter who tries to rape Florence, who murders a blackmailer and gets away with it, and who holds a wild party to which he invites old pals—carnival clowns— and lavishes bootleg booze on these guests. The party scene provides a particularly grotesque centerpiece to the movie. The guests are attired in costumes that make them look like jesters or the joker in a card deck. One reveler in a low-cut black dress rides on the backs of two men who are costumed like an ass. This partygoer later gives a drunken oration on the beauties of White Rock over ginger ale. (These were two popular mixers; White Rock, a bottled water, was ordinarily advertised as effervescent, flowing from natural springs.)

Although Florence ultimately renounces her lies, joins the Salvation Army, and promises to marry a blind Great War aviator John Carson (David Manners, in a beautifully understated performance that could easily have turned maudlin), we have no assurance that their world together will be any better than it was when Florence was ruled by Hornsby. Certainly, Florence will have less money coming in, living on Carson's government pension as she must. And by the film's end, we see that Hornsby is still rich: that he has continued on his self-promoting way, neatly avoiding arrest for murder. In this world, the evil remain unpunished; the Hornsbys and their friends—the bootleggers and their customers—continue to enjoy their illegal activities.

Lost Victims of the Great War and After

Another group of unfortunates depicted in movies of this period are the military of the Great War and immediately after. Three outstanding pictures of this genre are the silent *Wings* (1927), *All Quiet on the Western Front* (1930), and the part-talking *Men Without Women* (1930). All have the same tone of fatalistic determinism characteristic of naturalism. All show young, doomed fighters enjoying alcoholic pleasures as a prelude to disaster. *Wings* contains a superb scene that features World War I aviators drinking in a nightclub in France. The episode is made especially poignant by the viewer's knowledge that these young flyers are likely to be killed very soon when they take on the formidable German air power. Highlighting the scene are the frantic efforts of Red Cross ambulance driver Clara Bow, desperately trying to tell the staggeringly drunk Charles "Buddy" Rogers that his unit is being called out, even as she attempts to pull him away from the clutches of a young woman.

Likewise, the formidable Germans are the focus of *All Quiet on the Western Front*. Like their American foes, these young men are destined for aborted lives. By the time the soldiers settle into a bar in France, they have already endured the spirit-numbing experience of the western front: the sight of comrades ripped apart so that only their hands are left clinging to barbed wire; the hopeless terror of watching gas shells drop into the earth; the struggle with hunger and lice; the knowledge that the enemy soldiers they are engaged in slaughtering are mere teenagers about their own age. But once they gather into the bar and join in singing while they drink mug after mug of beer, they can briefly leave the horror behind. Two young comrades—Paul Baumer (Lew Ayres) and Himmelstoss (John Wray)—swear to one another that they will get desperately, fully drunk; in addition, while thinking of other pleasures they have lost, they see on the wall a poster featuring a beautiful French dancer. They rise unsteadily in order to offer a toast to the young lady, their faces shown only as the reflection in a mirror hanging next to the poster. Carried away by the passion of the moment, Ayres voices the hope that this lady might be available to cheer them up. However, Wray reminds his friend that the poster is dated May 1917, which was four months earlier, and that the woman is therefore a long way off by now. The mise-en-scène established here is evocative: the mirrored reflection of the two young soldiers, mugs of beer poised in the air next to an imaginary girl never to be found, becomes a symbol of the ephemera of their doomed lives—a lesson about the futility of war.

Another visually stunning film, which centers its action around sailors who will eventually be briefly trapped in a submarine beneath the China Sea, is John Ford's *Men Without Women*. But before the sailors descend on this fateful trip, they visit a Shanghai bar where they drink and amuse themselves with opium-addicted prostitutes. Their young, eager, hopeful faces are highlighted in a tracking shot that takes the viewer the length of the bar. These sailors are there to forget, at least briefly, that soon they must descend ninety feet under the China Sea. At one point, their radioman (Stuart Erwin) reminds them that there are only two hours remaining for them to get drunk. We later remember this scene when the young sailors in the submarine collide with a ship and are stranded, their air and their lives slowly running out.

Falling and Spinning: The Last Flight of the Lost Generation

One of the most memorable motion pictures of the early 1930s tells the harrowing story of what happens to those who have somehow managed to survive the Great War. *The Last Flight* (1931) is an excellent film, deserving of more attention than it has ordinarily received. The story was adapted for the screen by John Monk Saunders, who had originally written it as a magazine serial, then as a novel called *Single Lady*, and then adapted it for the stage under the title *Nikki*. In order to give his wife Fay Wray a part in the stage adaptation, Saunders had taken one of the male roles in the story and made it into a woman's part. Also in the stage production was a young Englishman named Archie Leach, who played Cary Lockwood; he would soon take the first name of that character when he signed with Paramount and became Cary Grant.[31] Although *Nikki* ran for only thirty-nine performances, closing in November 1931,[32] and the movie version is seldom seen today, *The Last Flight* contains some fine acting, trenchant dialogue, and a feel for the disillusioned Lost Generation of the 1920s.

Much of the action of *The Last Flight* occurs in Paris just after the Great War. Since there is no Prohibition in France, legal liquor is in evidence everywhere: alcohol is the central focus of everyone's lives, a reason for living and, with two of the characters, a reason for dying. The four flyers (David Manners, Richard Barthelmess, John Mack Brown, and Elliott Nugent), whose odyssey is chronicled in the film, are scarred both physically and psychologically from the terrors of war in the air. Following the Armistice, after they have come crashing back down to earth, they embark on another last flight, this one not in the fields of France but in the streets of Paris. As they attempt to flee from the world as well as from themselves, they make their final descent through a mist of alcoholic forgetfulness. As they do so, they meet Nikki (Helen Chandler), a wealthy American who is as aimless, rootless, and airborne as they. John Monk Saunders's screenplay keeps the action moving, as he traces the fragile lives of these five Lost Generation members. Saunders himself knew much about the impermanence of existence, for his own career was tragically cut short in 1940 when, at age 44, he succumbed to alcohol and drug addiction by committing suicide. While it is tempting to think of this movie as nothing more than a minor imitation of Hemingway's *The Sun Also Rises* (1926), the film is worthy of attention for its own considerable virtues.

And included among its most distinctive virtues are the excellent performances by all of the leading actors. Helen Chandler is especially touching as the lonely Nikki. One contemporary reviewer observes: "Helen Chandler, excellent as Nikki, gives the picture its chief charm."[33] In fact, Chandler moves far beyond charm. She projects pain without self-pity; desire without lust; love without possessiveness. She looks as though she might collapse at one unkind word, but it is Nikki who holds together the four tragic veterans. They become her protectors even as she becomes their redeemer. With a voice that seems always on the verge of breaking apart and soundlessly shattering, Chandler's Nikki nonetheless communicates beautifully: soothing and comforting the broken souls and wasted bodies of her comrades as she accompanies them in search of a meaning on their last flight. Though she frequently speaks in non sequiturs and though, as Barthelmess maintains, she is the "kind of girl who sits down on phonograph records," Nikki is straightforward, honest, and vulnerable: three qualities that appeal to the world-weary flyers. She keeps two turtles in her bathtub that she lovingly tends; these small, simple creatures in need of protection give the soldiers another connection to a world that has sadly gone by them. In short, Nikki is their lost innocence, and they reach out to her because she provides hope within their moral vacuum. And in the background is the omnipresent liquor to help them all forget where it is they are going and where it was they have been.

Where the four flyers have recently been is a military hospital. The movie's story begins in 1919; Shep Lambert (David Manners) and Cary Lockwood (Richard Barthelmess) are leaving the hospital to go out into a very inhospitable world, one that has no place for them any longer. When Cary asks Shep what he plans to do now, Shep replies that he intends to "Get tight. Stay tight." So they pick up two other recently released fellow soldiers, Bill (John Mack Brown) and Francis (Elliott Nugent), and head for the bars of Paris. According to one critic, these are "four survivors who choose a life of cosmopolitan expatriation rather than face a return to their families and conventional American values."[34] In fact, we know nothing of the families that these veterans have left behind nor are we given any clue as to what such "conventional American values" might be. These soldiers seem not to be rebelling against any particular values; rather, they appear disembodied, floating without anchor and without roots; nevertheless, in a very earthly fashion, each of these veterans is maimed in some way. Shep has developed a facial tic that causes him to have eye trouble. Cary is extremely self-conscious because he has suffered burns on his hands and can no longer do simple but important tasks, such as hold a cocktail glass with only one hand. Before the war, Bill was a college football hero; now he has an irresistible urge to tackle four-footed animals. Francis carries a chiming watch because he is always dozing off and is convinced that he has an appointment somewhere. All eagerly follow the resolution found in the words Shep had vowed to Cary on Armistice Day; all proceed to get tight and stay tight.

Shortly after these four lost souls arrive in Paris, Nikki becomes their companion in this drinking debauchery. They discover her in a bar, where her gaze is fixed on a cocktail glass that she is tenderly holding. She informs them that the glass contains teeth, which she has told a kind gentleman that she will hold for safekeeping. She relates this bizarre story with no trace of surprise or self-consciousness. By the time the stranger has returned for his teeth, the four flyers have adopted Nikki has a kind of lucky mascot and insist on accompanying her back to her hotel room so that they may resume drinking there. Joining them is a fifth man, Frink (Walter Byron). Frink is a newspaper reporter who persists in attempted sexual assaults on Nikki and who consequently represents a threat to Nikki's innocence. In fact, a major source of tension in the film lies in the conflict between Nikki's four protectors and the outsider who hangs around in hopes of finding Nikki at last compliant. When all six land in Nikki's room, Bill and Cary dissuade the reporter from his amorous advances by placing on each of his hands, palms down, a full cocktail glass. Their disabling gesture is only one of a series they impose on the predatory reporter as they try to preserve the virtue of this seemingly lost lady. Furthermore, Frink's awkward pose vis-à-vis the cocktail glasses carries symbolic significance: the indefensible position in which he has been placed implies just how paralyzed all are by alcohol.

A further illustration of the paralyzing effects of booze, of the catatonic states in which all of them aimlessly wander, may be seen in the timepieces associated with a number of the characters. Francis keeps winding his watch so that it will chime and awaken him, but he has nowhere to go and nothing to do when he gets there. Bill notes that, although all of Nikki's clocks are set at eleven o'clock, he himself prefers to be frozen at two o'clock a.m. Like the self-destructive novelist, F. Scott Fitzgerald, all of them have their own individual dark nights of the soul where time has stopped, and now all they can see within the void is the white logic of alcohol.

And yet, in the character of Cary as played by Richard Barthelmess, we can see beyond the booze to a wounded but cautious, sensitive soul. A 1931 reviewer of *The Last Flight* wrote to criticize Barthelmess's Cary, arguing that when Shep, Bill, and Francis disappear from the movie, "the picture lets down suddenly. Johnny Mack Brown, David Manners, and Elliott Nugent, Dick's pals, overshadow him."[35] While it is true that Barthelmess has a less showy role than his costars, his performance gives greater depth and greater insight into the emptiness of their lives. Like the world of his comrades, his is also a society of heedless disillusionment and low expectations. But unlike the other veterans, Cary is a sensitive fellow who wants desperately to understand what has gone wrong. Indeed, he offers a sharp contrast to the cynicism of Shep, to the utterly foolish bravado of Bill, and to the brooding, melancholy vacancy of Francis. And Nikki, for all of her seeming flightiness, senses this intensity, this caring side of the aptly named Cary. Consequently, it is Cary whom she finally falls in love with.

Yet initially Cary wants to flee from Nikki; her naïve frankness exacerbates the pain that stems from his brittle ego. Nevertheless, when he decides to run away from her by going to Portugal, the others refuse to let him off so easily and follow him to Lisbon. Their train journey gives them another opportunity to drink; it also provides Frink with another chance to attempt an assault on Nikki when he follows her into her compartment. Here the four comrades heed her screams for help and rescue her from Frink's advances, but their conflict with Frink is not quite over; that will come just a little later. The gently confused Francis will be the violent finish of Frink, yet at this point, on their train journey, Francis is determined to fulfill the mission that Nikki has assigned him: he is to care for the turtles by sprinkling them every few minutes. This duty Francis performs quite seriously and assiduously by applying small amounts from a champagne bottle to their shells. He is determined to do his job well and to give the best possible care to these little creatures.

Once they arrive in Lisbon, all six immediately head to a bar. Shep, who seems to be the heaviest drinker among a group of professional inebriates, can no longer remember what day or what month it is. This time, their drinking is a prelude to their attendance at a bullfight. Bill, still reliving his glory as a football half back (a position that John Mack Brown actually played for the University of Alabama), vows that he can prove his all–American courage by tackling a bull. Having previously brought down a carriage horse in Paris, Bill is convinced that a bull will present no problems either. But Bill discovers that a horse and a bull are not the same; he is fatally gored, though he has time enough left in the hospital to joke with the companions who have come to tell him goodbye.

However, they do not linger too long over their farewells, for a short time later the five remaining expatriates find themselves at a carnival, and once again they are getting drunk. Liquor seems to prevail at all of the public places they visit in Paris and Lisbon. While they are temporarily without a drink in their hands, they visit a shooting gallery where Francis demonstrates that, drunk or sober, his aim is dead center. And, when Frink pulls a real gun on the group, Francis reveals that his aim is no less accurate when it is directed at people, for he shoots and kills the troublesome Frink. Sadly, Shep gets caught in the line of fire, and he too is mortally wounded by the zombie-like, automatic actions of Francis, who subsequently disappears into the crowd, never to be seen again. And Shep lingers in a taxi with Nikki and Cary, dying little by little, accepting this fate, even pleased about it. As he ruefully tells his friends, "It is the best thing that ever happened to me."

So all that remain are Nikki and Cary. The final scene of the picture shows them seated together in a train compartment; furthermore, as if both realize the significance of their status as the last of the lost and wounded, neither one is drinking. In a rare moment of openness, Cary allows himself to show grief and compassion for Shep; he even lets Nikki see the comforting letter that he is writing to Shep's mother. Moreover, both Nikki and Cary agree that Bill, Shep, and Francis — wherever he might be — are now all at peace. Cary tells Nikki that Bill doubtless had been a success in the hospital, where he could proudly display his new blue shorts. These were among the last items Bill had bragged about shortly before his friends had left his room — and had left him there to die. Sadly, regretfully, Cary suggests that perhaps now Bill will "tackle the angel Gabriel and be a big success again." Of Shep, Cary confides to Nikki his melancholy resignation that Shep's death was, in fact, an unconscious suicide: "Shep Lambert spent his life in the war. He had died once. He was ready to die again." Cary's final observation is reserved for Francis. Like Hornsby in *The Miracle Woman*, Francis has demonstrated a type of criminal success seldom found in early films. In the shooting of Frink, he has murdered with impunity. Cary muses on the killer's possible fate: "Maybe Francis will forget to wind his chiming watch one day and go on sleeping — till the end."

In this final scene, Cary and Nikki have tentatively expressed their love for each other while their train takes them on to a possibly more hopeful future. Perhaps it will be a future without alcohol. Perhaps not. But in the deaths of their friends, they have lost an important part of themselves and of their past. As *The Last Flight* constantly reminds us, there are some things that can never be reclaimed.

3

Gangsters and Prohibition

... we have found indubitable evidences ... that Prohibition has worked quite well. Prohibition ought to be far better enforced than it is, and ought to have more public sentiment behind it. But what has been accomplished is substantial, and the present public sentiment in favor of going forward, not backward, is, to say the least, strong and determined.

— Irving Fisher, *Prohibition at Its Worst*, 1927

Prohibition in the United States became law at midnight on Saturday, January 17, 1920. The National Prohibition Act, more commonly known as the Volstead Act, set forth how the rules were to be enforced by Congress and the states. It did not take long, however, for the lawless to discover just what a great business opportunity could be had in the illegal booze racket. At 12:01 a.m. on January 17, 1920, a shed at a Chicago railroad yard became the target of six gun-wielding hoodlums who broke in, tied up the guard, and carried off two alcohol-filled freight cars; the liquor was valued at $100,000.[1] "Shortly afterward, across town, four barrels of grain alcohol were stolen from a government warehouse. In a third incident in the predawn hours of that first official 'Dry' day, a gang hijacked a truck full of whiskey that had just been stolen from another site. Already, the gangsters were feeding on each other."[2] Moreover, in an excellent illustration of the way in which art imitates life, gangster movies of those Prohibition days demonstrate just how deadly such warfare between rival gangs could be.

Is This the End of Rico?

One of the most famous of the early talking gangster pictures from the Prohibition period is *Little Caesar* (1931). It is also one of the best. It has excellent cinematography that fosters a good, impressionistic feel for the era, and some fine acting — chiefly from Edward G. Robinson, Douglas Fairbanks Jr., and Glenda Farrell. Moreover, individual scenes stand out as memorable set pieces. These scenes are combined with effective use of jump cuts to give a sharp staccato feel, corresponding to the repeated gunfire that underscores the action.

For instance, the opening shot is powerful yet understated. A car enters a gas station and a figure steps out. It is Edward G. Robinson's Little Caesar, seen in a long shot. He fires at the station owner, apparently killing him. Cut to a shot of the car in which there is someone waiting for him. Then we jump to the next scene, where we see the stick-up men themselves, Caesar Enrico Bandello (Edward G. Robinson) and Joe Massara (Douglas Fairbanks Jr.), eating spaghetti at a diner and bemoaning their unhappy lot as petty, small time hoodlums. They know that there is little profit in gas station holdups. Like his later counterparts in gangsterdom, Robinson's Caesar is ambitious for more, so he heads for Chicago to try to ease his way into an organized, efficient, lucrative mob. He takes with him the reluctant Fairbanks, who has promised himself that he will go straight and return to his profession as a dancer once he has made some big money.

Indeed, the city offers much that is alluring to these two small-timers. Women of dubious virtue as well as speakeasies filled with customers drinking from hip flasks are the primary attractions. The Bronze Peacock, which is a front for various illegal activities, Little Arnie Lorch's Gambling House, and Club Palermo are establishments that feature prominently in the gangsters' lives. In truth, the film moves so quickly from one of these businesses to the next that the viewer is often hard pressed to determine just where in the city the action is occurring.

Yet location is not terribly important to an understanding of the gangsters' activities. What is notable is that these enterprises provide convenient sites for gangland shootouts, a fact made especially evident when Little Caesar and Joe celebrate their new bonds of friendship with the Sam Vettori (Stanley Fields) gang by shooting up The Bronze Peacock at midnight on New Year's Eve, thus interrupting the booze-filled celebration carried on by unwary partygoers. In fact, before the holdup begins, we see the celebrants chatting and throwing streamers about. These ribbons not only fill the nightclub's main dining area but also float out into the cigarette and liquor concession counter. Prominently displayed on this counter are dozens of liquor bottles. Clearly, there is no hiding of these: the law has been paid off. A parallel shot occurs somewhat later in the film when we see the interior of Little Caesar's apartment; among the well-appointed furnishings is a sideboard filled with liquor bottles. The connection between The Bronze Peacock and Caesar's recent attainment of wealth via this particular club is shown through the similarities of these two set pieces.

Among the New Year guests at The Bronze Peacock is the police commissioner, Alvin McClure (Landers Stevens), but McClure's time as a guest at the club is quite brief, for he is shot and killed by Little Caesar; in addition, McClure's fate will reverberate within the Sam Vettori gang. One of the prominent features of the Prohibition era gangster genre involves the fighting among the gang members for control of the territory staked out by each mob; often it is an underling who muscles in on the big boss and his terrain. *Little Caesar* offers an early instance of such an occurrence. When Little Caesar returns from the New Year's Eve party to inform his chief Vettori that the holdup went just fine but that he "had to take care of a guy," namely, McClure, Vettori reacts with a mixture of horror and sarcasm: "A million guys in this town, and you had to pick the crime commissioner." In the meantime, Little Caesar proudly displays a bag filled with bills: the take from that evening's holdup at the Bronze Peacock, most of the loot undoubtedly from the sale of bootleg liquor. Little Caesar's successful heist empowers him to challenge Vettori for the rule of the mob. Even Vettori's "boys" are not willing to take on such an imposing figure as Little Caesar presents here.

It is not long before Caesar has undeniably become the boss, as evidenced by a banquet held in his honor at the Club Palermo. The celebration scene is one of the most entertaining in the movie, for it satirizes both the banal pretentiousness of the gangster organization as well as those interminable retirement dinners held for lifelong employees of one estimable firm or another. Here is the gangster as the quintessential Organization Man.

The scene begins with an effective panning close-up that moves across the table, followed by a long shot of a horseshoe table with the banquet guests throwing streamers and enjoying their illicit booze. The celebratory view one sees is a deliberate reminder of the earlier and very abbreviated New Year's Eve party, shortened with the compliments of Little Caesar himself. Prominently displayed on the wall behind the speaker's dais is a banner that proclaims, in the Rotarian spirit of good fellowship and brotherhood: PALERMO CLUB—FRIENDSHIP—LOYALTY. The major recipient of this heartfelt welcome is, of course, Little Caesar. Furthermore, in a parody of retirement celebrations, Caesar is presented with a watch that, in a nice touch, we soon discover has been stolen.

"I never touch the stuff," Edward G. Robinson (right) as Little Caesar tells Sidney Blackmer as Big Boy, after Big Boy has offered Little Caesar a drink to celebrate Caesar's promotion as a gangland boss. The ornate surroundings and the formal clothing signal Caesar's rise to power in *Little Caesar* (Warner Bros./First National, 1931) (Photofest).

Little Caesar also gives a pleasant little speech. Edward G. Robinson always had the ability to mock himself with a straight face, to look at the world with a jaundiced eye, as if he were saying, "Hey, I'm aware of the implicit contradictions inherent in our expectations of reality. The world is full of such absurdities. Here they are, but they need no moral commentary." So it is with this, Little Caesar's lecture to the mob members and their ornamental lady friends, as he gives both an appreciation and a warning: "The liquor is good — so they tell me. I don't drink it myself." He continues with the admonition not to get drunk "and raise a lot of Cain because that's the way a lot of birds get bumped off."

In fact, a rival gang led by Little Arnie Lorch will soon try to bump off Little Caesar; fortunately, Little Caesar follows his own advice and remains perfectly sober and consequently agile enough to escape with only a superficial wound to his arm. Now it is Arnie who will be the subject of retaliation, for Caesar hightails it to Arnie's establishment and addresses

him with the taunting reminder that Arnie had unfortunately hired amateurs to take care of Caesar, and that they had missed. Arnie is through,
continues Caesar; furthermore, "If you ain't out of town by tomorrow
morning, you won't ever leave it except in a pine box. I'm takin' over this
territory. From now on, it's mine." And so he does, moving farther and farther uptown into a posh apartment with gold inlaid furniture.

But no matter how much wealth they accumulate in their pursuit of
the ever elusive American Dream of success, revenge is always on the minds
of these Prohibition gangsters. Though Caesar cannot bring himself to shoot
his old partner in crime Joe Massara, when Joe announces that he wants
out, Caesar has no such qualms about his very nervous getaway driver Tony
(William Collier, Jr.). Tony is blasted as he climbs the steps of a church,
where he is about to confess his gangland misdeeds to a priest. Tony's tumble down the church steps will be echoed nearly a decade later in *The Roaring Twenties* (1939) when formerly successful bootlegger James Cagney takes
a similarly symbolic fall in the final scene of the film. But Caesar does not
have much time left for revenge. His fall is swift and definite. What precipitates his end is the fact that the cops are constantly watching his place,
thus leaving him unable to be reunited with his cash and therefore strand-
ing him in a penniless condition.

In one of the most haunting moments of the movie, Robinson's Little
Caesar is shown in a flophouse with other down-and-out men, where beds
are to be had for fifteen cents a night. In this scene, both the set design by
Ray Moyer and the cinematography by Tony Gaudio contribute to the sense
of helplessness felt by those Depression-era unfortunates who have lost all.
And a stunning close-up of an unkempt, unshaven Robinson reveals the
pain and despair of a man who, like an ancient warrior, extended himself
too far, who felt an omnipotence that inevitably dissolved in the smoky
gunfire.

Incredibly, Caesar is still clad in a suit and tie — or what now passes
for a suit and tie. But his face is soaked in perspiration: his eyes not just
moist, but encrusted and running water. He is clearly suffering from a res-
piratory ailment, perhaps pneumonia. Furthermore, in spite of his admonition to his followers in headier times, Caesar has decided to sample that
illegal booze. No cocktail glasses for him now, however; he is drinking
straight from the bottle. Robinson's expression in this scene conveys a
tremendous amount of emotion, exemplifying much about the power of
Edward G. Robinson as an actor. In fact, his performance throughout *Little Caesar* vividly illustrates what Andrew Sarris means when he observes
that "Edward G. Robinson was the most deserving movie star who never
was even nominated for an Oscar."[3]

Rico dies, of course, shot down by the cops as he staggers from the flophouse in a vain attempt to assert his power and authority one more time. His exit line — "Mother of mercy, is this the end of Rico?" — is one of the most famous in movie history.

Doorway to Hell *and the Emerging Rackets*

In his book *The Drunken Journalist*, Howard Good has observed: "During the long, supposedly dry years of Prohibition, films were never wetter."[4] We have seen the validity of this observation in our examination of *Little Caesar* as well as of other the Prohibition movies made between 1919 and 1931. Furthermore, we have also seen that the gangster genre of the early 1930s is a unique type in that most films of this genre demonstrate quite succinctly the importance of alcohol as the way to wealth for those who are not concerned with moral niceties.

One of the most significant features of these Prohibition-era gangster movies is their basic plot similarities. The most common plot structure, one that we have seen as a notable aspect of *Little Caesar,* revolves around the fact that gang members who deal in bootleg booze are in as much danger from rival gang members as they are from the cops. The opening scene of *Doorway to Hell* (1930), a film that is decidedly inferior to *Little Caesar*, sets the pattern for gangland shootings in later gangster films of the decade. Louie Ricarno (a miscast Lew Ayres: not nearly as menacing as Edward G. Robinson) and his fellow thugs drive to a house, lure one of the inhabitants out, and fill him with bullets. Louie's racket is beer, and there is no room for anyone who will not play by the rules established by the gang boss.[5]

When Louie is brought in for questioning by the law, he protests his innocence to Captain Pat O'Grady (the laconic Robert Elliott) by insisting, "I'm in a legitimate business, I am." Legitimate — no; a business — yes: a detail that is shortly made clear when Louie summons Chicago's bootleg gang leaders to a meeting, declares that they need to consolidate their activities into one, and make him the boss over all: the company president, as it were. But in a rather sudden change of heart, Louie, finally deciding to do something legitimate, gets married, and leaves his second-in-command Steve Mileaway (James Cagney in his second motion picture) with the onerous task of riding herd on the various factions fighting over control of the beer revenue. While it is clear that, in the past, Cagney has had a romantic relationship with Ayres's new bride Doris (Dorothy Matthews) and that he continues to eye her for possible diversion, Ayres is also effective in his determination to be faithful to his wife and to go straight. In truth, Ayres is more believable as a man in love than as a gangland boss. Despite his clean-cut, college boy appearance, he always had a fiery sexuality about him, even as a character actor in his forties and fifties.[6] So from this point on, sixth-billed Cagney takes over the rackets as well as the picture.

He also tries, with little success, to take over Louie's slowly disintegrating gang. Shortly after Louie leaves town, one of the gang members protests to Cagney: "I was hijacked last night for twenty barrels." Louie had promised to pay protection money for his pals, but that is no longer coming in, even as rival gang leader Rocco (Noel Madison) is moving to increase his territory. Cagney, who had already perfected his belligerent, taunting style, tells Louie's former allies to quit squawking, that Louie isn't coming back. Newspaper headlines summarize the story of deadly Prohibition rivalry, spearheaded by Rocco, who has hired hijackers to eliminate his competition: GANG WAR BREWING AS RIVAL BOOTLEG FACTIONS IMPORT OUT-OF-TOWN HOODLUMS. LOUIE RICARNO'S DISAPPEARANCE CAUSE OF SPLIT IN BOOTLEG RING. RIVAL MOBS THREATEN WAR TO FINISH. In short, the mobs have started double-crossing each other.

But how to get Louie back to Chicago? Cagney tries with a phone call to the honeymooning erstwhile gangster in Florida, but even Cagney's insistent style is ineffective. Then two of Louie's thugs decide on a plan that turns tragic: they try to kidnap Louie's kid brother Jackie (Leon Janney), who is attending a military school in another part of the state. When Jackie tries to escape by running away through the streets, he is run over and killed by a truck. Now Louie has reason to get revenge against the two whose attempted kidnapping led to his brother's death. Returning to Chicago, he finishes off one himself, while Cagney disposes of the other. Both are learning that the rewards of the illegal liquor traffic are at best transitory; the picture ends with Cagney in jail and Louie killed by the Rocco gang. In fact, police captain O'Grady, as played by Robert Elliott, who has some of the wittiest, most ironic lines in the film, summarizes why he doesn't arrest Louie. Having found Louie's hideout and knowing that Louie will die, courtesy of the Rocco mob, just as soon as he exits the building, O'Grady goes to this seedy apartment to tell Louie that Rocco is waiting for him outside. But that's all right, says O'Grady calmly, because "you're a menace to society, and this is the easiest way to get rid of you."

At the time that he was given the leading role in *Doorway to Hell*, Lew Ayres had appeared in only five movies, none of which had indicated that he would be suited to this particular role as a bootleg gangster. Most of his earlier movies had been grade B pictures, but one, *All Quiet on the Western Front* (1930), would become a classic. Shortly before the release of that movie, one film critic, doubtless at the urging of Universal Studio publicists, visited the set of this picture about the Great War and wrote a feature article on this diffident young actor:

> Lewis is about the quietest boy among the many youngsters on the "All Quiet" set.... Lew is friendly with everybody, but his own natural aloofness would preclude many warm friendships.
>
> Naturally, a great deal depends upon the outcome of this picture. Lew is not the type that will go on for years as a moderate success. He will either be a tremendous hit or a failure....
>
> If Lewis is the success that Universal predicts of him, a great deal will be written about him. Not many people will understand him, for Hollywood has little time or patience for people that are hard to know. He will be called "high-hat," of course. He will have few friends because not many people will take the time to batter down that wall which he has built around himself. And he will be unhappy most of the time, the usual reward for people who build such a wall.
>
> But he will be one of the most interesting young male stars in pictures. At least he will have the courage to be himself.[7]

This early commentary on the twenty-one-year-old actor was to prove prescient. Although Ayres was not exactly a failure, most of his movies throughout the 1930s were forgettable ones.[8] However, Ayres did indeed receive excellent notices for his featured part as the naïvely earnest young German soldier in *All Quiet on the Western Front* (1930), and the studios subsequently tried to find more parts to suit his clean cut, handsome type. Unfortunately, *Doorway to Hell* was not one of these roles.

Nonetheless, despite the unsuitability of Ayres for such gangster parts, we are still led to believe that Lew Ayres's Louie meets his fate with style and resignation. Although we are spared the sight of Louie's demise in that last scene, we are obviously supposed to learn a lesson from his bootlegging misadventures; the epilogue to *Doorway to Hell* intones moralistically: "The Doorway to Hell is a one-way door." But James Cagney was waiting just outside this door, ready to open it and find his way to stardom in another Prohibition-era gangster movie.

Beer and Blood in The Public Enemy

Shortly after he made *Doorway to Hell*, Cagney was cast in *The Public Enemy* (1931). The movie's screenplay was based on the story "Beer and Blood: The Story of a Couple o' Wrong Guys," written by Kubec Glasmon and John Bright, who had offered it to Warners in 1930. In its early draft, this coauthored novel ran for three hundred single-spaced pages and drew upon the experiences of the authors, both of whom had grown up in

Chicago and had personally known a number of Chicago gangsters.[9] A relatively inconsequential but competent actor named Edward Woods was slated to star as Tom Powers, the hoodlum who rises and falls with great swiftness. Cagney was scheduled to appear in a supporting part as Woods's buddy, just as he had backed up Ayres in *Doorway to Hell*. However, according to Cagney's forthright, somewhat immodest recollection, the movie's director, William Wellman, had seen the earlier picture and persuaded studio boss Darryl Zanuck that Cagney and Woods should reverse their roles. As Cagney remembered it:

> The story was about two street pals—one soft-spoken, the other a really tough little article. For some incredible reason, I was cast as the quiet one; and Eddie Woods, a fine actor but a boy of gentle background, well-spoken and well-educated, became the tough guy. Fortunately, Bill Wellman, the director, had seen *Doorway to Hell*, and he quickly became aware of the obvious casting error. He knew at once that I could project that direct gutter quality, so Eddie and I switched roles after Wellman made an issue of it with Darryl Zanuck.[10]

The switch, of course, was significant and historic: one that made Cagney a star. His "direct gutter quality" comes through from his first scene to his last. And the type of picture that Zanuck knew that *The Public Enemy* should be was the kind that was perfectly suited to the Cagney persona. Zanuck was determined to include a lot of sex and violence, both of which Cagney combined in abundance. So in keeping with the type of movie Zanuck wanted to film, he spent much time on the set, giving instructions to the director. According to one young assistant who followed Zanuck around the lot and wrote down Zanuck's instructions to various subordinates:

> He [Zanuck] was all hyped up about it, and kept repeating to [director] Willie Wellman and his crew that they mustn't let a drop of sentimentality seep into the action. "Everyone in this movie is tough, tough, tough," he kept saying. "People are going to say the characters are immoral, but they're not because they don't *have* any morals. They steal, they kill, they lie, they hump each other because that's the way they're made, and if you allow a decent human feeling or a pang of conscience to come into their makeup, you've lost 'em and changed the kind of movie we're making.[11]

Zanuck did in fact succeed in making a tremendously amoral movie, built around the premise that gangsters and booze can make ideal urban bedmates. The opening shots of *The Public Enemy* (1931) show the slums of Chicago in 1909. Prominently featured in this setting are shots of beer pails as they are being filled; these are transferred into large barrels and are then carried away in horse-drawn carts. We next cut to a busy intersection where there are a number of saloons. Entering this scene is a man carrying about a dozen of these pails, or *canisters* as they were known at the time, which are hung from a large pole. Their destination is unknown, but wherever the booze is going, chances are it will wind up in the homes, factories, taverns, and restaurants frequented by immigrants, whose few pleasures include daily consumption of immoderate amounts of alcohol. As the man toting the booze leaves the frame, a Salvation Army band enters, playing inspirational music to reform the souls of those who are about to enjoy their cheap beer. The juxtaposition of alcohol and religion is a deliberate one and sets the tone for the naturalistic underpinnings of the film. The movie's anti-hero is inevitably destroyed by the criminal world he so eagerly joins: a world filled with rival gangs vying for the liquor trade in Prohibition-era Chicago. As with *Doorway to Hell*, in the world of *The Public Enemy*, there is no religion, no God, and no way out save death. Though *The Public Enemy* was destined for cinema immortality not because of its portrayal of alcohol but because of its demonstration of an original use for grapefruit, nonetheless it is alcohol that propels the narrative and ultimately leads to the death of its protagonist, Tom Powers, played, of course, by the young, feisty, chillingly brutal James Cagney in his first starring role.

When Cagney received the American Film Institute Lifetime Achievement Award on March 13, 1974, he made a gracious, understated, thoughtful acceptance speech in which he offered a number of thanks to those people from his youth who had influenced his acting style. Among them were childhood acquaintances from the environment of his boyhood: New York's Lower East Side. Cagney ended his speech with a tribute to them:

> And the names, the names, the names of my youth: Lager-head Quinnlivan, Artie Klein, Pete Leyden, Jake Bodkin, Specks Toporcer, Brother O'Mara, Picky Hooli-han! They were all part of a very stimulating early environment which produced that unmistakable touch of the gutter without which this evening might never have happened at all.[12]

Indeed, forty-three years earlier, we can see clearly this unerringly accurate "touch of the gutter" in every gesture he makes. In addition, *The Public Enemy* is a fast-moving narrative, thanks largely to Cagney's presence. Of Cagney in this picture, one critic has written: "Fortunately there are so many high points in Cagney's kinetic performance that the entire picture is carried along at a rollicking pace."[13]

For the first nine years or so depicted in the film, Cagney and his boyhood pal Matt Doyle (Edward Woods) amuse themselves as small time thugs, engaging in such ordinary criminal activities as sticking up a fur warehouse and stealing large shipments of cigars. But with the coming of Prohibition, their opportunities for other business enterprises expand tremendously.

Some of the most memorable, humorous moments in *The Public Enemy* occur in the hours before the enforcement of the Volstead Act, before the ensuing reality of Prohibition descends upon the country. It is now 1920 and we cut to a sign on an establishment with the curious name of the Family Liquor Store: "Owing to Prohibition, our entire stock must be sold before midnight." And what a wild time these alcohol lovers have in those hours before midnight. The streets are packed with hundreds of people, all determined to stockpile as much booze as possible before the deadline. Some are blowing celebratory horns as they gather up bottles of liquor, like so many trick-or-treaters celebrating a Dionysian Halloween. When one fashionably dressed man tries to put a sack load of bottles into a very expensive-looking car, he drops one of the bottles on the sidewalk, shattering it and spilling its contents on the concrete. A speedy, nimble lady decked in fancy fur exits the car and tries to retrieve what is left of the bottle. A van labeled *Florist* drives to the curb; the drivers open the rear doors and carelessly toss fresh flowers onto the ground. The van is then quickly restocked with bottles. Meanwhile, a couple strolls by, pushing a baby carriage filled to the brim with bottles; the wife is carrying the infant.

The scene showing this last-minute mania before the dawn of Prohibition is, in fact, drawn from history. In various cities, mock funerals—complete with coffins filled with empty bottles—were held in honor of legal alcohol's demise. Many towns featured buglers who played taps. On the other hand, for those who wanted a more tuneful send-off, a new musical hit could be heard around the country as mourners stood on street corners and sang "The Alcohol Blues."[14]

Once the dreaded Prohibition becomes law, Tom Powers and Matt Doyle find that they have a new and illegal money-making avenue, courtesy of their old friend Paddy Ryan (Robert Emmett O'Connor). He tells them how their success is guaranteed: "Don't you think that booze isn't going to be valuable. I heard today that alcohol is going to thirty dollars a gallon." Tom and Matt do not need much convincing, so they make an upward career move that has its beginnings when the childhood chums use a stolen gasoline truck to siphon liquor from a bootlegger's warehouse. Their new enterprise selling illegal booze nets them tremendous rewards. Reaping an important fringe benefit from these rewards, Cagney gets fitted for a custom-made suit. In this brief scene, Cagney demonstrates his frightening, disquieting, sexually charged sense of humor as he smugly watches the effeminate tailor measuring his waist and chest. Pulling knowingly on his waistband, Cagney suggestively commands the tailor, "Don't forget, plenty of room in there." He smiles complacently as the tailor comments on the robbery the previous day at the booze warehouse, which had taken place "right under their very noses." Then Matt, who has been sitting on the sidelines with a self-satisfied expression, reminds the tailor to put six buttons on the cuffs. At this, Cagney retorts, "Be careful, Matt, or you're going to cut the nose right off ya." Here he steps down, makes a motion as though wiping his nose, flips his head in a mocking gesture at the clueless tailor — who has obviously missed the phallic implication of Cagney's nose allusion — and saunters out.

Tom and Matt go into business with Paddy Ryan; the nature of their enterprise involves delivering their brand of beer to speakeasies. The fact that the speakeasy owners do not want to pay the high prices for this beer is irrelevant. Indeed, their new boss Nails Nathan (Leslie Fenton) had ordered them to dictate to the owners upon delivery, "Here's the beer you ordered." And how Cagney does, in fact, energetically follow these orders. He bursts into a speakeasy with the energy of one who has been catapulted out of a cannon; he orders a beer, takes a drink, and spits it back into the

In *The Public Enemy* (Warner Bros., 1931), James Cagney (second from right) as Tom Powers uses his most persuasive techniques to convince the speakeasy owner that he needs to change beer distributors and buy from Cagney's mob instead. Lee Phelps is Pete, the unfortunate owner. Edward Woods is Matt Doyle, Cagney's nicely dressed partner, posed with gun in hand in front of the bar. Another partner, Clark Burroughs as Dutch, stands watch. Dutch's scruffy attire shows his lack of social standing in the mob pecking order.

owner's face: "That ain't our beer," he snarls. Then, after swirling around
to the back of the bar, he turns on every spigot and lets the liquid gush onto
the floor. He slaps the owner around a bit, then asks him how much beer
he wants. When the owner nervously replies "two kegs," Cagney orders that
five be delivered. Cagney had begun his career on stage as a dancer, and
this early training served him well in films. His actions are precise and
rhythmic; he always moves as though he were balancing on his toes, and
the gracefully brutal measures that he takes in this scene are no exception.

The rise of Cagney's Tom Powers is a rapid one, in part because, unlike
his dour, moralistic brother Mike (Donald Cook), Tom did not take time
out from business to join the army in the Great War. Indeed, when Tom's
brother returns from the fighting, wounded, he is even more solemn, more
serious, more straitlaced than ever before, with an obsessed look of mad-
ness about him. The dark circles under his eyes highlight the staring expression; the welcome-home wreaths surrounding him heighten the funereal
atmosphere. However, Tom and Matt are in a festive mood as they carry
in a gigantic beer keg and, in a nice homey touch, place it on the dining
table on top of one of Ma Powers's upended cooking pots. There it sits, a
grotesque centerpiece for Mike's homecoming dinner, so large that the diners have to crane their necks to see one another. It is a bizarre scene, made
even more so by the lively obtuseness of hosts Cagney and Edward Woods,
both seemingly oblivious to Mike's tenuous hold on sanity. Ma Powers was
played by Beryl Mercer, a peculiar character actress whose voice sounded
like chalk scraping on blackboard. In manner, she always appeared mentally estranged from the characters she was creating, and, in this scene, she
looks insanely cheerful as she eagerly awaits her children's next move.

Meanwhile, Mike has been ignoring his mother's dimwitted chirping
in order to focus his half-crazed vision upon Tom and Matt. But Matt
appears not to notice the gathering clouds, for he turns to Mike and declares,
"Say, we haven't drunk to your health yet. This is a *swell* celebration." Here
he pours drinks for all the guests. When he notices that Mike is still staring vacantly ahead, he urges, "Why don't ya drink, Mike? Come on, it's
only beer." But Mike only glances sideways at Matt, seething with aversion
to everything that is occurring and insisting that he doesn't want any. In
the interim, Cagney's expression reveals his thoroughgoing disgust at his
stuffy, holier-than-thou brother. Their ensuing conversation is one of the
most unforgettable dialogues in the film:

TOM: What's eatin' you?

MIKE (*emphatic*): I'm not interfering with your drinkin'. If you want to drink it,
go on. If I don't want it, I don't have to.

TOM (*grimacing*): So beer ain't good enough for you, huh?

MIKE (*jumps up, wide-eyed, nearly hysterical*): You think I'd care if it was just beer in that keg? I know what's in it! And I know what you've been doing all that time — how you got those clothes, those new cars. You've been tellin' Ma that you've gone into politics, that you're on the city payroll.... You're murderers! There's not only beer in that keg — there's beer and blood! Blood of *men*!

Following this frenzied speech, and, despite the obvious wound to his arm, a testament to his sacrifice in the Great War, Mike grabs the heavy keg, lifts it over his head, and smashes it against one of Ma Powers's tables in the corner, thus destroying both the furniture and the decorations upon it. Ma whimpers slightly. Cagney as Tom has been listening to the message and he is convinced that his brother is screwier than ever. He slowly stands and faces Mike, whose hair is now disarranged and partially covering his face. Cagney then attacks Mike by delivering a line that would continue to have significance to a later generation: "You ain't changed a bit. Besides, your hands ain't so clean — you killed and liked it! You didn't get them medals for holding hands with them Germans!"[15]

Yet, despite Cagney's belligerent anti-war statement, Tom and Matt are fighting a war that they will ultimately lose. They are in an ongoing turf battle with another speakeasy bootlegger, Schemer Burns, and it is the Burns gang that kills Matt in a shootout on a street corner. Determined to avenge his old friend's death, Cagney tries to take on the whole rival gang single handed and he is shot in the process. Bandaged from head to toe, he improbably makes peace with his family, all of whom gather at his hospital bedside. But he is later kidnapped by the Schemer Burns mob: taken from the hospital, bandages and all. He is then killed and delivered to his mother's doorstep, his body propped up against the door, "as though it were the day's supply of meat."[16] The final shot of Cagney in this movie even now has the power to startle: When the bell rings, Mike rushes to the door, happily thinking that his brother is coming home — alive. What he sees instead is a standing corpse, still wrapped in bandages, looking like a mummy unceremoniously tossed out of its tomb. When Mike opens the door, Cagney falls forward on his face, his feet bouncing grotesquely in the air as he tumbles inside, while the Powers's phonograph plays the cheerful "I'm Forever Blowing Bubbles," the same eerily inappropriate tune that has been heard over the film's opening credits. The movie's naturalistic and moral messages are clear and echo those of the previous year's *Doorway to Hell*: No one survives who becomes a part of the criminal world; all must pay with their lives.[17]

From the Yiddish Theater to Gangster Movie: Scarface

In 1929, the Austrian-born stage actor Paul Muni attempted motion pictures and appeared in two, *The Valiant* and *Seven Faces*. Although *The Valiant* is an affecting film in many ways, albeit suffering from the static qualities that afflicted many early talkies, Muni was disappointed in both ventures and subsequently returned to the East Coast where he was well known in both the English and Yiddish theater. So when director Howard Hawks visited him in New York sometime the following year with an offer of the lead in *Scarface*, Muni was not at all receptive to the idea. He protested that he was wrong for the role of the gangster Tony Camonte; according to Hawks's later statements, Muni was pleasant but adamant, asserting that "he was not physically strong enough.... Besides he protested that Cagney had made *Public Enemy* and Robinson had made *Little Caesar*. What more could be done in *Scarface* that hadn't already been done?" But Muni's wife Bella[18] always kept a careful eye on her husband's career, and she persuaded him to take the part.[19] It was a wise decision, for *Scarface* is, in my opinion, one of his three best films, along with *I Am a Fugitive from a Chain Gang* (1932) and the largely overlooked but beautifully crafted and haunting *We Are Not Alone* (1939). In *Scarface*, Muni's Tony Camonte is chilling, humorous, perverse, reckless, vengeful, cruel, animalistic. Even his walk is ape-like, as though he has just walked out of one jungle and into another: this second one made of concrete, automobiles, and tommy guns. Furthermore, Muni invested a lot of time into preparation for the part. He read as much as he could find on the life and career of Alphonse "Scarface" Capone, and he experimented with his character's arrogant walk. He also tried a variety of accents until he and director Howard Hawks mutually agreed on one that would work realistically. Hawks would later say that Muni perfected a vocal "rhythm [with] a subtle oily lilt which worked beautifully through the whole picture."[20]

However, our first glimpse of Muni in *Scarface* is a voiceless and sinister one; he is seen only in shadow and in profile, whistling an eerie tune that will become his identifying mark throughout, a signal that he is approaching his next victim. The shadow then draws his gun, greets a rival, and finally speaks, uttering the nonchalant, "Hello, Louie," as he kills the unfortunate Louie. As with the opening of *Doorway to Hell*, a murder occurs because a fellow mobster has not been playing fair, has been muscling in on the beer-running business that another, stronger gang leader wants to control.

And Muni hopes to be the controlling force in this trade in illegal liquor. His very demeanor from the outset reveals a man at odds with the world and in love with himself. Likewise, when we first actually see his face, we can clearly witness these anti-establishment characteristics. Sitting in a barber chair with a towel covering his face, he pulls the towel away when a cop approaches to question him about Louie's demise. What he exposes in so doing is a countenance with a long scar on the cheek, accompanied by a deceptive expression, both quizzical and astonished. He looks like a man who has been caught off guard in a traffic accident: a victim who has recently been run over and still has the tire tracks on his face. When the cop asks him about what he knows of Louie's death, Muni's Tony Camonte is arrogant and belligerent as he refuses to answer. Instead, he mocks the law by striking a match on the cop's badge. He knows that the mob members and their lawyers have protected him before and that they will undoubtedly continue to do so. Indeed, though Tony is taken into custody, he is soon released and available to rejoin his boss, Johnny Lovo (Osgood Perkins).

As is the case with many characters of the gangster genre, Tony's relation to Lovo is based on mutual suspicion and distrust. One point of contention concerns Tony's ambition, which has grown out of his excessive hubris. Tony is itching to take over the North Side beer-running territory, but this particular turf belongs to a man called O'Hara, who, says Lovo, is too powerful to mess with. Nonetheless, Lovo has his own agenda, which is beginning to develop nicely, thanks to Louie Costello's auspicious death. In a scene reminiscent of Lew Ayres's gathering of hoodlums in *Doorway to Hell*, Lovo meets with Costello's men and informs all who will listen that he is now running Costello's South Side domain. Those who demonstrate a desire to go out on their own are quickly stopped by a well-placed punch administered by Tony. Like Ayres, Lovo considers himself to be a legitimate entrepreneur, as he tells those assembled: "Running beer ain't a nickel game anymore. It's a business and I'm gonna run it like a business. Three thousand saloons on the South Side. Half a million customers. Figure that out."

Lovo does have everything pretty well figured out, at least for the moment. He sends Tony and Guino Rinaldo (George Raft) into the South Side territory to take orders for beer from speakeasy customers who are already buying their beer from rival businessmen. In a scene reminiscent of the one in *Public Enemy* where Cagney bullies the speakeasy owner into buying beer from his organization, Muni and Raft beat up bar proprietors, and, like Cagney and Edward Woods, turn on the spigots to let their rivals' beer pour onto the floor and talk these owners into buying from them barrels they don't need at inflated prices they cannot afford to pay. Moreover, when Muni and Raft fear actually entering a saloon, they throw bombs through the windows, thus preventing any future profits for the owners. A more overtly violent film than *Public Enemy*, *Scarface* consistently demonstrates the brutality and casual amorality of the people who engage in such urban warfare.

Nor is it only the men who evidence such moral relativity. Lovo's mistress Poppy (Karen Morley) is hard, ironic, opportunistic, and terribly sexy as she drifts away from Lovo in order to tempt and tease a willing Tony. The twenty-two-year-old Morley gives a remarkable performance; she is both saucy and alluring in her eagerness to help Tony in his illegal activities. In addition, after Raft has killed her former lover Johnny Lovo in order to avenge Lovo's unsuccessful murder attempt on Tony, Poppy spends no time mourning Lovo's death, but instead eagerly follows Tony out of the apartment she has shared with Lovo. The other woman in Tony's life is his sister Cesca (Ann Dvorak), who futilely joins him in their fatal stand off with the law in the film's final moments. Unlike Poppy, Cesca is truly in love with Tony: incestuously, perversely so. Dark, wild-eyed, vulnerable, and achingly slender, nineteen-year-old Dvorak also gives a superb, evocative performance as the woman who marries Guino only to witness his murder by Tony, who does not know that Cesca and Guino are married but thinks that Guino is simply taking advantage of his sister.

Following Guino's shooting, Tony realizes that he has betrayed both a loyal friend and a sister for whom he has physical yearnings. It is at this point that Tony metamorphoses into a zombie-like creature, even ignoring Poppy when she calls. By this time, Tony and Cesca have retreated to the house that Tony has turned into a fortress, complete with shuttered windows made of reinforced steel. Armed with a revolver, Cesca had earlier entered this hideaway, planning to kill Tony and avenge Guino's murder. But blood will tell, and she quickly becomes his helpmate as she loads his machine guns for Armageddon. Yet Cesca is mortally wounded by a cop's bullet, which has come through a steel-fortified window that Tony had not shuttered quickly enough.

Once again, the censorship dictates of the time remind us that Crime Does Not Pay and that the road to wealth, built as it is upon the violent bootleg trade, is paved with vile dust and dead bodies. In this final scene, Muni reveals what a sick coward Tony truly is as he hysterically tries to keep Cesca from dying, protesting that she cannot leave him because "I'll be here all alone! I'm no good without you, Cesca. I'm no good by myself!" Cesca, of course, succumbs, and Tony is forced out of the building by tear gas. No longer armed, he cringes and pleads with the cops not to shoot. They oblige him until he tries to run from them, at which point the staccato sound of bullets careening off his body mark the end of Tony Camonte. As he falls, a panning shot toward the sky leads to a clear view of a brightly lighted advertising sign that Tony had earlier pointed out to Poppy as a fortunate portent, a credo by which he intended to live. The first line reads: THE WORLD IS YOURS; the second: COOK'S TOURS. As with *Doorway to Hell* and *Public Enemy*, the final scene discloses a fitting irony associated with the finish of the beer-running gangster protagonist.

Yet there are a number of significant differences between Tony Camonte and his predecessors. Whereas both Lew Ayres and James Cagney at times demonstrate a fairly decent side — for instance, Ayres is devoted to his younger brother and Cagney to his mother — Paul Muni, to his credit, never makes Tony Camonte sympathetic, never shows Camonte to be anything but a heartless, crude, ignorant, animalistic thug. By the same token, as critic James Harvey has pointed out, unlike Cagney's Tom Powers in *Public Enemy*, "Muni's Tony Camonte seems almost explosively sexual — an id on the loose — swinging his arms from his shoulders as he walks, with the taut, straight back that seems never to relax, as unrelenting as the eyes.... Scarface himself is a spectacle, unnerving and riveting at the same time."[21] In short, Muni's performance is a superb, disquieting one, perhaps the best of the early 1930s gangster genre.

Not only has *Scarface* withstood the test of time, but contemporary reviewers also recognized the film's importance. One 1932 critic, writing for a woman's magazine, praises the film, but seems to have missed the incestuous nature of Tony's excessive interest in and jealousy of his sister:

> Virtue takes an awful beating in *Scarface*, the latest saga of the underworld, and, I should think, would probably clean up that cycle for good. Here is the gangster, brutal and pitiless, and, as played by Paul Muni, he becomes a new low in monsters. His desire for power is his motivating force, and his concern for his coquettish little sister occupies what there is of his heart, and in the end brings about his death.[22]

This same reviewer also adds an informative cultural comment, one that provides some facts about 1932 movie audiences and their seeming inability to be disturbed by onscreen violence:

> Whether as a nation of spectators we've become so hard that we are interested, rather than appalled, by such continuous devilment, or have developed a calm that we reserve for the afflictions of others, it is interesting to note that only a mild gasp greeted the throwing of the dead body from the taxi.[23]

In hindsight, perhaps, we can better understand that the desperate economic times of the Depression combined with the cynicism, which accompanied the continued violations of Prohibition, doubtless led viewers to be inured to such gangland slayings. Nonetheless, censors did hold up the release of this film until a number of changes were made in the script; such alterations included a dialogue deploring the tendency of the public to glorify the gangster and his brutal methods of Prohibition evasion. The 1932 reviewer alludes to these censorship difficulties:

> The story is a little jerky now and then, having had a long and tough struggle with the censors, and you feel that expediency alone could account for the little moral lesson that is sandwiched in at the end. But it is absorbing and exciting — almost too exciting — and I can't imagine a better actor than Muni in this blood-curdling role ... the story is a potpourri of some of the more spectacular front page crimes, and it has a gruesome authenticity.[24]

Another 1932 review, this one in *Photoplay*, contains the following superlatives about *Scarface*: "The gangster picture of all time. A masterpiece that belongs to no cycle. Horrible and fearless, with Paul Muni in one of the great characterizations of the screen."[25] In the same *Photoplay* issue, Sidney Skolsky, in a feature article on Paul Muni, offers the following opinion: "Certain parts of 'Scarface' make other gangster films seem sissy."[26] In short, *Scarface* is indeed perhaps the most brutal of the early gangster pictures.

World War I Veterans and Prohibition

By the late 1930s, Prohibition was dead; however, the end of the Noble Experiment had begun many years earlier. Indeed, from the beginning of the lawless era that immediately followed passage of the Eighteenth Amendment, scofflaws had been hell bent on circumventing the law. By 1932, when the Democrats met in Chicago to nominate their Presidential candidate, they were certainly listening to their constituents throughout the United States, many of whom were clamoring for a return to safe, legal liquor. On July 1, 1932, when Franklin Roosevelt was nominated on the fourth ballot, Democrats who supported the "Wets" knew that they had a strong ally. Roosevelt's acceptance speech, which contained the famous line — "I pledge you, I pledge myself, to a new deal for the American people" — offered as a part of that new deal the repeal of Prohibition. Roosevelt took office in March 1933, and by December 5, 1933, the requisite three-fourths of the states had ratified the Twenty-First Amendment to repeal the Eighteenth Amendment.[27] Organized crime, which had so prospered with the traffic in and manufacture of illegal booze, now had to find another means of revenue.

Thus, because of recent historical events, *The Roaring Twenties* (1939) represents a break with earlier gangster movies set during Prohibition. These earlier films, made when Prohibition was actually the law, must necessarily tell a different story than does *The Roaring Twenties*, made six years after

Prohibition's repeal. By the end of the decade, this picture purported to tell the saga of a bygone era. But the early drafts of this story displeased some members of the cast and crew. James Cagney, the star of *The Roaring Twenties*, later claimed that the initial script was such a poor one that various interested individuals were always dropping their own little touches in it to liven up a bland story.[28] Among those who contributed suggestions was the director Raoul Walsh, who had replaced Anatole Litvak.[29] Walsh, a versatile craftsman who was one of Cagney's favorite directors, would direct the star ten years later in *White Heat*. In addition to giving Walsh credit for story enhancement, Cagney, with his comment, also reveals a good deal about his own perennial tendency to alter scripts. In most of his movies, he improvised and inserted personal bits of dialogue during filming, especially if he thought the picture lacked humor.

Yet, for all its plot weaknesses, the movie contains many outstanding, nostalgic moments in it. Such moments include social commentary that focuses on the readjustment problems facing the returning veterans of the Great War, specifically on their inability to find a job once they get back home. When Cagney's character, Eddie Bartlett, returns to the garage where he had worked as a mechanic prior to the war, he is surprised to learn that his former boss has no intention of rehiring him; moreover, to make matters worse, the garage's current employees— men who had not gone to war — mock him. So he accepts the offer of his old prewar pal Danny Green (Frank McHugh) and splits the earnings he makes from driving Danny's cab part-time. Unlike the amoral Tom Powers of *Public Enemy*, Eddie Bartlett is basically a decent sort: optimistic, honest, and hopeful that his world will soon return to normal. But as we saw in *Public Enemy*, with the passage of the Volstead Act in 1920, liquor traffic goes undercover; as a result, Eddie's life goes awry.

But unlike Cagney's Tom Powers, Eddie Bartlett initially gets sucked unwittingly into this underworld. A passenger in his cab asks him to deliver a package to a speakeasy. Though the brown paper bag clearly looks as though it contains a bottle, Eddie naïvely carries it into the building and loudly announces that he has a package for Panama Smith, the proprietor (Gladys George.) Though Panama pretends that Eddie is carrying meat, the cops inside are not fooled — the package is definitely the wrong shape — and arrest both her and Eddie. Eddie covers for her, goes briefly to jail, and then is bailed out by a grateful Panama. By the time Panama rescues Eddie, she is already smitten by him and curious to know more about this odd kid who, unlike her usual associates, seems on the level. There is a sexual chemistry that radiates out whenever Cagney and George share a scene.

In fact, Gladys George combined toughness with vulnerability, qual-

Frank McHugh as Danny Green ladles bathtub gin into an authentic-looking bottle, while James Cagney as Eddie Bartlett watches intently lest some of their precious, carefully concocted wood alcohol be wasted. As bootlegging partners during Prohibition, Green and Bartlett become very prosperous in *The Roaring Twenties* (Warner Bros., 1939).

ities which enabled her to hold her own against Cagney's energy. In addition, she had a voice that was both sensual and soothing, even as her New England accent contributed a harshness to her vocal resonance. She looked and sounded as though she were always on the verge of cracking.[30]

Thus the characters of Panama Smith and Eddie Bartlett are certainly attracted to each other, though Panama leads Eddie into the sort of life that will finally destroy him. But she is infatuated with him and, feeling that she owes him for taking a rap for her, she persuades him to become a bootlegger. Since he has been living on the edge of poverty from the time he returned from the Great War, Cagney enlists McHugh's Danny Green and they go into the liquor running business together, even making their own gin. In one especially amusing scene, the pals stand over the bathtub, stirring a concoction that looks as though it contains fifty percent gasoline. According to the voiceover announcer (John Deering), whose intonations give *The Roaring Twenties* a documentary-like feel, this wood alcohol, which has become so popular with Prohibition drinkers, is cooked again and sent back out onto the street. In no time at all, Cagney is on his way to becoming wealthy by slowly poisoning a thirsty public. The returning soldier, who had been told that there was no room for him at his former auto mechanic's job, soon owns a whole fleet of cabs.

But the cabs are only the beginning. Cagney and his employees hijack a boat carrying illegal liquor and owned by a rival syndicate boss, Nick Brown (Paul Kelly). Working for Brown is Cagney's old acquaintance from the war, George Hally (Humphrey Bogart). Though they are rivals, and though they understandably do not trust one another, they decide to go into business together in order to take some of the trade away from Nick Brown. And they are immensely successful. But the stock market crash of 1929 and the repeal of Prohibition in 1933 are two catastrophic events that leave Cagney broke, with no alternative but to return to his old job of driving a cab. For reasons not explained in the narrative, Bogart continues to live a life of illegally gained luxury, until Cagney kills him in a confrontation concerning another friend from the war, Lloyd Hart (Jeffrey Lynn). Lloyd is a district attorney who, Bogart knows, has enough dirt on Bogart to send him to prison for several life terms.

Once Bogart has been eliminated, Cagney's death is guaranteed.[31] Shot several times by Bogart's mob, Cagney staggers out of Bogart's elegant apartment and stumbles toward the steps of a nearby church, improbably knocking over a mailbox on his way. He begins to ascend the steps, then falls backward. Panama runs after him and crouches next to him as a lies on his back on the church steps. Although he is already dead, she sits on the steps and gently holds his head in her lap. Ironically, this is the closest that they have ever come to physical intimacy. Interrupting this tender moment is a cop who strolls by, his nonchalant manner indicative of his lack of interest in what appears to be just another body, one of many in an environment where gangland slayings are an everyday occurrence. But he knows that he must make a report anyway, so he asks the usual questions, though he is clearly not interested in rounding up the usual suspects:

COP: Who is this guy?

PANAMA: This is Eddie Bartlett.

COP: How are you hooked up with him?

PANAMA (*sadly, ruefully, still in love with him*): I could never figure it out.

COP: What was his business?

PANAMA: He used to be a big shot.

With this line — Panama's resigned summation of Bartlett's life and of her small, unhappy part in it — the movie ends on a melancholy, naturalistic note. Not only did Prohibition fail to work as a social experiment, but it also doomed those movie gangsters who at first, tried to thumb their very wealthy noses at it and then, following its repeal, attempted to find other means of livelihood.

4

The White Logic
of W. C. Fields

Somebody sure spilled the whole bag of nuts this time.

— Review of *International House*, *Photoplay*, 1933

"Ambrose! Wake up! There are burglars singing in the cellar!"

— Kathleen Howard to W. C. Fields in *Man on the Flying Trapeze* (1935)

A Desire for Respectability

Like many popular film personalities of the 1930s, W. C. Fields would later spark a revival of interest among the young during those iconoclastic, rebellious days of the late 1960s and early 1970s. Indeed, in retrospect, Fields appears to have been ideally suited to the cynical, never-trust-anyone-over-thirty anti-establishment, anti-materialism of the Vietnam era. However, unlike the truly anarchic Marx Brothers, there is something decidedly middle class about W. C. Fields. For instance, the Marx Brothers' *Horse Feathers* (1932) contains a lunatic scene in a speakeasy, where Groucho, Chico, and Harpo go in search of hunks who can play football. None of their actions make any sense: Harpo plays the slot machines; Groucho and Chico drink and leave without paying. Chico also works there, taking orders for various brands of bootleg liquor, all of which he dispenses from the same bottle. On the other hand, when W. C. Fields goes into a speakeasy, his purpose is to escape his wife, and to spend the time drinking. Fields is, after all, a man who, despite his drinking proclivities, has a respectable occupation, a comfortable but unostentatious house, a wife, children, and exceedingly noxious in-laws. In addition, unlike the Marx Brothers, who never aspire to normality, there is a sad, even despairing quality to all of Fields's wistful efforts at respectability. Richard Schickel has captured quite accurately the dilemma of the Fields persona:

> Prickly guardian of a few pitiful possessions (the contents of a moribund grocery or drugstore, a sad automobile of uncertain vintage, a flat barely evading classification as a slum), sour protector of the virtue of a family unit which he loathes and which unmercifully deflates his every attempt at dignity, nourisher of some hopeless dream of power and wealth, endless inventor of a past infinitely more appealing than the present, Fields was, par excellence, the *lumpen bourgeois* at bay. One was always certain that, just off screen, the minions of the chain stores were constructing a supermarket that would reduce him to penury.[1]

In addition to his worry over the ever-present possibility of bankruptcy, Fields very much craves the loyalty of his family, even in the face of the stridency of his wife and the physical cruelty of his children. His wife, in-laws, and younger children cozy up to him only on those occasions when he manages to succeed financially through sheer good luck. Yet one family member forever remains loyal; there is one person in the family unit whom Fields does not loathe. Fields always displayed a gentle tenderness toward his onscreen adolescent daughters. Such strong father-daughter bonds are evidenced by a longing on his part to do more for them than he fears he is able to do. For instance, in both *Running Wild* (1927) and *The Man on the Flying Trapeze* (1935), he intercedes between his daughter (played by Mary Brian in both films) and her stepmother, for he is trying to shield his daughter from the anger and indignation that his second wife lays quite heavily upon her stepdaughter.

According to Fields's biographer Simon Louvish, one of the most important results of Fields's appearance in *Running Wild* was the opportunity it gave him to meet Mary Brian, for she was to become his favorite screen daughter, a young girl who often protected him from himself and from his alcoholic excesses.[2] They appeared together in three films, including *Two Flaming Youths* (1927), and they remained friends and neighbors long after their professional association had ended.

The loyal relationship, both onscreen and off, that eventually developed between Fields and Mary Brian was similar to friendships that had been apparent earlier and others that would subsequently be echoed in affinities between Fields and other young women who would portray his daughters. It is possible that Fields longed for a daughter, but it is equally clear that the fictional daughters he treats with the most tender love and respect undeniably fall into a narrow category: they are young women who have outgrown the pesky brattiness of girlhood but who have not yet begun to approach the deteriorating effects of middle age. These petite, attractive young ladies are also the ones who tolerate — even sympathize with — his drinking.

Louvish speculates that it was Fields's appearance in the 1923 stage production of *Poppy* that established the recurring Fieldsian pattern of the young woman/older father figure: the two-against-the-world motif. Set against a nineteenth-century carnival background, *Poppy* is a melodramatic tale of an orphan girl who takes up with and is unofficially adopted by an often inebriated carny con man: the quintessential W. C. Fields's character. Though the story is a hoary sentimental tearjerker, both Fields as the con artist and Madge Kennedy as Poppy captured good notices from the New York theater critics. Moreover, Ms. Kennedy received letters from around the country; lonely old couples were so touched by her plight that they wanted to adopt her as their own. These proposals emanated directly from the emotional pain of strangers:

> This raw nerve which Poppy touched in certain lonely or unhappy old people was clearly echoed by the nerve it touched in Fields; it is from *Poppy* that we can date the fantasy relationship of father and daughter which was to become a staple of so many Fields films. The self-sacrificing father with the beautiful and vulnerable daughter stood in contrast to the real-life sundered relationship between the father and his estranged son. The long-dead mother-wife was so convenient a substitute for the very alive and very demanding Hattie [Fields's real-life, long-estranged wife].[3]

Likewise, in *It's a Gift* (1934), *Poppy* (1936) and *The Bank Dick* (1940), Fields clearly reveals a sentimental attachment to three other actresses who play his daughters— Jean Rouverol, Rochelle Hudson (the adopted daughter in *Poppy*), and Una Merkel, respectively. In addition to this longing for a stable family, another ambivalent tone is struck in Fields's attachment to the bottle. Throughout his film career, even in the many episodes that demonstrate Fields's public and private obsession with drinking, Fields the auteur and Fields the actor come together to suggest that his alcohol addiction is as much a subject for anguish as it is for laughter.

It Ain't a Fit Night Out for Man nor Beast

The Fatal Glass of Beer (1933) was not particularly well received by theater owners upon its initial release. J. E. Weber of the Princess Theater in Chelsea, Michigan, complained: "Two reels of film and 20 minutes wasted."[4] J. J. Medford of the Orpheum Theater in Oxford, North Carolina, concurred:

"This is the worst comedy we have played from any company this season. No story, no acting, and as a whole has nothing."[5]

I suspect that *The Fatal Glass of Beer* is a film more in tune with the twenty-first century than it was on its first appearance in the early twentieth. What these harsh critics referred to as "wasted" minutes and as "nothing" is, in truth, an excellent illustration of Fields at his absurd best. *The Fatal Glass of Beer* moves quickly, with people, animals, and objects appearing and disappearing apropos of nothing. The dialogue is nonsense, with no transitions between sentences. Nothing connects. By the same token, ours is a fast age, accustomed to instant access to information and communication via the Internet and text messaging. Yet most of what we see and hear pops up in fragments. We process information in bits and pieces; as a result, our lives tend toward incoherence and compartmentalization. Even our email has its own abbreviated language. So it is with the illogical, staccato pace of *The Fatal Glass of Beer*, which is perhaps the most blissfully insane short film ever made. In it, W. C. Fields plays Mr. Snavely, a man whose brain is happily disconnected from anything resembling reality. Although the movie is set somewhere up North, Fields actually lives nowhere; he is disengaged from both time and space.

The picture's title comes from a deliciously awful ballad that Snavely croons to a visitor, a man who has come calling on Snavely in his remote, snowbound cabin. His guest is Officer Posthlewhistle of the Canadian Mounted Police (Richard Cramer), who suddenly bursts into the remote Snavely cabin and improbably wants Snavely to entertain him. Like Snavely, he is bundled for subzero weather; what is more, he wastes no time in requesting that Snavely play his dulcimer and sing a tender song, which, insists Posthlewhistle, must have a good moral lesson. At first, Snavely demurs, claiming that his voice is not at its best because, as he seriously explains, "we can't get ipecac in this part of the country." But Snavely decides to accommodate his friend, so he opens a chest, out of which he first pulls a small electric fan, followed by a dulcimer. Although Snavely is wearing oversized mittens, he doesn't bother to remove them as he strums the chords and croons in an off-key quaver to Officer Posthlewhistle.

The song itself, such as it is, deals with the evils of drink. And, like all good ballads, it has a little story. This one tells of a poor country boy who goes to the city to look for work after promising his mother that he will lead a sinless life and "always shun the fatal curse of drink." But, alas, the luckless country boy goes to a tavern and falls in with some sinful, worldly college students, who tempt him to drink until at last he takes "the fatal glass of beer." When he discovers to his horror that he has taken that awful drink, he throws the glass upon the floor and staggers through the door "with delirium tremens." Once upon the sidewalk outside, he meets "a Salvation Army girl and wickedly broke her tambourine." However, this is no ordinary young crime victim, for she retaliates by delivering a graceful, high, balletic kick to the young country boy's head. It is, continues the singer, "a kick she'd learned before she had been saved." So, concludes Snavely, this earnest warbler, here is the moral for all young men who go to the city and fall victim to the terrible lure of alcohol, "Don't go around breaking people's tambourines." Poor Officer Posthlewhistle is reduced to tears by this sad saga of the horrors of life in the Big City.

All the while Snavely is singing this tale to the accompaniment of his dulcimer, we see the story enacted on screen: from the temptation in the tavern, to the consumption of that fatal glass of beer, to the young man's encounter with the athletic Salvation Army lass. The young man shown in these scenes is the sad-eyed, slow-talking George Chandler, who reappears later in the picture as Snavely's son, the horrible Chester: the prodigal returning home after spending three years in prison for embezzlement. When Fields and his tough-looking, aggressive wife discover that Chester has indeed stolen the bonds for which he did time and that Chester has subsequently thrown the "tainted money" away, they are enraged. Without those stolen bonds, the Snavelys no longer want dear Chester under their snowbound roof. Fields accuses him of coming back only "to sponge on us for the rest of your life" and hits the hapless son with a pitcher and washbasin. Mrs. Snavely joins in the attack by striking Chester with crockery. Then they toss the pajama-clad ex-convict out into the snow. The fatal glass of beer has long been forgotten.

Louvish has observed of this movie: "This is Fields at his most surreal, parodying the Frozen North and, probably, his rival Chaplin's rendition of it in *The Gold Rush*, in 1925.... All attempts to analyze the sketch's 'social significance' disappear into the buzz of its anarchic play on meaningless postures and juxtapositions.... Mark Twain would have rolled on the floor, had he seen it."[6] Certainly, Mark Twain would have appreciated the brilliant unpretentiousness of W. C. Fields. Furthermore, *The Fatal Glass of Beer*, in its dazzling incoherence, is one of the best short comedies of the 1930s.

In his analysis of many early short sound comedies, Andrew Sarris believes that the pacing can be exasperating but that with Fields, the pacing was nonetheless somehow appropriate: "With the coming of sound there was a tendency to let the spoken voice reverberate before cutting to the next action. But in the jumble of Fieldsian sadism represented in these shorts, the deliberateness of the pacing seems to add to the pain of the poor wretches whose fingers, toes, teeth, beards, and heads of hair fall into the path of Fields's malevolent muse of mangle."[7]

Wu Hu!

International House (1933) is a delightful, episodic mixture of music, romantic comedy, and vaudeville skits. In addition to W. C. Fields, the movie features the notorious man-chaser and many-times-married Peggy Hopkins Joyce, who plays herself and who plays around with the ever-alert Fields. The movie also includes such well- known players of the thirties as Stuart Erwin, George Burns, Gracie Allen, Franklin Pangborn, Bela Lugosi, Rudy Vallee, Baby Rose Marie, and Cab Calloway. The latter, in an upbeat rendition of "Reefer Man," pays tribute to the beauty of getting high on pot. In one of the early episodes, we see W. C. Fields also getting high. As he prepares to take off in his autogyro, several men are helping him in these preparations by hoisting boxes and beer kegs onto this relatively small flying contraption. Fields is shown sitting in the plane, blowing foam off beer mugs that are being handed to him by the crew on the ground. As we watch the scene, a voiceover narrator seriously intones: "Professor Henry R. Quail takes off from Juarez, Mexico on a secret mission." Weighted down with such a vast amount of beer, the autogyro wobbles dangerously as it takes off, relentlessly swinging from side to side, stumbling through the air, a drunken correlative to its unsteady pilot.

Yet Fields manages to become airborne and stay airborne; a short time later, we see a newspaper photo of Fields, smiling in close-up, smugly sitting in his plane. Underneath the photo is a headline and brief note about his shaky progress:

PROFESSOR QUAIL STILL EN ROUTE

Reports from various cities state that numerous people have been injured by empty bottles tossed from the plane by the Professor. All are resting comfortably as can be expected. The Professor's flight will go down in history as one of the outstanding events in aviation.

Accompanying this little tidbit is a map of the world that shows various countries throughout the globe being intersected with squiggly lines going in all directions. The map looks as though a small child has taken a crayon and marked haphazardly through it. Under this illustration is a caption: "Chart of Professor Quail's Flight in Autogyro."

Though it is a long way from Mexico to China, especially in a primitive kind of helicopter that appears to be flying nonstop, Fields takes no time at all to approach the fancy Roof Garden of the International House Hotel in Wu Hu, China. The garden is filled with guests who are dining in elegant surroundings. But their dinner is interrupted by the intrusion of a beer bottle that falls straight down, smashing a vase and landing upright.

Like an intrusive centerpiece, it sets itself down at a table occupied by the fussy Franklin Pangborn. Hovering over the Roof Garden, the autogyro gets close enough for the curious diners to hear the lost occupant yell down at them, "Hello below? Is this Kansas City, Kansas? Or Kansas City, Missouri?" Fields then lowers his autogyro neatly onto the center of the dance floor, exits his flying machine, and asks, "Hey, where am I?" The ensuing dialogue between Fields, Peggy Hopkins Joyce, and Franklin Pangborn, is marvelously absurd:

JOYCE: Wu Hu!

FIELDS (*eying her with much interest*): Wu Hu to you, sweetheart.

FIELDS (*calling to Pangborn*): Hey, Charlie, where am I?

PANGBORN: Wu Hu.

FIELDS (*looks at Pangborn's prissy expression, looks down at his lapel and removes the flower, tossing it away*): Don't let the posy fool you. Where am I?

PANGBORN: This is the Roof Garden of the International House.

FIELDS: Never mind the details. What town is it?

PANGBORN: This is Wu Hu, China.

FIELDS: Then what am I doing here?

PANGBORN (*exasperated*): Well, how should I know?

FIELDS: What is Wu Hu doing where Kansas City oughta be?

PANGBORN: Maybe you're lost.

FIELDS (*in his best bombastic manner*): *Kansas City* is lost! *I am here!*

At this point, Fields slides awkwardly out of his autogyro and lands clumsily on the Roof Garden dance floor. Mistaking Fields for someone else, a Chinese gentleman bows politely and greets him: "Honored visitor, I welcome you. I was afraid you might not arrive." Fields's reply is to the point: "Me too. I ran out of the last bottle of beer just a minute ago." Yet Fields's attention wanders momentarily from his obsession with drinking, for he has already spotted the provocatively-attired Peggy Hopkins Joyce and decided that she is going to be his partner for the evening. After allowing Fields to lead her to a table, she offers seductively, "Won't you join me in a glass of wine?" Ever ready to play, Fields quickly replies, "You get in first and if there's room enough, I'll join you." Yet here Peggy Joyce rebuffs all of Fields's romantic overtures, so he is forced to leave the dining area by himself — yet he is not quite alone. After the other guests have left, he moves easily from table to table, collecting quite a number of half full liquor bottles. By the next morning, we see what has happened to these bottles. Now empty, they are carefully nestled by the bed of the still slumbering Fields. When he awakens, he is greeted by one of the many manservants

W. C. Fields definitely needs another drink as he listens with growing irritation to Gracie Allen's nonsensical monologue in *International House* (Paramount, 1933). Fields plays Professor Henry R. Quail, who has just landed his autogyro on the rooftop garden of the International House Hotel in Wu Hu, China. By the time Quail lands, he has consumed his entire cargo of liquor, so he is delighted to find more liquid refreshments in Wu Hu (Photofest).

who are lurking about the elegant International House. "Water, sir?" inquires the man, addressing the still groggy Fields. Fields's reply is not at all surprising: "A little on the side. Very little." When the servant later brings Fields a tray with liquor and soda water, Fields is true to his request. He fills an eight-ounce glass with liquor and tops it off with a squirt of water.

This particular Fields's movie has an unusual plot twist: in this one he has no wife, no mother-in-law, and no children to nag him about his drinking. In fact, Fields is as airborne as his autogyro, with nothing at all to tie him down into frustrating domesticity. Although he flies off with Peggy Hopkins Joyce and their passengers Tommy Nash (Stuart Erwin) and Carol Fortescue (Sari Maritza), we can assume that Joyce is merely a passing fling and that soon he will once more take off— alone and lost again — on another "secret mission." Film critic Michael Sragow, in a capsule review of *International House* for *The New Yorker*, observes of Fields in this film: "Fields gives off a hilarious air of entitlement; in this film he's at the peak of his dirty old manhood."[8] And so he is.

Enter the Nagging Wives

As *You're Telling Me!* (1934) opens, we see W. C. Fields as the budding inventor and part-time optometrist Samuel Bisbee, who is wobbling his way up the walk to his house. There are only a few steps leading to his front porch, but he hesitates in front of them, unable to decide the best approach for his ascent. Finally, he sits on the bottom step and removes his hat, jacket, and shoes, apparently on the assumption that divesting himself of this attire will make him more mobile. Once Fields has managed to navigate the steps, he is faced with his next hurdle: opening the door. He dimly spots the keyhole, he has his key in hand, yet he finds that connecting the two is problematic. All is not lost, however, for he summons enough mental acuity to recall that he has a handy instrument to guide his way. Thus, he pulls out a metal contraption, one end of which fits neatly over the doorknob, the other end circling the keyhole. With such a tool to guide him, Fields at last manages to find the keyhole and get into the house.

Awaiting him upon his entrance is Mrs. Bisbee (Louise Carter), his disapproving wife: one in a long line of harridans who are determined to make life hell for the aggrieved Fields. Nevertheless, he is always wont to put the best face on these confrontations, so he assumes the most nonchalant attitude possible under the circumstances as he asks, "Is the dinner on the table, dear?" Mrs. Bisbee's reply reveals that she is not impressed with his false air of normality, however: "On the table and off—five hours ago." Still trying hard, Fields attempts once more to argue: "Oh, don't exaggerate. It's only the shank of the evening. Half past eight." Here he surreptitiously looks at his pocket watch, which displays the correct time: two minutes until midnight.

And Mrs. Bisbee is only too well aware of the time. Their ensuing argument focuses on Fields's blundering inability to make a good impression on his daughter and on his daughter's friends. She notes with bitter sarcasm her husband's disreputable physical appearance, "with your shoes off, your suspenders down, and your breath smelling of cheap liquor." Yet Fields naturally takes exception to her observation. His response is indignant: "Cheap? Four dollars a gallon." A short time later, he tries to make a dignified exit from the room but gets entangled in some drapery tassels. Trying to extricate himself, he flails his arms about as though he were an inept boxer fighting an invisible opponent, all the while muttering, "Worse than flypaper — might as well have flypaper curtains in the house."

Fields's place of business has a soothingly daffy atmosphere, which serves him as a retreat from the stultifying rigors of his home. On the window is a sign that announces his professional versatility; in descending order we read: *Samuel Bisbee*, followed by a large illustration of an eye. Then we see the various vocational hats Bisbee dons: *Optician, Optometrist, Oculist, Glasses Fitted*. Needless to say, Fields is never shown in any of these professional capacities. He does, however, have a back room in which he socializes with his cronies and brags about the stupendous inventions he is devising, including his amazing puncture-proof tire. The most prominent feature of this room is a keg of liquor that Fields keeps in the middle of the table around which he entertains his friends. At one point, he fills a glass from the wrong keg, drinks it, grimaces, and then discovers that he has sampled some roach exterminator. Nonetheless, his misstep appears to have been a minor one, for his insides are apparently inured to various forms of unhealthy liquids. In fact, after one of his pals realizes the error and provides him with the correct keg, Fields samples it and decides he prefers the rat poison.

Fields's drinking escapades are also well known to people of the town. In one episode, Fields has decided to board a train and run away from family troubles; he has determined to end it all by drinking iodine (an action that doubtless would not have caused his stomach any serious distress.) As he is stumbling down the train aisle on his way to do the deed, two old ladies recognize him and cluck disapprovingly at his unseemly progress:

FIRST OLD LADY: Hmp. There goes Sam Bisbee — drunker than a hoot owl.

SECOND OLD LADY: Is he a hard drinker?

FIRST OLD LADY: Hard? It's the easiest thing he does.

Naturally, all ends happily for Fields. His financial and personal problems are solved when he sells the rights to his puncture-proof tire and becomes a wealthy landowner whose wife and in-laws now at last consider him to be proper company. Yet Samuel Bisbee's character has changed only in outward appearance. In the final scene, Fields packs his family off and summons his buddies to join him in having "the first real drink I've had in months."

As the unfortunate Mrs. Bisbee, Louise Carter is an effective foil for the bumbling, but ultimately lucky, Fields. Also appearing in *You're Telling Me!* is Kathleen Howard as the supercilious mother of Larry "Buster" Crabbe, who wants to marry Fields's daughter Pauline (Joan Marsh), even though Pauline is from the "wrong" side of the tracks. Kathleen Howard would subsequently play Fields's wife in two of his best films— and the two that, incidentally, are my personal favorites—*It's a Gift* (1934) and *The Man on the Flying Trapeze* (1935). A former opera singer who had performed with both the Royal Opera Company of London and the Metropolitan Opera in New York, Kathleen Howard had a stunning vocal range, her contralto moving effortlessly from the lower range to an excruciatingly high pitch that must have certainly reverberated in Fields's head. So when she speaks indignantly to Fields, she sounds like she is viciously striking a metal bar with an iron pipe. And in *It's a Gift*, she has many such occasions to strike at him, for not only is he a tippler but, as in *You're Telling Me!*, he also dabbles in various unsuccessful money-making plots. In one early scene from *It's a Gift*, Howard raucously complains: "Remember that scheme to revive the celluloid collar you had a couple of years ago? Well, *that* was going to make you a *fortune.*" On her next line, her voice rises to an uncomfortable pitch, one calculated to inflict impalpable pain on its listeners: "*Where* is it?"

But Kathleen Howard as the long-suffering Mrs. Amelia Bissonette has good reason to complain about Mr. Harold Bissonette's reckless improvidence. After inheriting some money from his Uncle Bean, who has passed away while eating an orange ("I didn't know that oranges were bad for the heart," muses Fields), Bissonette buys a nonexistent orange ranch in California. Once again, Howard's Amelia Bissonette berates her husband. Fields has assumed one of his most typical positions: lying curled up on his side on the sofa, his left hand under his lead, the right on his hip. Ignoring the fact that Harold is trying very hard to relax, Amelia accosts him with her usual tirade. Standing menacingly over him, hand on hip, she complains, "The only real money you'll ever have and you threw it away before you could get your hands on a penny of it." Then, noting that Harold is trying to ignore her, she snaps at him: "Why are you lying down?" He meekly, sensibly replies, "I'm tired." Reaching for the upper octaves, Howard retorts, "Why don't you go to bed?" Fields tries hard to explain, "I thought I'd lie down and take a little nap first."

But naps are out of the question, for Amelia continues her harangue, as she wonders aloud how Harold ever got the bank to loan him money on the strength of his inheriting from his Uncle Bean's estate. Then, surmising that her husband must have summoned gumption from somewhere, she offers the following accusation, "Probably stopped in at the saloon on the way there." At this challenge, Fields partially raises himself, stammering in protest, "No, I didn't *tonight* ... I didn't." But as usual Amelia is not paying attention to her husband. She offers the following paradoxical challenge: "Are you listening to me? Wake up! Wake up and go to sleep." However, sleep is out of the question for Fields, who spends the remainder of the night outside on the porch in an uncooperative swing; he is harassed by the noise of the milkman, by the antics of Baby Leroy in the upstairs apartment, and, above all, by the intrusion of an obstreperous insurance salesman (former vaudevillian T. Roy Barnes). Barnes, in one of the most memorable few moments ever enacted in a film comedy, announces to Fields in a splendidly excruciating nasal voice that he is looking for Karl LaFong. When Fields evidences a lack of interest in Mr. LaFong, the persistent Barnes takes the trouble to spell the name for him: "capital *L*, small *a*, capital *F*, small *o*, small *n*, small *g*."

Despite these domestic setbacks, Fields hauls his family off to his newly purchased orange ranch in California. In addition to his wife, two children, a pesky mutt, and a dilapidated car, he takes along his flask to have ready whenever he is lucky enough to be away from Amelia's prying glances. When they set up their tent for the night, he hides behind its spacious folds while he sneaks a nip. But the ever-suspicious Amelia, ascertaining that his silence bodes ill, demands, "Har*old*! Are you drinking?" On the defensive once again, a chastened Fields replies, "No I'm not dear; I was thinking." Unconvinced that her husband could really have adopted a pensive mood, Amelia announces that, since there is little room inside the tent, he will have to put wood on the fire and sleep outside in a folding deck chair: "And no more *drinking*," she reminds him. Somewhat uncoordinated as a result of his continual sips from the flask, Fields gamely tries to set up the folding deck chair, but it remains neatly collapsed. "Don't forget to put the wood on the fire!" remonstrates an offscreen Amelia. "I won't, dear," responds Fields meekly, as he obeys her commands by throwing the obstinate chair on the fire and, flask still in hand, joining a nearby group of men who are singing "On the Banks of the Wabash." Yet he has no sooner joined the chorus than Amelia discovers the fate of the folding chair and throws a large object in Fields's direction, knocking off his hat and convincing him that it would be a prudent idea for him to return to their tent.

But a worse fate is awaiting Fields and family when they finally arrive at the California ranch, for which Fields has sacrificed both his inheritance and his small general store: the ranch is a lean-to that is about to fall in. As Fields sits disconsolately on the shack's front stoop, still drinking from an apparently bottomless flask, he is warned by a neighbor that some buyers want his particular property for a racetrack. The helpful neighbor also suggests that Fields hold out for as much money as possible. When the potential bargain hunters appear, the forewarned Fields continues his imbibing, all the while making a deal that ultimately gains him a fortune. The heretofore crabby Amelia, unused to good news where her husband is concerned, faints; however, the helpful Fields revives her with a shot of booze.

As in *You're Telling Me!*, Fields becomes a wealthy man of leisure through a series of serendipitous circumstances. By the movie's end, he no longer has to drink surreptitiously from his flask; instead, he has settled comfortably into his sumptuous orange ranch, complete with a table loaded with liquor bottles and all the oranges he can squeeze to add flavor to his ample supply of alcohol. And his whole family, now basking in the eternal sunshine of wealth, has readily forgiven him his former trespasses.

The Unfortunate Demise of Mrs. Nesselrode

In *Man on the Flying Trapeze* (1935) W. C. Fields plays Ambrose Wolfinger, a dependable fellow supporting a wife, mother-in-law, brother-in-law, and a daughter. In truth, Ambrose is so steady and predictable that he has not missed a day of work in twenty-five years; that is, not until the day he asks his boss for the afternoon off, telling his employer that he needs to attend the funeral of his mother-in-law, Mrs. Nesselrode (Vera Lewis, looking like a buzzard that has donned a dowdy dress). The fact that the old lady is still very much alive does not bother Ambrose in the least because he wants to go to the wrestling matches, and he has consequently had to think fast in order to come up with a feasible excuse for missing one half day of work. However, by the time Ambrose has told his whopper, we have already become so thoroughly acquainted with his dreadful family that we would not be unduly concerned were Mrs. Nesselrode to actually pass out of the scene forever.

Once again, Kathleen Howard plays the formidable wife. As Mrs. Ambrose Wolfinger, she continues to provide an indomitable counterpoint to the perpetually harassed Fields. In the opening scene, she is sitting up in bed, gazing quizzically at the empty bed next to hers. "Am*brose!*" she yells in her most challenging tone, her voice rising loftily on the second syllable as she continues: "*What* are you doing in the bathroom?" What Ambrose is doing in the bathroom, of course, is sneaking a drink. But he merely replies meekly, "Brushing my teeth, dear." In order to add credibility to his response, he takes his toothbrush and vigorously rubs it against the side of the cabinet, hoping that the brushing noise will quiet his suspicious wife. Additionally, he reveals his dexterity, doubtless polished through years of practice, by drinking from his glass all the while he is making brushing motions. From off camera come the dulcet tones of Kathleen Howard: "I don't know *what's* come over you lately! You're *always* in the bathroom brushing your teeth!" Then the camera cuts to a close-up of Howard, whose shrewd expression reveals that she doesn't trust Ambrose for a minute: "Are you *sure* you're brushing your teeth?"

Since Ambrose does not have a satisfactory answer to that query, he instead climbs into bed, satisfied that his bottle is well hidden somewhere in the vicinity of the bathtub. But even as he is settling in for a snooze, two burglars (Walter Brennan and Tammany Young) are seen entering the Wolfinger cellar, where they immediately discover Wolfinger's supply of applejack, help themselves to a generous drink, and subsequently begin singing "On the Banks of the Wabash," their inharmonious voices carrying very nicely through the floor vent into the Wolfinger bedroom. "*Ambrose*," interrupts Howard as Fields is trying to sleep, "Did you leave the radio on?" Getting no response, she goes to the vent and listens in increasing dismay, finally returning to her husband to announce in a panic: "Ambrose! Wake up! There are burglars singing in the cellar!" To his wife's total exasperation, Fields expresses his lack of concern with a marvelous non sequitur; he wants to know what the burglars are singing. "Oh, what does it matter what they're singing!" protests Howard. When she demands that he go down to investigate, he suggests that he get another hour or so of sleep first. When he finally lands in the cellar, having tumbled down the stairs, he finds that there are now three singing intruders: the two burglars and a cop who has joined them in drinking and vocalizing. Fields naturally decides to link up with them in their merrymaking; then, having had their fill of applejack and "On the Banks of the Wabash," the four finally stumble down the street to the police station, with the cop carrying a keg of the applejack to present as evidence. The consequence of this evening of frivolity is that Fields is put into the pokey for manufacturing applejack without a license; in the cell with him is a homicidal lunatic who torments Fields by going into great detail about how he has murdered his wife, though he reassures Fields that he had killed only one of his wives. ("That's certainly in your favor," the increasingly panic-stricken Fields encourages his cellmate.)

After his daughter comes to his rescue by dipping into her meager savings and bailing him out, Fields's Ambrose Wolfinger is now free to approach his boss President Malloy (Oscar Apfel) to ask for the afternoon off. Although Wolfinger has not had a day off in twenty-five years, Malloy still wants to know the reason for Wolfinger's odd request. Digging fast and quickly into his store of possible reasons, Wolfinger comes up with a sad tale of the death of his beloved mother-in-law, Mrs. Nesselrode. Naturally, Malloy is sympathetic, wanting to know how the old lady died. Still thinking of possible scenarios, Wolfinger begins to relate the story of how the old girl took a chill, of how he offered her a drink, and of how she refused it. But unfortunately, Malloy does not allow Wolfinger to finish the story; he neglects to hear the last part about Mrs. Nesselrode's refusal of stimulants. Instead, he hears only the part about how Wolfinger offered her a drink. Consequently, Malloy does a bit of conclusion jumping and assumes that poor Mrs. Nesselrode has been the victim of what he refers to as that well-known curse of modern society: poisoned liquor. Naturally solicitous of Wolfinger family's feelings, Malloy asks his employees to send flowers and notes of condolence to Mrs. Wolfinger. So, to the great consternation and puzzlement of both Mrs. Wolfinger and the not-yet-deceased Mrs. Nesselrode, floral wreaths and sympathy notes begin arriving at the house, unbeknownst to Ambrose, who is contentedly on his way to the wrestling matches.

Yet his contentment is to be short-lived, for Mrs. Wolfinger calls his office and discovers that her errant husband has taken the afternoon off to attend his mother-in-law's funeral. Nor is her mood improved when she receives the evening paper and shares the headlines with her mother:

AGED WOMAN VICTIM OF POISONED ALCOHOL

Mrs. Cordelia Nesselrode Takes Drink and Dies

As luck would have it, Ambrose encounters a series of unfortunate occurrences on his way to the matches and subsequently misses them altogether. Or he almost misses them, for, as he is standing outside next to the ticket window, he is hit by a flying wrestler who has just been picked up, tossed out of the ring and out of the building. Ambrose's secretary (Carlotta Monti, Fields's real life mistress) has also taken the afternoon off to see the wrestlers; when she finds him lying on his back, she kneels over him, offering him sympathy and comfort. Unfortunately, another wrestling match spectator, Fields's brother-in-law Claude (Grady Sutton), sees the two of them in this compromising position, and chuckles as he remarks with some amusement, "Drunk again. And lying in he gutter." Not content just to observe, he hurries home to report Ambrose's foul deed to his mama: "Took his secretary to the wrestling matches where they drank themselves into imbecility and fell into the gutter."

Yet as usual, in the end all turns out happily for Fields. Fired for lying, he gets his job back through the intercession of his loyal daughter; furthermore, he is taken back into the fold by his wife, who still cares for him after all. And Mrs. Nesselrode? Despite headlines to the contrary, she will remain true to her lifelong philosophy as a teetotaler.

One Good Dishonest Turn Deserves Another

W. C. Fields as Professor Eustace P. McGargle, carny barker and con man, is pouring drinks for attorney E. G. Whiffen (Lynne Overman). McGargle's hospitality is not altogether altruistic, however. He is hoping to get Whiffen so potted that Whiffen will divulge information about the extent of the fortune of the Countess Maggie Tubbs DePuizzi, played by the silly, simpering Catharine Doucet. ("Countess DePussy," Fields's McGargle at first gallantly addresses her, before she hastily corrects him. Fields delighted in getting such names past the censors.) Whiffen takes one gulp, sputters, and exclaims: "Land o' Goshen! That's hotter'n a depot stove, ain't it?" McGargle's reply is matter-of-fact: "Yes, it is. Ninety-eight percent alcohol and two percent sweetening. Very fine for your stomach, though. Let me help you to a little more here."

Poppy (1936) has a number of such humorous moments, most of which center around McGargle's penchant for drink and duplicity. The old carny man makes and peddles alcohol to sell at a dollar a bottle, but he always has a scheme up his sleeve or under his very ample hat. One luckless townsman (Bill Wolfe) is a notable victim of McGargle's machinations. After falling for McGargle's spiel about the health benefits of the bottled elixir, of which McGargle just happens to have many on hand, the sucker decides to buy just one and gives McGargle a five dollar bill. In place of the expected change, however, he gets in return five bottles of the stuff. Many of the film's ensuing episodes show the hapless fellow armed with those bottles and chasing after McGargle, all the while swearing that he doesn't want that many. At one point, McGargle snatches all five away from him, but naturally gives him no money in return.

In another one of his scams, Fields's McGargle goes into a bar and orders a whiskey; with him is a stray dog that he has just found. He places the dog on the bar and does an adroit ventriloquist turn, thereby convincing the bartender that the dog can talk. After he sells the talking dog, he rushes for the exit. But as he departs, the bartender hears the dog declare that he will never talk again. The skit is an old one — the talking dog gag doubtless a familiar one to moviegoers — yet Fields pulls the joke off and makes it appear rather fresh and funny.

Despite these humorous bits, *Poppy* finally descends into sentimentality, with Poppy (Rochelle Hudson) discovering that she is really and truly an heiress and marrying the callow young man she loves (Richard Cromwell). In the meantime, her adopted father McGargle saunters out in search of more scams, leaving her to live happily-ever-after.

Egbert Sousé Foils a Holdup

In *The Bank Dick* (1940), W. C. Fields's Egbert Sousé, resident of a Norman Rockwall-type town called Lompoc, has perhaps the all-time nastiest family ever recorded on film. His wife, Agatha Sousé (Cora Witherspoon), is ill mannered, crude, piggish, self-centered, and cruel. Unlike the musically inclined Kathleen Howard, who occasionally shows a gentleness and a soft spot for her dithering husband, Witherspoon gives no quarter at all to Fields. She epitomizes boorish vulgarity. His mother-in-law, Mrs. Hermisillo Brunch (the hefty, imposing Jessie Ralph), is equally terrifying; she is especially fond of tormenting Egbert with endless and loud commentary about his manifest limitations. Egbert's younger daughter, Elsie Mae Adele Brunch Sousé (Evelyn Del Rio), is a sly, manipulative, aggressive child of about eight who sadistically delights in kicking her father and throwing large objects at him. In the movie's opening scene, these three are seated at the breakfast table, cramming their mouths with food. As usual, the two older ladies are complaining about Egbert, who has not yet come down to eat. Mrs. Brunch bleats in stentorian tones: "Imagine a man trying to take care of his family by going to theater bank nights, working puzzle contests, and suggesting slogans." Into this unpleasant family gathering comes Egbert's older daughter Myrtle (Una Merkel), a soft-spoken whiner who loves her father but who has an annoyingly obsequious manner about her. She joins the others and begins sobbing. She proffers the reasons for her distress, as though anyone is listening, as though anyone cares: "My Sunday School teacher, Mr. Stackhouse, told me that he saw my father coming out of a saloon the other day and that dad was smoking a pipe." Her blubbering suggests that such a tragedy is almost too much for such a sensitive soul to bear. Nonetheless, Myrtle then regains her composure and announces resolutely: "Oh, I'll kill myself. I'll starve myself to death. That's the easiest way out. It's not so difficult to do." Then, completely calm and collected, she offers the following confession: "I tried it yesterday afternoon."

Naturally, the three buffoons at the table are not paying attention, for it is clear that Mrs. Sousé, in a tremendous display of poor table manners, is still cramming food into her mouth as she mumbles abruptly: "What's the matter with her?" Meanwhile, Mrs. Brunch continues her griping with respect to Egbert: "There he goes again. Drinking and smoking. House just reeks of liquor and smoke." At this summation of his bad habits, Egbert, descending the stairs, hastily swallows his cigar. Were it not for the devoted Myrtle, Egbert's life would be a complete hell. The report of her Sunday School teacher notwithstanding, Myrtle remains steadfast in her desire for her father's approval. For instance, at few moments later she proudly introduces her boyfriend, Og Ogilbey (Grady Sutton). "Og Ogilbey. Sounds like a bubble in a bathtub," observes the unimpressed Sousé. (Name is pronounced "Soosay" Fields keeps reminding Lompoc citizens.)

One of Fields's favorite refuges from this hideous family is a bar with the intriguing name of the Black Pussy Cat Café. Fields had originally wanted to call the establishment the Black Pussy Café, but the censors would have none of that. However, in this movie, Fields was able to slip a number of things past the cutting room floor; for one, whenever he refers to this hideaway, as he frequently makes a point to do in the course of the movie, he calls it the Black Pussy Café, clearly omitting the word *cat*. In addition, on all of the signs that display the name, *Pussy Cat* is not written as one word, contrary to traditional spelling expectations. Moreover, in one especially humorous scene, Fields is photographed in the foreground, sitting at the bar; the background shot, however, is in perfect focus as well, allowing the viewer to see the window and only one word of the bar's name as it appears painted on the outside. The word is naturally backwards with the letters themselves reversed, but the single word PUSSY is painstakingly printed in large capital letters. In a subsequent episode, when bank examiner J. Pinkerton Snoopington (Franklin Pangborn) is seated in the café, clearly printed behind him in the booth are the letters USSY. They provide a fitting backdrop for the persnickety, effeminate Pangborn and provide ample evidence of Fields's offbeat sense of humor and delight in foiling the censors.

One of Fields's favorite people in this little burg of Lompoc is the bartender (Shemp Howard) at this café. At one point, Fields asks him earnestly and confidentially: "Was I in here last night, and did I spend a twenty dollar bill?" When the bartender replies in the affirmative, Fields sighs happily: "What a load that is off my mind. I thought I'd lost it." Turning away to leave the bar, he picks up four cocktail glasses, being especially careful not to spill their contents. As he does this, he reassures the bartender: "I'll bring the glasses back later."

The Black Pussy Cat Café is also the place where Fields consummates a number of big deals and carries out some grandiose schemes. It is here that he listens to Mackley Q. Greene (Dick Purcell), movie location scout, complain about how his shooting schedule in Lompoc has been held up by the drunkenness of the director, A. Pismo Clam (Jack Norton). Not one to pass up an opportunity, Fields gives him a lengthy history of his directorial efforts with the likes of Keaton, Chaplin, and Fatty Arbuckle: "Can't get the celluloid out of my blood. Nights I used to tend bar." So Fields is naturally hired to replace the ailing director who, according to one character he meets on the movie set, "is as tight as a snare drum." When Fields inadvertently halts a bank robbery getaway by falling on top of one of the robbers at an opportune moment, he relaxes the next morning in the bar, retelling his exploits, all the while proclaiming that he deserves a good snort: "After the bout I put up with those two crooks, I'm still arm weary." His subsequent boasting about the bank president's gratitude, about the promise of a vice presidency, prompts an alert bar patron by the name of J. Frothingham Waterbury (Russell Hicks), a stranger to the area, to offer Fields a surefire deal on the purchase of some valuable beefstake mine stock. Fields listens attentively, all the while drinking shot glass after shot glass filled with booze. He finally orders a glass of water, only to use it as a miniature finger bowl into which he daintily dips his fingers. Fired with enthusiasm and liquor, Fields goes to the bank and tells one of the cashiers, his daughter's boyfriend Og — the bathtub bubble — about this great proposition. The chubby-cheeked and slow-witted Og is so convinced by Fields's palaver that he "borrows" five hundred dollars from the bank to buy the stock, promising himself that he will pay back the "loan" when he gets his bonus in four days.

However, Og's plans are set askew when bank examiner Snoopington arrives that same day to go over the books. But Egbert Sousé is always thinking, so once again the Black Pussy Cat Café becomes the setting for Fieldsian shenanigans. Determined to keep Snoopington away from the bank ledgers until Og gets his bonus and can repay the money, Fields leads the reluctant Snoopington to the Black Pussy and orders two whiskey highballs. However, Fields has mischief in mind, for he asks bartender Joe (Shemp Howard): "Has Michael Finn been in here?" Joe's conspiratorial reply shows confidence: "No, but he will be." Of course, once Snoopington has enjoyed his Mickey Finn, he almost immediately begins to feel its effects. He slumps backward against the wall, eyes glazed over. He announces to the pleased Fields: "I feel deathly ill." Ever ready to take advantage, Fields commiserates, adding the helpful suggestion that what Snoopington needs is food, perhaps some "nice chili con carne." This idea naturally makes Snoopington's stomach churn even more dangerously. At this point, with his prominent pince-nez highlighting his wide-eyed expression, Pangborn looks like a tired owl. Moreover, he even tries to fly, for after Fields props him up and returns him to his hotel — The New Old Lompoc House — and leads him up the stairs, Pangborn tumbles out the window. "Drat, drat, drat, drat," mutters Fields as he races down the stairs, through the lobby, and out the door in order to collect the unlucky Snoopington, retrieve him, usher him back into the lobby and up the stairs again. "Friend of mine caught him on the first bounce," Fields announces to the dumbfounded clerk. Watching the inebriated guest stagger, a frumpy old lady accosts the hotel clerk with her displeasure: "I shall make it my business to see that the Lompoc Ladies' Auxiliary will be informed. I thought this was a family hotel." When the clerk reassures her by repeating Fields's information that the guest is only suffering from ptomaine, the respectable lady is unimpressed: "Hmph. Didn't smell like ptomaine."

But Fields isn't through with Snoopington yet. Having got the bank examiner comfortably settled in bed, he decides that he must call a doctor, his old friend Dr. Stall (Harlan Briggs). The aptly named Dr. Stall will, of course, delay the return of Snoopington to the Lompoc Bank. When Fields telephones Dr. Stall to explain why a doctor's service is necessary, he is careful to explain that the man in question is a bank examiner, "an old friend of the family" who has been "on a bender. He is full of nose paint." (Frankly, the meaning of "nose paint" in this context escapes me, unless it possibly refers to a reddening of the nose as a consequence of too much alcohol.) Meanwhile, Pangborn's Snoopington is in agony, clearly suffering from an acute upset stomach: a distress exacerbated by Fields's insistence on suggesting to Snoopington all of those good things that Snoopington might want to eat. Among these are "breaded veal cutlet with tomato sauce" and "a chocolate éclair with whipped cream." As Fields continues to recommend such tantalizing food, Snoopington keeps placing his hand over his mouth, leaping from bed, and racing to the bathroom.

Enter Dr. Stall, smoking a pipe and looking quite self-satisfied. "How's business" queries Fields. Stall seems resigned to a recent dearth of clients: "Fair. I don't suppose we'll ever get another whooping cough epidemic again." Despite his gloom over a lack of prospective patients, Stall appears determined to add Snoopington to his list of customers. He begins his torture of the bank examiner by edging close to Snoopington's bedside and blowing smoke directly into Snoopington's face. "Do you mind showing me your tongue?" asks Stall, while Snoopington, already sick and dizzy, recoils from the smoke. After briefly staring at Snoopington's obliging tongue, Stall confidently affirms his remedy: "You must eat more solids— meats and sauces. You need iron: liver and bacon. You lack vitamins A, B, and C." Next, Stall produces a large jar of pills that look like big mothballs, and explains what Snoopington is to do with these balls: "You take two of these in a glass of castor oil for two nights running. Then you skip one night." Fields adds encouragement, explaining to Snoopington that the pills are "perfectly tasteless. Very good with goulash."

All the while Snoopington is being subjected to Stall's excessive zeal, Fields is trying to make it clear to Stall that Snoopington must remain where he is for four days, since that is "when the boys at the bank get their bonus." After the obliging Stall leaves, Fields also exits, but on his way out he reassures Snoopington: "I'll have the missus bake you a coconut custard pie with saveloy pudding." The prospect of eating a pudding of cooked dry sausage made from pigs' brains sends Snoopington right back into the bathroom.

However, all of Fields's strenuous, imaginative efforts to keep Snoopington from examining the bank records come to nothing; later that same day, Snoopington recovers enough from the ministrations of Fields and Dr. Stall to enter the bank in search of an audit. Never one to give up, Fields reiterates to Snoopington the absolute necessity of bed rest, for, according to Fields, Snoopington has that dread disease: "mo go on the ga go go." Yet once again, all turns out happily. Snoopington never gets around to checking those books. Og's beefstake mines are really and truly worth a fortune, so Og won't have to go to prison and can return the bank's money. Fields makes a mint by selling a screenplay; furthermore, he adds to his wealth by catching another bank robber and getting the reward. His nasty family members remain nasty, but that's O.K. because now they are rich and nasty; consequently, they no longer care when the family patriarch wants to leave their newly acquired mansion and venture outside to engage in his happy pursuits.

Supporting Actors

At this point, it is appropriate to discuss the style of two character actors who provided able support for Fields in a number of movies. Franklin Pangborn was ideally suited to be Fields's foil in both *International House* and *The Bank Dick*. Pangborn's fussbudget characters in these movies provide a perfect counterpoint to the Fieldsian chicanery, with Pangborn's exasperated eye-rolling and "you-really-mustn't-do-this-to-me" protests providing a tidy counterbalance to Fields's subversive plots. Fields's "posy" line in *International House* implies knowledge of Pangborn's homosexuality, as does the PUSSY sign clearly displayed behind Pangborn's back in the bar scene in *The Bank Dick*. Writing about Pangborn, Anthony Slide comments: "The characters he portrayed were generally 'sissified,' with arched eyebrows and mincing walks. He could be prissy and pompous, and he was the ultimate screen 'pansy.'"[9] Furthermore, like so many gay movie actors of the first sixty years or so of the twentieth century, Pangborn led a discreet private life, though he would become a regular, along with other members of the gay colony in Hollywood, at Cole Porter's soirees in the 1930s and 1940s.[10]

Yet, to his credit, Fields had no qualms about working again and again with closeted gay actors, including the round-cheeked, whiny, but faintly likable Grady Sutton. One film historian has called Sutton "nearly everyone's favorite prissy bungler."[11] Off screen, Sutton, like Pangborn, was circumspect about his private life; even in old age, near the end of his life, he would hang up on inquisitive interviewers and "maintained a stony silence about the gay subculture of Hollywood."[12] Yet both Pangborn and Sutton capitalized on the effeminate types with which they were usually identified. In so doing, they were the perfect complements to the commanding but often intoxicated presence of W. C. Fields. In addition, even today, a reevaluation of these two comedic character actors continues to provide added insight into Fields's perennial penchant for drinking. When they allow themselves to be assaulted, both physically and verbally, by Fields at his bombastic best, they also expose that Fieldsian weakness for alcohol. Here is a sad, world-weary man who remains forever tied to the knowledge that the world — as represented by such oafs as Pangborn and Sutton — is probably even more absurd than he fears. Therefore, Fields's understanding of the white logic of alcohol only serves to confirm and reinforce his nihilistic suspicions.

Eddie Cantor, who had worked with Fields in the Ziegfeld Follies early in the twentieth century, remained friends with the comedian until Fields's death on Christmas day in 1946. The day before, Cantor had visited his dying friend in the hospital. As Cantor later related the story, Fields, too weak to talk, whispered to his fellow vaudevillian: "I wonder how far I might have gone if I had laid off the booze?"[13]

It is doubtful if Fields would ever have been truly content as a teetotaler. He was too aware of the grin of Jack London's Noseless One, of the allure of the White Logic. Fields always knew of life's impermanence, was ever aware that death is never optional. Ultimately, then, it is tempting to imagine Fields as the quintessential Modern Man, transported into the twenty-first century: to see him seated at a computer, a large bottle of gin balanced on the pullout shelf next to the keyboard, chuckling merrily and muttering maledictions at the screen, all the while hitting the DELETE key again and again.

5

Alcohol and the
High Life in the 1930s

CARY GRANT: Maybe what you need is some time out from what
you've been doing — day in, day out.

KATHARINE HEPBURN: You mean time out from what I've *not* been
doing —*days* in, *years* out.

—*Holiday* (1938)

By the mid–1930s, approximately one-third of the nation remained unemployed and unsure of where their next meal was coming from. Rural America was hit especially hard by the Depression. In 1934, the per capita income of a farm family was only $167; however, the national median, at only $1500, was not much better.[1] Yet many of these struggling poor, whether farm or city workers, were often willing to spend a nickel or dime in order to go out on the town on Saturday night to see a movie. And what they often saw was a world that was as remote from their own as the North Pole, for many of these pictures satirized those who had the good fortune to be rich.

Depression-era audiences were not only eager to look at fancy clothing and elegant Fifth Avenue mansions complete with elevators, but also happy to observe the manifest flaws inherent in the empty lives of the rich — lives that most could only imagine.

Bing Crosby Plays Bing Crosby

The Big Broadcast (1932) is an entertaining Prohibition era musical starring the immensely popular Bing Crosby as a radio singer named, of course, Bing Crosby. He has legions of female fans who constantly chase him through the streets, occasionally causing him to miss a big radio broadcast. One evening, he settles into his favorite speakeasy, where he meets a Texas millionaire, Leslie McWhinney (Stuart Erwin). McWhinney is aptly named, for he is seated behind rows of empty cocktail glasses and drunkenly whining about the inconstancy of women, one of whom has just relieved him of $100,000. But McWhinney is not worried about the loss because he is worth over one million dollars which, by 1932 standards, makes him terrifically rich.

Crosby, who has a few dollars himself, and McWhinney immediately become the best of pals and continue their imbibing much later that night at Crosby's fancy penthouse apartment; here they moan together over the fickleness of women and subsequently decide to End It All by closing the windows and turning on the gas. But their determination is thwarted by two late-night visitors who light a match and blow up the place, leaving the two stupefied buddies none the worse for wear: their lives and their fortunes and Crosby's penthouse intact.

Even Married Couples Can Have a Good Time

While the Crosby-Erwin relationship borders on slapstick, many depictions of depression high life have a more polished tone. Sophisticated romantic comedies of the 1930s often showed the pleasures of alcohol consumption within a setting of casual elegance. The rich continued to be satirized in these movies, their stylish manners and morals both scrutinized and envied by Depression audiences. Such skilled actors as William Powell, Myrna Loy, Cary Grant, Constance Bennett, Katharine Hepburn, David Niven, and Lew Ayres would spend many happy hours in these lavish, carefree settings, drinking but apparently — and unrealistically — suffering no obviously dire consequences.

The Thin Man (1934), along with its many sequels, is an excellent illustration of the fun that a wealthy yet happily married couple can have with cocktails and with each other. In this film, Nick and Nora Charles (William Powell and Myrna Loy) project the quintessential image of the perfectly coiffed, nattily attired Important People About Town. That Nick Charles is also a clever sleuth becomes secondary to the bon vivant style he effortlessly maintains. When we first see William Powell's Nick in this, the first onscreen incarnation of *The Thin Man*, he is standing at a nightclub bar, a place where he is clearly well known. In the background, we can hear an orchestra playing an upbeat tune. With a few rhythmic motions designed to be in step with this tune, Nick Charles is cheerfully demonstrating to some of the club's employees the proper way to shake a Manhattan: he declares that the shaker's movements should be synchronized to the beat of a fox trot.

To the accompaniment of this particular beat, in hastens Nora Charles (Myrna Loy), loaded down with Christmas packages and further burdened by something attached to the end of a leash. Indeed, Nora's urgency is underscored by the fact that she is being pulled onto the dance floor by the clever Airedale, Asta. Because Mrs. Charles, like Mr. Charles, is already slightly tipsy, Asta has no trouble in upending her and her unwieldy boxes. Once several helpful bystanders have pulled her up, Nora gains enough self-possession to spot her husband and explain her ungraceful entrance. Looking accusingly at Asta, she tells Nick: "He's dragged me into every gin mill on the block." Nick's next observation demonstrates that Nick understands Asta's homing instinct: "Yea, I had him out this morning." To this, Nora replies dryly: "I thought so."

Next, Nora proceeds to show that she can match her husband with actions as well as with words. She sits with him at a table and inquires as to how many martinis he has drunk. When he answers "six," she looks at the one cocktail glass in front of her and orders five more martinis. She is clearly having a good deal of fun with these playful games of one-upmanship. But the entertainment appears to have ended — at least temporarily — by the next scene, which shows Loy back home, stretched out in the bed, painfully, but not regretfully, hung over. She complains to her solicitous spouse, "What hit me?" Buoyant as always, Powell replies with a sly smile, "The last martini. How about a little pick-me-up?" However, this proffered hair of the dog is too much for Loy, who gives out with a most emphatic, "NO!"

When Nick and Nora Charles are not wandering about with drinks in their hands, they get involved with a number of murders. After the discovery of the first body, they host a cocktail party, ostensibly to celebrate Christmas, though any excuse for a gathering of drinking friends will do. Present at this event are dozens of people, many of whom Nick and Nora do not know. In fact, Nora makes a disingenuous call to the operator of the apartment lobby, instructing her listener about potential guests: "Don't bother to announce anyone. Just send them all up. They're all his friends." Meanwhile, Powell's Nick makes a continuous circle of the room, cocktail tray in hand, genially handing out drinks to increasingly inebriated guests. As the evening passes away, the celebrants' mood becomes more and more festive. Finally, they show their camaraderie by screeching a discordant rendition of "Oh, Christmas Tree." Meanwhile, one of the partygoers blubbers into the phone his frustration at his inability to connect with someone very important at the other end of the line: "I wanna talk to *mother*."

The evening's festivities finally ended, Nick and Nora retire to their cozy twin beds. Also present in their bedroom is a large supply of liquor bottles, conveniently placed in a corner of the room. These come in handy when one or the other or both awaken in the middle of the night and feel the need for refreshment. Such an occasion soon presents itself when a crazed assailant enters their bedroom and shoots Nick. After the cops arrive and nab the culprit, Nora asks the slightly wounded and somewhat dazed Nick if he would like a drink. But her question is as unnecessary as his reply, "Whadda *you* think?"

In spite of his penchant for alcohol, Nick Charles pulls himself together sufficiently enough to solve the three murders that occur in the course of *The Thin Man*. Moreover, the next-to-last scene in the picture is the traditional one involving all of the principal players brought together for the purpose of listening to the sharp-eyed detective tell them which one of those present is the murderer. In keeping with his overall sociability, however, Nick gathers all the usual suspects around a sumptuously outfitted dining table, complete with candles, liquor, and butlers. As he neatly, confidently summarizes the actions of the assembled company and the often deadly events that have ensued as a result of these actions, he brandishes his liquor glass. Finally, he proposes a toast. In so doing, he misquotes an old cliché, one that is fraught with meaning and potential disaster for those who have been so intimately involved with the three deceased persons: "Let us eat, drink, and be merry, for tomorrow we die." Then, as Nick coolly describes those occurrences that have preceded the murders, Nora interrupts his speech at the table by leaning over to him and beginning the following sotto voce dialogue with her husband.

NORA: Is this true?

NICK: I don't know.

NORA: Then why are you saying it?

NICK: It's the only way it makes sense.

With this observation, Nick raises his glass and takes another drink. Of course, his identification of the guilty one is correct. So all ends happily, with Nick and Nora in the last scene comfortably easing themselves into a train compartment's lower berth. Both are blissfully tight and ready to play.

The director of *The Thin Man*, W. S. Van Dyke II, took only twelve

Myrna Loy and William Powell as Nora and Nick Charles strike a typical stylish pose with cocktail glasses raised as they host a Christmas party in *The Thin Man* (MGM, 1934). Nick is a super sleuth who always solves the mysteries that fall his way; Nora is his cool helpmate. They seem supremely content at this tipsy gathering, even though they are unacquainted with most of their guests (Photofest).

days to complete the picture. A director who had earned the nickname of "one take" Van Dyke, he was probably responsible for the fast paced air of spontaneity and fun that pervades the picture.[2] Indeed, Powell and Loy are obviously enjoying themselves throughout as the always tipsy Nick and Nora.

More Murder Among the Rich

The opening of *After Office Hours* (1935) gives the viewer every indication that what follows will be a movie of the drunken reporter genre. We are introduced to Clark Gable — the quintessential hard-boiled reporter — and Stuart Erwin, the quintessential good pal of the leading man. Gable is in the newsroom and is chastising Erwin, a news photographer who has been missing from his job for a number of days. When Gable asks Erwin where he has been for the past three days, Erwin replies "Brooklyn." Gable's next question makes a natural assumption about newspaper people: "Drunk again?" To this, Erwin replies sarcastically, "How can I get drunk in three days?"

But *After Office Hours* is not a picture about alcoholic reporters but rather about alcoholism among the rich and notorious. In this film, the reporter is the detective and the accused murderer is Henry King Patterson (Hale Hamilton), a famous, wealthy alcoholic who is falsely accused of murdering his cheating wife; the murder accusation comes about precisely because, in his upscale society circles, Patterson has a well-deserved reputation as an aggressively dissolute drunk.

Clark Gable as reporter James Branch first meets the cantankerous alcoholic Patterson at a posh drinking establishment called the Riverview Club. Also at the club that evening are Mrs. Julia Patterson (Katharine Alexander) and Tommy Bannister (Harvey Stephens), the playboy with whom Mrs. Patterson is scandalizing society by having an affair. Mrs. Patterson is obviously annoyed that her husband is among those present at the nightclub. Moreover, Henry Patterson is making embarrassingly belligerent remarks while in his customary drunken state. Increasingly irritated by her husband's comments, Julia Patterson observes sarcastically to those present: "Henry says the cutest things when he's drunk. And he's always drunk." To this, the angry, cuckolded Henry, aware that his wife is flaunting her lover in public, retorts: "Why shouldn't I be drunk? I got more right to be drunk than anyone else in the world." As if to reinforce the reasons for Henry's righteous indignation, Julia starts to leave the nightclub with Bannister. At this, the increasingly disturbed Henry orders Bannister to take his hands off Julia. Trying to salvage some dignity in the face of a good deal of curiosity on the part of those watching (among them reporter Gable, who just loves a tantalizing scandal), Julia determines to steer her husband away from any more humiliation: "I think we'd better go home, Henry. You're in no condition to entertain guests." But, as usual, Henry is in denial: "My condition is my own affair."

Much later that evening, Mrs. Patterson is found dead in the family mansion: murdered by a person or persons unknown. Even so, her husband is naturally arrested for the murder. Not only had the maid seen the Pattersons violently quarreling earlier that evening, but Henry Patterson himself has no recollection of what he had done in his fuzzy-brained condition in the course of that night. Consequently, the hapless Henry concedes that, yes, he might very well have been the murderer. But sharp-eyed reporter Gable suspects Bannister, who does indeed turn out to be the true killer. All loose ends are tied up as Bannister is captured, Gable and Constance

Bennett — a very rich lady whom Gable has been pursuing throughout the picture — are married, while Patterson undoubtedly resumes his drinking — but minus his nagging, now deceased wife. And after the first scene, no one ever again mentions that news photographer Stuart Erwin might have a drinking problem.

Although *After Office Hours* was a relatively minor picture, it received good contemporary notices. Clark Gable was a major MGM star in 1935, and reviewers took note of that fact. So too, Constance Bennett was a favorite of moviegoers: "She [Bennett] is in training to be a newspaper woman and already can hold her liquor. There isn't much story but a lot of smart lines and situations."[3] In hindsight, of course, we can see that these "smart lines and situations" revolve around the drinking proclivities of the "smart," upper class set.

Drunken Ghosts

By 1937, Cary Grant had become one of the most popular stars in Hollywood. He had broken away from the spineless, pretty boy parts that the studios had forced him to play in the early 1930s and had begun to develop the sophisticated, detached, ironic, yet darkly comic persona that would characterize his roles for the remainder of his career. His portrayal of the wealthy, dissolute George Kerby in *Topper* (1937) typifies the beginnings of such maturity. From the opening scene, we know that George and his wife Marion are heading for disaster. They are riding in a fancy, custom-built convertible; however, they are decidedly not *driving* this car, for George is sitting on the car trunk, happily steering the auto with his feet. His wife Marion (Constance Bennett in another sophisticated role) is seated next to him; both are cheerfully intoxicated and singing loudly and off key. They are, of course, on their way to a nightclub where they plan to have more fun with alcohol. In keeping with their elite financial status, they visit a chic and innovative club where the only way in is by way of a slide like those found on elementary school playgrounds. George observes this bizarre means of access and wryly comments to Marion: "Honey, you slide in and they *carry* you out."

Indeed, by the time they close the club, they are nearly ready to be carried out, though they manage to stumble to their car and drive to the bank run by their friend Cosmo Topper (the slyly perplexed Roland Young). George, who is on the bank's Board of Directors, has an appointment with Topper the following morning and has decided to get there early, park, and settle with his wife into an alcoholic-induced sleep until the bank opens.

It is long past closing time, but Cary Grant and Constance Bennett (both leaning on piano) as George and Marion Kerby do not seem concerned. Although in
this scene from *Topper* (MGM, 1937) the Kerbys have not yet become ghosts,
they are still well on their way to entering fantasyland. Here they are reluctant
to leave the nightspot where they have spent the evening drinking. Hoagy
Carmichael is the pianist; George Humbert is the impatient nightclub owner;
Donna Dax is the bored hatcheck girl (Photofest).

By the next morning, they have naturally drawn a crowd, but they seem not
to care. Both have a deliberate insouciance that carries them through even
the most potentially embarrassing of episodes.

Nowhere is this studied casualness more evident than in the next
episode where George and Marion invade the staid respectability of the
Topper bank and create a good deal of internal havoc in the orderly existence of Cosmo Topper. Both of the Kerbys are still clad in their evening
clothes from the night before, yet they are at least momentarily sober.
George manages to disrupt the Board of Directors meeting with his inappropriate comments, but he doesn't distract Topper as much as Constance
Bennett's Marion does. While George is holding forth with the Board, Marion sneaks into Topper's office and, still hung over, she falls asleep on his
couch. Yet she awakens when Topper enters and proceeds to do her best to
tantalize and arouse him. Her formal nightclub gown is low cut, tight fitting,

sleeveless, and revealing. So too, her high heels are designed to show her slender legs to their best advantage. Taking full advantage of her slender, fashion model figure, she sits in Topper's swivel chair behind his desk, raises her legs provocatively, and places her feet on his desk. In so doing, she is careful to make certain that her dress is pulled up to her knees. Then, sure that her wardrobe is just the way she wants it, she moves the chair back and forth, swinging her legs in such a way that Cosmo can easily see up her dress. The scene is daring — one that obviously got past the 1937 censors.

In addition, Marion's conversation with Cosmo is geared towards making Cosmo less uptight; she playfully teases him not only with her body but also with her words. She calls him "Toppy," encouraging him to lighten up and enjoy life more. She also astutely comments playfully on the fact that he is staring at her knees. (Actually, he appears to be staring elsewhere, somewhat higher on her anatomy.) When Cary Grant's George Kerby enters, he does not seem at all concerned about the fact that his wife is trying to seduce Topper. Rather, Kerby spends a few fruitless minutes looking for a bottle, assuming that Topper must naturally keep one in his office. He finally gives up and asks Topper where it is. Topper is indignant: "There isn't a bottle. This is a *business* office." To this reply, George patiently explains to Topper about where one should put one's priorities: "Listen, business is all right in its place, but don't you think that's carrying business a little too *far*?"

Though George and Marion are droll sophisticates while they are alive, they are even more amusing after they are dead, having been killed in a car crash shortly after they leave Topper's bank. *Topper* is, after all, a movie about dead people arising from their physical bodies and the fun that ensues from their ghostly — and inebriated — invisibility. When George and Marion realize that they have emerged from the accident as ghosts, they decide that they must do something constructive, a good deed, to redeem themselves in the afterlife. And who better to perform this good deed upon than Cosmo Topper? The Kerbys resolve to save Topper's soul by showing him that life can be exciting if only one will get rid of inhibitions, will divest oneself of boring routines and daily schedules. And the way in which to accomplish this lifestyle betterment is to cast off convention by drinking to excess.

So, in due course, they capture the bewildered, confounded Topper and take him to their exclusive penthouse apartment. George is especially delighted to be back home again because, as he tells Topper, "I haven't had a drink in days." George proceeds to remedy this neglect and also to begin Topper's rehabilitation by offering Topper a generous cocktail. Topper confesses that he once took a drink, but that it wasn't much fun, for he got dizzy and had to keep one eye shut. However, having gotten used to the idea that the Kerbys are indeed ghosts who have been sent to tantalize him, the poor repressed banker is game for anything now. Dressed in a gray business suit and looking like a puzzled beaver, Roland Young is so right as the repressed businessman that it is hard to visualize anyone else in the role. Very solemnly, Young's Topper finally makes an eventful decision as he announces to George: "Maybe I do need a drink. Maybe I've needed a drink all these years and haven't known it."

Certainly the alcohol has a rejuvenating effect on poor Cosmo. After one drink, he begins acting squirrelly. While seated next to George, he suddenly declares that he feels like singing and dancing. As though taking on a life of their own, his feet begin moving erratically in an odd sort of sit-down dance. Grant assumes a quirky, quizzical expression — one for which he was to become well known — and questions Topper's out-of-character movements: "What is this dancing complex?" The query about his "complex" is indeed too complicated, too abstract a question for Topper, who simply replies, quite seriously, "Look here, would you mind if I just got up and danced around about on my tiptoe?" Topper then proceeds to do just that, as he waltzes effortlessly and gracefully about the room, holding tight to an imaginary partner. As he completes a circle, this dancing beaver announces confidently to a bemused George: "I think I could learn how to live after all." Moreover, he credits his new-found ability to live with his new-found interest in the benefits of alcohol. In addition, as a byproduct of his knowledge that he can drink with no difficulty, he is convinced that he will be able to sing as well. So far, George and Marion are well on their way to "redeeming" Topper from his former, boring life choices.

But Topper's redemption is short-lived. Following his efforts to practice waltzing with the ghost of Marion, Topper collapses on the floor and assumes an interesting, quasi-fetal position: He is lying on his stomach, but his feet are propped on a chair; his hands are folded under his head, his butt sticking straight up. George's observation is an understated one: "Poor Topper. I don't think he knows how to drink." Soon, however, the fun-loving, ghostly Kerbys haul Topper down to the penthouse lobby. Since the Kerbys can dematerialize at will, and since they do so before taking Topper out of their penthouse, the stupefied, staggering banker looks mighty odd to the other apartment residents seated in the lobby. One perplexed bystander wonders aloud: "What's the matter with that man? Why doesn't he fall?" His wobbly, jerky appearance resembles that of a marionette operated from above by an unseen handler using invisible wires; he even spooks the elevator operator (a pre–Dagwood Arthur Lake), who deserts his post and runs down the stairs. After a frantic dash to the lobby, Lake catches up with Topper, who is not moving anywhere nearly as quickly as his slender, energetic pursuer. Demonstrating a good deal of righteous indignation, Lake confronts the befuddled Topper: "What's the idea of stealing my elevator?" Then, compounding Lake's confusion, Marion's voice comes from somewhere out in space: "We haven't got your elevator, silly." Finally, as if to add more insult to Lake's already acute mental distress, the apartment manager fires him for insulting a guest.

Still in a semi-conscious state, Topper is carted outside by the Kerbys. Here the blissfully distraught banker gets into a fight with some curious onlookers and is subsequently arrested and hauled away to court where he pays a fine and is dismissed, even though he arouses the curiosity of the judge, who watches in amazement as Topper's hair is rearranged and his clothes tidied through the intervention of an unseen agent. Moreover, notoriety sits well on the erstwhile nondescript banker, for once his antics make the headlines, his staff members become exuberantly friendly, his secretaries flirt with him, and his wife receives social invitations from snooty ladies who had heretofore snubbed her and who represent some of the best families in the city. Yet all of this is too much for poor Cosmo, who decides to escape from his jealous wife (the wonderfully elegant and daffy Billie Burke). Nevertheless, there is no escape from the persistent Marion, who materializes in Topper's car and insists on his taking her to the Seabreeze Hotel for a little fun and frolic. By this point, Topper's redemption is nearly complete. He eagerly takes Marion to the hotel nightclub and orders quite a number of pink ladies— to be served all at one time. Yet by now, George has become jealous of Marion's and Topper's attentions to one another, so he intervenes and jumps into the car with them as they leave the hotel. Once again, there is a wreck; this time Topper is injured, but, unlike the Kerbys, he survives. So all ends happily; Topper is reunited with his wife, George resolves to quit drinking, and George and Marion go on their ghostly way, having completed their good deed for Topper. Presumably, Topper will be a more carefree man, now that he has learned how alcohol can loosen inhibitions; in addition, his teetotaling wife is so happy to have him back alive following his auto accident that we are led to believe she will now allow him to live a less structured, less sober life.

Although *Topper* has not worn particularly well with the years, Grant, Bennett, Young, and Burke give earnest, believable performances. Writing about Cary Grant, Andrew Sarris has astutely observed: "*Topper* (1937), with Constance Bennett as his after-life consort, and with Roland Young as the eponymous survivor of this otherworldly farce-fantasy, helped establish a certain high society gloss for his persona, but was otherwise by far the least endearing and enduring of the 'classic' screwball comedies."[4] Yet

Cary Grant also has a resilience about him that is evident in *Topper*. Charles Champlin summarizes this aspect of Grant's character:

> The other paradoxes which have surfaced in the Grant characterizations over the years include his special blend of worldliness and naiveté and his ability to mix polish and pratfalls in successive scenes. Grant is also, refreshingly, able to play the near-fool, the fey idiot, without compromising his masculinity or surrendering to camp for its own sake. His ability to play off against his own image as the strong and handsome romantic hero-figure is, as a matter of fact, probably unique among the superstars. No one else comes even close to mind who could similarly toy with his own dignity without losing it.[5]

In *Topper*, Grant does engage in some silly acts and carries them off with comic aplomb. On the other hand, another film historian has persuasively argued that something forbidding and dark also lingers in the Cary Grant character: "And there is something feline about him ... a hint of danger, a look of sheathed-claw contentment."[6] In addition, the suggestion throughout that alcohol can solve all problems associated with a boring lifestyle is never quite convincing. Nonetheless, the happy-go-lucky attitude taken throughout the movie toward the pleasures of drinking decidedly reinforces a fact of life established by Nick and Nora Charles several years earlier: that married couples can have fun while staying pleasantly plastered.

The Rich Are Very Different

Three Blind Mice (1938) is in many ways a forerunner of *How to Marry a Millionaire* (1953), a popular movie made two decades later. In both movies, three women have as their lifetime goals the snatching of wealthy husbands. In this early version of the gold digger's tale, the three predators, who also happen to be sisters, (Loretta Young, Pauline Moore, and Marjorie Weaver) must first lure their prey into a good position for the kill. In order to accomplish such a task, they choose to pose as members of the wealthy set themselves and enjoy the fringe benefits that such high living offers. Leaving their farming community in Kansas and taking with them a small inheritance, each sister assumes a different pose: now Pamela Charters (Loretta Young) has become a wealthy woman, who is traveling in style with one sister, Moira (Marjorie Weaver) playing her maid and the other sister, Elizabeth (Pauline Moore) playing her secretary. Their scheme works and, in short order, Young becomes engaged to Steve Harrington (David Niven), a wealthy estate owner with an eccentric sister Miriam (the formidable Binnie Barnes), whose favorite beverage is beer.

It is Miriam who is the focus of the inebriated fun in the family. She first enters the scene while her brother and the three Charters sisters, two of whom are still disguised as working class drones, are dining at the family table. She breezes cheerfully in and introduces herself to the three ladies, all the while appearing befuddled about which of the three is engaged to her brother. Following her is a man of indeterminate nationality (Leonid Kinskey); he looks furtive, puzzled, and loyal — not unlike a pet hamster that has just been let loose from its cage. After sitting at the table, the brazen Miriam notices his presence just across from her. Curiously, she questions him, almost as an afterthought: "Where did I find you?" Not surprisingly, he answers, "At the bar. At the Del Monte Hotel." Now Miriam appears relieved to be on familiar ground as she proclaims: "You know, the funniest thing. I always meet the nicest men in bars." Then, puzzled once more by his presence, she wonders aloud: "How did you happen to come home with me?" Kinskey's reply is matter-of-fact: "You said you were afraid to drive after you had so many highballs and would I drive for you please." Now truly delighted with this enlightening bit of information, Miriam happily exclaims: "Oh, was that *you!*" Here Miriam raises a full glass of beer and cheerily toasts the three husband-hunting ladies as well as her ever-tolerant brother.

Cut to the next scene, where Miriam breezes into a nightclub with Steve, Pamela, and Elizabeth. As usual, she is searching for a drinking companion to keep her amused and to drive her home if she indulges too much. As she leaves her companions at the table, she announces that she is going "big game hunting." A panning shot, following Miriam's line of sight, moves the audience down the bar. Miriam's hungry eye focuses on Van Dam Smith (Joel McCrea); she wastes no time in marking him as part of her territory. Maneuvering herself into a comfortable position, she aggressively pokes him on the shoulder and leads with an old come-on: "You're not big Robert from Seattle, are you?" McCrea as Van Dam looks surprised but somewhat apologetic: "No, I regret to say that I am not." Now amused enough at his response that she is willing to admit to the ancient game she is playing, Miriam confesses: "No, I didn't think you were. You don't look like him. Are you alone?" To Van Dam's quick "Absolutely," Miriam responds equally quickly as well as provocatively, "I can't see *why.*" With no hesitation, the imposing, no-nonsense Miriam aggressively steers Van Dam to her table. She is determined not to let the evening go to waste, especially if there is a good-looking man available.

In a later scene, we see Miriam still in a jovial mood, shaking cocktails at her own private bar while her brother is hosting a party in their elegant home. Her long-suffering companion Leonid Kinskey, he of the earlier scene when we had first met Miriam, looks wrung out as he begs of her, "*Please*, when do we stop drinking?" Having no answer to that peculiar question, she spots Van Dam as he enters and naturally inquires, "Oh, Van, how about a little nightcap?" After hesitating, he replies, "Maybe one just might help." Ever glad to be of service in this area, Miriam proudly announces, "I'll make it myself." When Van orders her to "load it up, I may need strength," Miriam replies with a tone both playful and ominous, "You're gonna get it." But the drink does not have the effect that Miriam had hoped for; Van leaves shortly after. Miriam ruefully complains to a stupefied Kinskey, "Well, I guess I didn't make that one right."

Never one to be deterred when it comes to mixing drinks, though, Miriam is again ready to be a hospitable bartender, so when her brother enters, she asks, "Steve, how about another little drink? I've got one all ready for you." What Miriam does not realize is that both Van and Steve are suffering from an affliction known as unrequited love, and that both believe that alcohol will make all of their woes go away. So Steve's reply echoes Van's as he takes the drink, "I'm gonna need strength." Since Miriam is still alert enough to remember recent conversations, she comes back with a perceptive observation, "Either someone else said that, or I'm *hearing* double." After Steve exits, Miriam decides to branch out and try another alcoholic beverage — something different from the beer she ordinarily carries with her from room to room. Yet she chokes and gasps after taking a swig of one of her own mixtures. The effect of this particular drink causes her to conclude — to no one in particular — "I guess they're better men than I am." Yet there is someone else present. He is the "no one" who remains slouched over the bar: Miriam's erstwhile escort Leonid Kinskey. Throughout this scene, his expression of intoxicated yet pained disgust never changes. He looks as though he were trying to keep his head from toppling off. He would like to find a way out. So, for all of her frenetic energy devoted to grabbing a man, Miriam is left alone at the picture's end, while all three of the Charters sisters admit their real identities and find True Love with men who adore them.

Unlike the very mellow William Powell and Myrna Loy as Nick and Nora Charles, Binnie Barnes as Miriam does not appear to be pleased with her lot in life, as evidenced by the sad little witticisms she throws out. She is wealthy, idle, spoiled, accustomed to being the center of attention, but altogether lonely and directionless. She epitomizes the world-weary wisdom that accompanies a person's acceptance of the white logic of alcohol. Liquor gives her a purpose and meaning, but it is not enough. Although Barnes tries hard to give a humorous spin to Miriam, she is unable to maintain this character's high spirits throughout the film. Ultimately, Miriam deflates due to inertia; no longer funny, she appears in the final scene as the odd one out in a room filled with three happy couples.

The High Life and the Fallen Woman

If one were to use one's imagination in order to picture Miriam some twenty years later, one might look to the title character of *Madame X* (1937) for a hint of things to come. There had been one earlier sound version of this old soap opera prior to its remake in 1937. The 1929 *Madame X* had starred Ruth Chatterton as the ill-fated victim of alcohol and the double sexual standard. Yet Gladys George as the eponymous protagonist in the 1937 incarnation is more credible than her predecessor, more poignant as the alcohol-drenched woman with a past. Gladys George was a fine actress: a New Englander with a hard edge but a soft spot — Bette Davis without

In *Madame X* (MGM, 1937), Henry Daniell plays Lerocle, a con artist who propositions Gladys George, portraying the woman who will come to be known as Madame X. He finds her in a seedy hotel, guesses that she had formerly been a lady of class, and invites the down-and-out, intoxicated woman to join him in his schemes. Cynical and tired of life, she agrees, for she figures that she has nothing left to lose.

the mannered posturing. George's portrayal of Madame X is an outstanding one. From the movie's first scene, where she appears as a sophisticated, wealthy lady, to the last, where she is a wasted, used up murderer, George is sad and believable. She is especially striking in the episode in which she cuts a deal with a con man and blackmailer, played by Henry Daniell. He finds her in a seedy hotel in South America, realizes that she had once been a woman of class, and decides to use her in a card-playing scheme to trap wealthy tourists. She is, of course, drunk, but it is clear that she knows enough to spot an exploiter when she sees one. It is also sadly obvious that she is too far gone to care, as she offers her body to him as well as what is left of her spirit.

In this version of *Madame X*, Gladys George embodies the darkest aspects of alcohol and the high life. An adulterer who has been undone by a cruel, unforgiving husband, she would have probably represented to Depression audiences an example — albeit a pitiful one — of how the high and the mighty could fall.

Time Out for a Holiday

In an early scene from *Holiday* (1938), Lew Ayres as Ned Seton, scion of the wealthy Setons of Park Avenue, emerges in a long shot and ambles down the long marble hallway of his family's mansion, eventually coming into close camera range. It is Sunday morning, and he is formally dressed in tie and tails. There is a large bandage above his left eye. We learn the reason for the formal attire when the downstairs butler (Thomas Braidon) speaks to him: "Your father has just left for church. Said he couldn't wait for you." Oblivious to this bit of news, Ayres's Ned asks what, for him, is a pressing question: "Did I get home all right last night?" The following conversation highlights both Ned's confusion and the butler's calm acceptance of Ned's customarily off-balanced state:

BUTLER: Everything's perfectly all right, sir."

NED: How did I get this bump on my forehead?

BUTLER: You slipped once or twice, sir, in your bathroom.

NED (*satisfied, now heading out the door, but with an important reminder*): I'll want a drink in my room just as soon as I get home from church.

But first he must get home, a challenge that appears daunting when he first exits the church with his very annoyed father, the wealthy, self-important Edward Seton (Henry Kolker). Father and son are stopped by some nosy parishioners, who cannot help but notice the large bandage on Ned's forehead. With no trace of irony, one solicitously inquires: "Did you have a little accident, Ned?" Ned's wry answer is both honest and self-depre-cating: "So they tell me. I don't seem to have been there when it happened."

But *home* does not contain the comfort that Ned had hoped for. Shortly after arriving back at the mansion, he bursts in on his sister, Linda Seton (Katharine Hepburn) and Johnny Case (Cary Grant), who are just getting acquainted in one of the house's smaller rooms on an upper floor. Ned has not been in this room since his childhood, but he is scouring the whole house: a man with a mission and a question for his sister: "Who took the bottle of Scotch out of my closet? It was in my riding boots. A full quart." Neither Linda nor Johnny knows where the missing liquor is, but Ned's trip to the old music room brings back memories as he finally takes note of where he is, looks wistfully around the room, and observes: "I haven't been up here in *years*."

It is from this point in the film that we gain insight into why Ned drinks; he has buried himself and his childhood dreams under a blanket of booze. As Ned looks around at the playroom of his youth, we learn that he is a frustrated artist: a musician and a composer who is completely cowed by his overbearing father, a man devoted solely to the acquisition of things. The elder Seton has brought the totally unqualified and uninterested Ned into the family firm and insists that he set an example for the other employ-ees. When he tells Ned to work each evening until 6 p.m., Ned feebly protests that he has nothing to do at the office after 3 p.m. But no matter: like Binnie Barnes's Miriam, Ned gets his revenge not only with the bottle but also with his caustic commentary about people, places, and events. Like Miriam, he shoots well-aimed arrows at a world in which all of his days stretch meaninglessly ahead.

In one particularly memorable scene, which takes place at a New Year's Eve party given by the elder Seton to celebrate his daughter Julia's engage-ment to Cary Grant, Ned is, as usual, drunk, but more than willing to edu-cate Grant's Johnny Case on the type of family that he is marrying into. Ayres plays the scene matter-of-factly; there is nothing maudlin or self-pitying about his lecture on the evil Setons and on his place in their grand scheme. As he talks to Johnny, he casually waves his highball glass, but his story is anything but casual. It is full of pain:

Father wanted a big family, so mother had Linda straight off to oblige him. But Linda was a girl, so she promptly had Julia. Julia was a girl — it seemed hopeless. The next year — well — they had me, and there was much joy in the land. It was a boy, and the fair name of Seton would flourish. Must've been a great consola-tion to father. Must've been very grateful to mother. Drink to mother, Johnny. She tried to be a Seton for awhile and then gave up and died.

Lew Ayres (Ned Seton) in the center is flanked by Cary Grant (Johnny Case) and Doris Nolan (Julia Seton) in *Holiday* (Columbia, 1938), as he assumes his usual position with a cocktail glass in hand, even as he defends his drinking in the face of the disapproving stares of his two companions. Ned Seton's defiant yet wistful expression reveals the pain of a wealthy young man trapped in a superficial world in which he feels outcast.

Following this, Johnny stares in disbelief and tries to calm Ned: "You're talking through your hat, Ned." But Ned just shakes his glass at Johnny and protests: "No, I'm not."

Ned's one friend in the family is his sister Linda, who, unlike their snooty sister Julia, understands him because she is also a misfit Seton. One of the reasons that Ned is on his way to becoming passed-out drunk is his pity for Linda, who had wanted to hold the engagement party to announce the forthcoming wedding between her sister Julia and Johnny. But as usual, the father has had his way, and he has made the engagement party an ostentatious, boring spectacle, complete with engraved invitations and footmen at the door. And plenty of liquor available for Ned, who, at least for this evening, doesn't have to hide the bottles. Convinced that he has not yet made his case against the Setons and that Linda needs all of the support he can give, he continues his complaints, turning on Julia with the accusation that both she and his father have turned Linda's "funny little shindig into a first class funeral." "Unlike me," he wryly observes, "Linda always hopes."

Ned's speech is too much for Julia, who berates her increasingly ine-briated brother, complaining that he has been drinking steadily since eight o'clock. It is now almost eleven, so we may assume that Ned's tolerance for alcohol is extremely high, perhaps because he has had so many years of practice. Moreover, Julia's nagging only exacerbates Ned's belligerence and defensiveness, a fact made even clearer as he turns on her: "Darling sister, I shall drink as much as I like at any party I agree to attend. And as much as I like is as much as I can hold. It's my protection against your tiresome friends. Linda's out of luck. She hasn't any protection."

Ned's constant self-flagellation is in decided contrast to Johnny Case's self-confidence. Both are products of their backgrounds and environment. Where Ned has been allowed neither to make his own decisions nor to build his own identity, Johnny has been forced to work from the time he was quite young in order to help support a working class family. Johnny knows who he is and what he wants. Ned knows nothing of the sort; in fact, he remains in a stupor most of the time. The movie's narrative makes clear that Ned is constantly tipsy because he has been made to feel worthless. Yet Lew Ayres never plays Ned for sympathy; he makes Ned a selfish, puerile whiner, one with not enough backbone to stand up to his father. Though Ned pities Linda, he does nothing to assuage her pain. He is too busy nour-ishing his own hurt to look out for the hurt of others. In short, Ned is a weak-willed character who will never change, will never grow up because it is too easy for him to make excuses for himself.

Yet for all his childishness, he is perceptive enough to share with his sister Linda an abhorrence of the stuffed shirt mentality that governs not only the lives of the Setons but also those of the Seton family and their snobbish social circle. He makes fun of the Seton cousin, Seton "Dopey" Cram (Henry Daniell) and his wife, Mrs. Laura "The Witch" Cram (Bin-nie Barnes as another unsympathetic, high society dame). The nicknames "Dopey" and "The Witch," coined by Ned and Linda, illustrate the decided lack of respect shown by the two younger Setons. When Ned's father, as usual, chastises Ned for his boorish behavior toward these important kin-folk, Ned responds by flippantly tossing off a sarcastic line: "Kindly walk, do not run, to the nearest exit." On this note, he aims himself forward and walks slowly out the door, as though he were walking down the aisle to a wedding or a funeral. To Ned's increasingly befuddled brain, the nature of the ceremony itself would be unimportant. Ironically, Ned's exit line is cal-culated and melodramatic, and has no effect whatsoever on his stuffy father.

Later, when Ned and Linda are alone together, each facing his/her own demons, Ned gives Linda a lesson in drinking. "Happy New Year!" he says as he ruefully toasts his sister. By now, Linda, who has fallen hard for her sister's fiancé, is suffering from unrequited love and is consequently in the mood to join him. The following dialogue reveals not only their mutual unhappiness but also the intensity of their brother/sister relationship. Moreover, their conversation demonstrates the way in which both Katharine Hepburn and Lew Ayres have the ability to get inside the skins of these particular characters and project a most paradoxical quality, one which involves a combination of worldliness undercut by naïveté:

LINDA: What's it like to get drunk, Ned?

NED: It's—(*curious, pauses to consider how to interpret her question*)— how drunk?

LINDA: Good and drunk.

NED: *Grand.*

LINDA: How is it?

NED: Well — to begin with, it brings you to *life.*

LINDA: Does it?

NED: Hmmm. And after awhile, you begin to know all about it — you feel — I don't know —*important.*

LINDA: That must be good.

NED: Yes. Hey (*He motions for her to sit next to him and adopts a conspiratorial tone.*) ... and then, pretty soon, the *game* starts.

LINDA: What game?

NED: A *swell* game. A terribly exciting game. You see, you think clear as crystal, but every move, every sentence is a problem, and it gets pretty interesting.

LINDA: You get beaten though, don't you?

NED: Sure. But that's good. And you don't mind anything — not anything at all. Then you sleep.

LINDA: How long can you keep it up?

NED: A long while. As long as you last.

LINDA: Oh Ned, that's awful.

NED: Think so? Other things are worse.

LINDA: Where do you end up?

NED (*desperate but resigned*): Where does everybody end up? You *die.* That's all right too.

And so Ned Seton ends up by giving up. When Linda finally determines to grab what she wants and sail with Johnny to Europe, she pleads with Ned, in the presence of their father, to come with her. Though it is clear that he yearns to escape, he lacks Linda's strength and spunk. He looks askance at his disapproving father, and he cannot do it. Furthermore, although Linda vows to return for Ned and spirit him away, Ned will never go. Sadly, he knows that the ennui and the inertia and the fear and the booze will finally beat him at the game.

Two other actors had been considered for the part of Ned Seton: screenwriter Donald Ogden Stewart, who had played the role on Broadway many years earlier and who coauthored the *Holiday* screenplay with Sidney Buchman; and Robert Benchley, who had played drunks onscreen but who was decidedly middle-aged by 1938. Columbia's Harry Cohn wanted Stewart, and director George Cukor wanted Benchley.[7] But both Stewart and Benchley were too old to be believable as the Seton scion; Stewart was forty-three at the time of filming and Benchley, forty-eight. So the final choice of twenty-nine-year-old Lew Ayres was an intelligent one. Not only was he the right age, but he was also right for the part. Yet *Holiday* did not do well at the box office and had mixed reviews. Hepburn's somewhat shrill, mannered performance was especially criticized. Moreover, the Depression-era message of the picture — that the rich are, by and large, a vacuous bunch — was a fairly worn out one by 1938.

6

Alcohol and the
Thwarted Artist

Why did they never get at the root of the matter, the thing that
drove him to do what he did, the thing that drove him to drink?

— Charles Jackson, *The Lost Weekend*, 1944

It is to be remarked, in passing, that when a man begins to drink
rationally and intelligently he betrays a grave symptom of how
far along the road he has traveled.

— Jack London, *John Barleycorn*, 1913

A Forgotten Actor Gets Invited to Dinner at Eight

John Barrymore was a brilliant, witty, hard-working, charming stage
actor: a perfectionist with a prodigious memory and a splendid vocal range.
He brought style and class to his two greatest stage roles—Hamlet and
Richard III. He was also an alcoholic, a promiscuous womanizer and adulterer, a man with a penchant for scatological remarks—both on and off the
stage — and an extremely jealous, paranoid wife beater. For much of his
adult life, he wasted his gifts and ultimately used alcohol to destroy his
mind, his body, and his personal relationships. In short, he delighted in self-
immolation and was apparently bent on self-abasement, especially in the
last ten years of his life. Nowhere is this self-mockery more evident than
in Barrymore's performance as the fading movie actor determined to self-
destruct in *Dinner at Eight* (1933).

Thanks to Barrymore's lack of inhibitions, one of the most insightful depictions of alcoholism on the screen occurs in this fine motion picture. The movie was well received on its initial release and still endures as a classic. It is a satisfying combination of many varying moods: droll, absurd, satiric, and melancholy. Mordaunt Hall, in his contemporary review for the *New York Times*, had praise for the screenplay:

> A strong line of drama courses through the story notwithstanding the flip dialogue. The picture runs along with a steady flow of unusually well knit incidents, which are woven together most expertly toward the end. This is owing to the fine writing of Mr. [George S.] Kaufman and Miss [Edna] Ferber, and it might easily be said that the wonder would be that anybody could go askew in turning such a play into pictorial form.[1]

This outstanding picture also deals with a number of serious topics along the way—adultery, chronic and incurable heart disease, bankruptcy, and alcoholism. The latter subject receives a noteworthy treatment through the memorable self-parody given by the complex genius John Barrymore. Those who had the good fortune to see him on stage have called Barrymore the best Hamlet of his generation, but he was just as well known as the frequenter of nightclubs, bars, and Prohibition speakeasies. This legendary performer was the scion of an acting family that, by the time of Barrymore's birth in 1882, had already spanned five generations. Barrymore was the son of actors Maurice Barrymore and Georgianna Drew Barrymore, grandson of actor/manager Louisa Lane Drew, great-grandson of the English music hall star Eliza Lane Kinloch, and great-great grandson of Thomas Haycraft Lane and Louisa Rouse, strolling country players in England during the reign of George III.[2] In the days when women who took up the stage were looked down upon as "fallen" women, John Barrymore's maternal grandmother, the redoubtable Mrs. Drew, was not only an actor but also the manager of Philadelphia's Arch Street Theatre, which she successfully ran for many years. One of her daughters, Georgianna, had married Maurice Barrymore, a hard-drinking, brawling, irresponsible, unpredictable, and charming Englishman born in India in 1839, the son of an army officer. John was the youngest of the three children born to Maurice and Georgianna Barrymore.[3]

But John Barrymore did not inherit his grandmother's ferocious, no-nonsense, disciplined, unemotional tenacity; rather, he resembled his witty, intelligent, but impulsive and often inebriated father. According to some accounts, John Barrymore had been a chronic drinker from the age of fourteen.[4] By 1933, when Barrymore appeared in *Dinner at Eight*, his career was on the decline: this, in spite of the fact that the previous year he had made five motion pictures for which he had earned $375,000.[5] Too many years of hard drinking — before, during, and after Prohibition — had resulted in his inability to concentrate on his roles, to get through his lines without a good deal of stumbling.[6] Thus, in this picture, Barrymore gives an autobiographical performance in his portrayal of Larry Renault, a self-deluded, alcoholic has-been actor: a disintegrating shell who chooses death when he is forced to confront both of his fading lives — the public one and the private one — as well as the disgrace of knowing that no one will hire him to play any kind of part anymore, no matter how minor. As *New York Times* critic Hall describes him: "His [Lionel Barrymore's] brother John is cast as Larry Renault, the motion picture actor who brags of having earned $8,000 a week at one time, while he has only seven cents to his name."[7]

Complicating Larry Renault's quandary as a man on a slippery slide is the fact that Larry Renault/John Barrymore is still a presence — albeit a shadowy, wavering one — and that he remains a fascination to younger women. He ruefully jokes to his infatuated, pining — and very young — admirer Paula Jordan (Madge Evans) that he has been the casualty of multiple marriages and that he currently has a wife to reckon with.[8] But Paula does not care, as she fancies herself in love with this fast fading screen idol, even though what she loves is nothing more than an ephemera, a phantom with no substance and therefore no future.

When we first see Barrymore/Renault, he is examining his photograph, which he has prominently displayed in a frame on the dresser in his hotel room. This is a room that he is for the moment sharing with Paula Jordan (Madge Evans). Meanwhile, Paula's scatter-brained socialite mother (Billie Burke), unaware of her daughter's liaison with Renault, has coincidentally just invited him to their home for dinner at eight. Yet Barrymore's apparent self-absorption is belied by the self-deprecating style that he demonstrates in each scene in which he appears. Ironically, even by 1933, John Barrymore still had the power to command the screen whenever he enters the scene. Contributing to the powerful force of the Barrymore performance is his insistence on playing his role throughout just a little off balance, as though he were constantly trying to keep his head from tumbling off.

One of the first displays of this balancing act occurs when he grabs a large empty decanter and casually, almost as an afterthought, tries to eke out one more drop into a cocktail glass, while Paula strains to look unperturbed. Then, temporarily resigned to an empty glass, Renault describes to Paula a minor play in which he is scheduled to appear. Boasting that he has an important part in the play, he looks confident and speaks to her in precise, clipped diction, as though he were already in rehearsal. Yet beneath this façade of supremacy lies an overwhelming insecurity. Alcohol has robbed Barrymore/Renault of his self-respect and, although he seems genuinely fond of Paula, he knows that their relationship is doomed. Indeed, the fact that she is the dominant one is made abundantly clear when she assumes the superior position by lying on top of him on their hotel room couch and kissing him.

But her ardor has its limits, especially when he receives from a cooperative bellboy (Edward Woods) another quart of liquor and, in the ensuing scene, pours glassful after glassful, as though he were drinking iced tea. Here, Madge Evans as Paula does a superb job of reacting to Renault's insatiable thirst. She plays her part accurately, simultaneously showing her disapproval but also enabling him to keep up the pretense that his behavior is perfectly acceptable, that it is just slightly socially askew. Paula Jordan is typical of all of those who try to cope with alcoholics by pretending that their addiction represents only a slight error that can be corrected through a quick, furtive erasure. Trying to get him to put down the glass, she adopts a most soothing, placating, tone; ultimately, however, her manner is both condescending and frantic, as she equivocates: "At mother's tonight, I want them to see you at your best." But Barrymore/Renault is not fooled. Like most alcoholics, he is sensitive, ever on the defensive about his drinking, so he tells her to mind her own business, that he will do as he pleases.

Moreover, in the accompanying dialogue, Barrymore/Renault follows a familiar pattern, one common among alcoholics, when he tries to rationalize his drinking: to blame the hard circumstances of his past life for the harsh truths of his present one. He begins his lecture to her by alluding to their striking age difference. In one of many instances where Barrymore/Renault derides himself, he wryly reminds her, "You're nineteen and I'm forty-seve — ... I'm almost forty." Since the real-life Barrymore was actually fifty-one at the time he made *Dinner at Eight*, his reference to his sense of time disappearing is all the more poignant.

But Barrymore/Renault does not stop at self-mockery. His ensuing speech is filled with self-pity and bitterness toward those who, he has deluded himself into believing, have had more breaks than he and therefore fewer reasons to drink. He maintains that everything has come too easy for Paula, that she has no idea what it is like to be "up against it," to have to keep fighting for everything. The more Barrymore/Renault winds himself up to pitch his hardball excuses, the more drinks he pours. He even metaphorically fancies himself a sort of mountain climber engaged in a precarious sport in which he is doomed to lose. He tells Paula that, when you are as unlucky as he is, you have to "pull yourself up, hand over hand, while they're waiting with a knife to cut the rope." Then, summoning all the bravado he can under the debilitating circumstances, he proclaims that he's not through yet.

But almost. Following Paula's exit and her declaration that she will shortly announce to her family her love for Renault, Barrymore's agent Max Kane (Lee Tracy) arrives with more disheartening news. The deal for the play is off, unless Renault agrees to play the minor part of the beachcomber. Tracy's performance in this movie is a curious one; his glassy-eyed, frenzied, hysterical exhibition suggests that he himself is under the influence of chemical stimulants.[9]

But in this scene from *Dinner at Eight*, it is Renault who is becoming increasingly intoxicated. The more he listens to Tracy's bad news about his proposed small part in a play, the drunker he gets. Finally, desperate for money to buy more liquor, he is reduced to searching among his personal belongings in order that he might find something to give the obliging bell-boy to sell on his behalf.

And his predicament is about to get worse, for later that day, Tracy as Max Kane returns with the play's producer Jo Stengel (Jean Hersholt). In the intervening hours, Renault has managed to dress himself for a formal dinner at the Jordans: he is now wearing tie and tails. On the other hand, his slurred speech contradicts his elegant appearance. Gone is the precise, crisp diction with which he had addressed Paula; equally missing is the gallant, deferential manner he had adopted with her. Renault is belligerent with his potential employer, arguing that if he is to play the beachcomber in the forthcoming play, it will have to be built up: "Now listen, Stengel, I'm a name." He also reminds Stengel that at one time he was making eight thousand dollars a week and that he is doing Stengel a favor to appear in his "ratty little show." These are not tactful maneuvers, but they are about to become even less polite. Renault sticks his face into Stengel's, grabs his arm, and declares unnecessarily, "I'm drunk and I know I'm drunk." Having had enough of Renault's truculence, Stengel, who had never planned on employing Renault anyway, exits. Throughout the entire scene, Tracy futilely tries to act as a peacemaker, to protect Renault from himself, but Tracy's actions seem even more feverishly glassy-eyed than they had been in his previous visit to Renault's hotel room. Tracy, who giggles a good deal and waves his hands wildly, gesturing at no one in particular, looks as if he is completely out of control.

And Tracy's Max Kane becomes even more frenzied in the next scene; he has just been humiliated by Renault's "performance" in front of the producer, and he plans to get even by giving Barrymore/Renault some facts. He begins by calling Barrymore a "cock-eyed, drunken fool." Throughout this confrontation scene, Barrymore is shot in profile; furthermore, though he is standing, he rocks unsteadily as he tries to focus on Tracy's words, which are not pleasant. Tracy begins by informing him that he owes Tracy

John Barrymore (right) as the aging star Larry Renault in *Dinner at Eight* (MGM, 1933) looks irritated at and suspicious of his agent Lee Tracy as Max Kane, who protests that he has had trouble getting the has-been actor even the most minor roles. Renault is already on his way to getting extremely plastered; by the end of the scene, still attired in that formal suit and thoroughly plastered, he turns on the gas and dies.

five hundred dollars— money that, we assume, went for booze. Tracy next cuts even more deeply with his announcement that it has been impossible for him to get any kind of part for Renault — old vaudeville producers, for instance, laugh at him for suggesting Renault. In the following speech, Tracy's voice is high-pitched and breaking; he sounds like Fred Allen playing a carnival barker, except that his "pitch" is aimed not at selling but at destroying: "You never were an actor. You did have looks, but they're gone now. You don't have to take my word for it. Just look in any mirror. They don't lie. Take a good look. Look at those pouches under your eyes. Look at those creases. They sag, like an old woman." As Tracy cackles at Renault, both characters can be seen reflected in a mirror; the image created by the astute cinematography of William Daniels is intriguing, since one can now see four characters lined up like an absurd chorus line. All of them seem in imminent danger of cracking up. But it is the Barrymore/Renault character who finally does crack. The end begins for the has-been actor with Tracy's exit line, which is a prescient one, for the agent leaves in disgust, but not before tossing the ultimate insult at Renault: "Go get yourself buried."

Alone again, Renault has the opportunity to contemplate his mirror image, his dismal future, and his agent's final line. Through the use of low-angle lighting, the fine cinematography here emphasizes the dark bags underneath Renault's eyes as his appearance is reflected in the mirror. Shadows fall across his face and move down to cover his neck. His apparition looks dark, gloomy, and sick. Terrified of being struck down by his own frightful image, he ducks his head. But he is not finished, not yet, as he slowly raises his head, his famous left profile still facing the camera. (Barrymore always insisted that the left side be emphasized. He deplored the appearance of his right profile.) He takes a few steps and collapses against a chair. The scene is reminiscent of one the previous year in *What Price Hollywood?* in which Lowell Sherman, an alcoholic, dissipated director, looks aghast at his shadowy visage in a mirror and subsequently fatally fires a gun into his chest. In fact, when director George Cukor complimented Barrymore on his excellent performance as Renault, Barrymore made an apt comparison: "Well it ought to be. This is a combination of Maurice Costello [Barrymore's father-in-law at the time], Lowell Sherman and me."[10]

But Renault, still proud of his aging face, chooses a different exit method than the one executed by Lowell Sherman in *What Price Hollywood?* His plans begin to crystallize at this point when his errand boy, a.k.a. the bellboy, enters with more bad news: he has been unable to pawn a pathetic gold picture frame that Renault had given him. At first, Renault becomes belligerent, calling the young man a liar; then he is reduced to begging the boy for money, as he pleads with him, pulling on the bellboy's uniform: "I gotta have it." Not only is the boy unmoved and adamant in his refusal, but another intruder is about to shoot the final arrow. Enter the hotel manager (Edwin Maxwell) and one of his cohorts (John Davidson), who has doubtless come along to give the manager moral support, for Renault is about to be evicted. Not wanting to embarrass himself and wanting to avoid a direct confrontation with this swaying drunk, the manager concocts a plausible lie about a distinguished couple who always reserve that particular suite of rooms when they are in town. So, of course, Renault will have to leave. The manager is kind enough to give Renault until noon the next day for this forced departure. Renault takes in all of this obvious fabrication, while his face registers horror, incomprehension, and disbelief. He leans unsteadily in the manager's direction, musters all of the dignity that he has remaining, and mumbles, "What other rooms can you give me?" The answer is obvious, and after the manager and his "second" leave, Renault collapses, now completely stripped of all pretense, all artifice, and utterly broken. The way in which Renault chooses to die was for the most part Barrymore's design.[11] Knowing that there is nothing left of himself to mend, Renault turns out the lights, stuffs his fancy dinner jacket and coat under the door, tears up a photo of Paula and tosses the scraps out the window, and turns on one floor lamp — one that splashes light over one chair. Then he turns on the gas and, with some satisfaction and resignation, settles into the chair so that the lamp is behind him. In a neat theatrical gesture, Renault creates his own final mise en scène, with the lamp's bright illumination spotlighting his face, which is still visible in left profile. Fade out on a long forgotten actor.

Following his direction of Barrymore in this film, George Cukor would become a close friend of Barrymore's and subsequently offered this assessment of the actor: "His ability to project himself into a dramatic character and then let that character completely transcend his own individuality; and then, to interpret it down to the last fine shade of mood — that genius is possessed by no other actor on the screen today."[12] Yet, by 1934, the year following his performance in *Dinner at Eight*, Barrymore was suffering more and more from the effects of alcohol poisoning, including acute memory loss, especially for recent events. His attention span became increasingly diminished. He would ask someone a question but would then be unable to follow the answer, so he might repeat the question over and over, as though he were asking it for the first time. Barrymore's good friend Gene Fowler — a pretty fair tippler himself — recalled Barrymore in the last years of his life: an actor who appeared to be in a sadder state than Larry Renault:

> He eventually suffered a peculiar type of amnesia, as if he were being intermittently lifted out of the contemporary flux of personal history. Then toward the end of his life he frequently experienced a disorientation of time and place. This defect caused Jack to resort to fabrications and grotesqueries to hide from others his lapses of memory. His affliction became varyingly acute, depending upon the degree of toxicity.[13]

Memory loss also affected Barrymore professionally as well as personally. By 1937, with his movie career on the skids, Barrymore needed help remembering even short bits of dialogue that were required of movie actors. His brain was so befuddled and his attention span so short that studio assistants would write his lines on a blackboard and hold the board aloft behind the cameras. Barrymore became quite adept at reading the lines from the board without appearing to be reading; he would never even move his eyes. Nor would he admit that his memory loss was the reason for these blackboards.[14]

Although Barrymore continued to stumble along through these movies from the late 1930s and into the early 1940s, and although he gave some inspired supporting performances in a number of them, most were second-rate pictures. *Dinner at Eight*, then, represents the culmination of a long career that ended with Barrymore's death on May 29, 1942. The primary cause was cirrhosis of the liver, although there were a number of contributing conditions, among them "failure of kidney function, chronic gastritis, ulceration of the esophagus which hemorrhaged, hardening of the arteries, and chronic eczema."[15] The final cause was pneumonia. Even as he lay dying, Barrymore reportedly grabbed a glass of mouthwash from a young nurse who was brushing his teeth and, to the young woman's great distress, swallowed all of the contents.[16]

W. C. Fields, one of Barrymore's best friends, served as a pallbearer at Barrymore's funeral on June 2, 1942. However, he did so under protest, claiming: "The time to carry a pal is when he is alive."[17] Fields was reportedly very distressed about Barrymore's death, for Barrymore had been a good drinking buddy. Yet Fields was resolved to carry on as best he could. In keeping with this determination, the great comic actor fortified himself at the funeral. Riding back from the cemetery, not in one of the undertaker's limousines but in his own touring car, Fields carried with him a portable refrigerator, which he had stocked with various ingredients for making cocktails.[18] No stranger to the bottle himself, Fields apparently believed in sending Barrymore off in style.

The Lost Weekend *and the Price of Self-Delusion*

Some twelve years after the release of *Dinner at Eight*, there appeared a reminder of the renowned Barrymore persona in another critically acclaimed movie. Shortly before taking a long-anticipated drink in *The Lost Weekend*, Ray Milland as the cynical lush, Don Birnam, observes to the bemused bartender the way in which alcohol makes him feel empowered, the way it apparently energizes his creative juices. He boasts that, when he is unpleasantly inebriated: "I'm John Barrymore before the movies got him by the throat."[19]

In fact, Charles Jackson, author of the enduring 1944 novel *The Lost Weekend*, felt that he had much in common with other creative artists. He thought of these comparisons as he wrote his riveting, semi-autobiographical study of an alcoholic's slow and steady mental and physical deterioration during one long, nightmarish weekend. Indeed, Jackson had based the novel on his own experience as an alcoholic. He had started drinking when he was a patient in a tuberculosis sanitarium in Switzerland, and his alcoholic odyssey lasted seven years.[20] Although Jackson writes from personal experience, he tells his story in the third person, solely from the perspective of Don Birnam, an educated writer and raconteur, but a man forever lost, not just for a weekend, but for all time. The novel's limited point of view heightens the overall claustrophobic effect of the narrative, as Birnam moves from a tenuous sobriety at the outset, thence to a subtle, controlled inebriation throughout much of the novel, and finally concludes his nightmarish wandering in an unsettling and unsettled hallucinogenic state. Ultimately, then, Jackson gives to his novel no happy ending, no definitive answers.

The 1945 movie version of this popular novel retains the basic story, but lacks the frantic, stream of consciousness intensity of the book. So too, the film also contains a relatively happy conclusion. Nor does the movie suggest some of the more daring, controversial aspects of the Birnam character hinted at in the novel. For instance, Jackson's narrative includes some obvious clues that Birnam is a homosexual, one who has had prior rendezvous with young men. These encounters have resulted in disgrace and subsequent drinking binges, both in the present time of the novel as well as in the past. Nowhere in the movie, however, is there any reference to Birnam's alternative sexual orientation; nevertheless, the character of the male hospital nurse as portrayed by Frank Faylen is definitely suspect in the way that he glances askant at the Milland character after he has been tossed into the alcoholic ward for a drying out. Clearly, 1945 audiences were not prepared for any references to homosexuality in mainstream Hollywood films, no matter how remote the allusions. Therefore, there is no suggestion whatsoever anywhere in the film that the Ray Milland character is anything but happily heterosexual. In fact, he eyes two women: one, of course, is Jane Wyman's Helen; the other is Gloria, a prostitute (Doris Dowling) who hangs around Nat's Bar, ever on the lookout for a handsome, well-heeled man. The only rival for Don Birnam's attentions to these two women is, of course, alcohol. But this is a serious rival, one that remains at the forefront, even by the end of the picture.

Despite the discreet fine-tuning of the novel's depiction of the darker side of Birnam's sexual predisposition, fine performances by Ray Milland as the smooth, charming, wily Don Birnam; Jane Wyman as his long-suffering girl; Phillip Terry as Don's unsympathetic yet codependent brother; and Frank Faylen as the unctuous, leering, serpentine nurse, contribute to the film's realistic tone. And for his stunning achievement as the sly but perpetually befuddled protagonist, Ray Milland transcended his usual charming but fluffy onscreen character and won the 1945 Best Actor Academy Award.

Ironically, Billy Wilder had originally wanted José Ferrer in the part of Birnam, but production executive Buddy de Sylva wanted an attractive protagonist, one with whom the audience would consequently be more in sympathy.[21] Moreover, Ferrer had long been associated in audience's minds with villains, and the Paramount executives thought that this negative image would run counter to viewer expectations. What was needed, according to the studio bosses, was a physically appealing man, a basically nice guy with the potential to be exceedingly likable if only he would give up the booze.[22] And ultimately, the studio's choice was a fortunate one, for Milland makes the novel's Don Birnam come to life. He is, by turns, charming, handsome, introspective, melancholy, and quite believable.

Though the character of the onscreen Birnam differs somewhat in style from the fictional Birnam, the filmmakers nonetheless retain much of the texture of the novel. For instance, as with the novel, the film version of *The Lost Weekend* has a Hitchcockian, voyeuristic quality about it, a feature that allows us to experience viscerally the slow disintegration of a sensitive, intelligent writer. In fact, the opening shots as set up by director Billy Wilder and executed by cinematographer John F. Seitz would be echoed by Hitchcock in the initial scenes of both *Rope* (1948) and *Psycho* (1960). As *The Lost Weekend* begins, we see a panning shot of the New York City skyline; then the camera zooms in on the open windows of a high-rise apartment building. Finally, the camera pans to a window that features an unusual decorative touch: a liquor bottle suspended from a rope and dangling from the window, like some perversely huge Christmas ornament. Then we look through the window and see Ray Milland framed by a window sash just over his head. The shot is established in such a way that the 'O' of the sash looks like a miniature noose. In the visual sense, then, the character of Milland's Don Birnam is established from the outset through the hanging liquor bottle and the strategically placed window sash. In the course of the movie, Birnam does, indeed, proceed to give himself enough rope to entangle and nearly hang himself via the bottle.

By the same token, this "O" hanging from the end of the sash creates a perfect circle, a symbol that will recur in a later scene in which we see Don seated at his favorite bar, where he spends many hours gulping the contents of numerous shot glasses. The rings left on the bar by these glasses create a mosaic of interlocking circles that resemble the encircling links of a chain. Once again, we are left with an image of capture, imprisonment, and death. In addition, the wet imprints of the liquor glasses on the bar are not in a straight line but fan out in every direction, like the randomly placed pieces in a half-finished jigsaw puzzle.

But from the opening shot of the movie, Milland shows that he is a man content to leave behind the missing pieces, to forgo the chance to make his life whole again. As he traces Birnam's spiraling, downward path, Milland gives a powerful, subtle performance as a charming man obsessed with the self-destructive power of alcohol. In fact, his behavior so authentically captures the mindset of the seasoned alcoholic that he appears to have sublimated his own personality into that of Don Birnam. Such a character type is summarized accurately by Jack London in his 1913 memoir, *John Barleycorn*. London knew from his own personal struggles all the tricks of the alcoholic: the self-deception, the secretiveness, the gradually increasing need for stronger and stronger drinks in order to attain the same effect. One sentence from this short autobiography not only captures the alcoholic persona but also, through its description, accurately anticipates Milland's interpretation of what makes Don Birnam run: "What the skilled and seasoned drinker achieves is a discreet and canny semi-intoxication."[23] Such canniness, coupled with the seasoned alcoholic's ability to look respectably sober and talk fairly coherently, is the hallmark of Milland's performance. In short, Milland does maintain an aura akin to such "semi-intoxication." He acts as though he is a man determined to walk on eggs without squashing the shells.

In addition, from the opening scene, Milland is exceedingly discreet, allowing us to see the wheels of deception already turning, as he tries to think of a way to make his ever wary and watchful brother (Phillip Terry, in an effective performance as the sanctimonious reminder of Don's moral lapses) and his solicitous girl (Jane Wyman) leave the apartment so that he can retrieve the bottled treasure hanging just inches away. Though Milland is temporarily sober, having just been released from a sanitarium, that sobriety will soon end, for he is primed for a change. Milland depicts Birnam like a chess player: on edge, cagey, contemplating his next move, but also anticipating his opponent's moves. But he receives a temporary setback when he is checkmated by his careful, suspicious brother, who discovers the hanging contraband and dumps its contents down the bathroom sink.

Once he is rid of both brother and girlfriend — those two sober nuisances—Milland's Don Birnam wastes no time in finagling a way to get booze to replace the liquid his brother has just wasted. Stealing the ten dollars that his brother has hidden — money earmarked for the cleaning lady — Don escapes from the dull sobriety of his apartment into the welcoming, peaceful haven of his favorite liquor store.[24] As with the opening scene, Birnam is framed again, but this time his self-imposed noose takes a different form: through effective use of deep-focus photography, he is seen standing behind rows of liquor bottles, which are neatly arranged in a foreground shot.

Emerging from this store, one of his favorite haunts, and carefully holding his two precious bottles upright in a sack, he hurries toward the local bar where he is well known to the world-weary bartender (Howard Da Silva). Milland hits just the right note as he sits awaiting his longed-for drink, savoring the fact that, when he has had his fill at the bar, he still has his two bottles in reserve, something to look forward to when he finally staggers back to his apartment. But he is not thinking so far into the future; right now, this moment is all that matters. Watch him impatiently tap his fingers on the bar, strike a match to light a cigarette, put the wrong end of the cigarette in his mouth and then hastily turn it around, look hesitatingly at the shot of rye — as though he is gloating over his immense reserves of self-control — pick the glass up, put it down, shake the flame from the match before it burns his fingers, then grab the shot glass and quickly finish it. Watch the subtlety of Milland's agonized movements, which are deceptively simple, but which are effective precisely because of their simplicity. His controlled, quiet desperation makes his characterization all the more credible.

Much later, fortified and emboldened by approximately ten shot glasses of whiskey and back in the security of his apartment, Milland must find a hiding place for one of the precious bottles that he had bought on his way to the bar. He demonstrates the typical secretive canniness of the alcoholic when he fastens his fuzzy vision upon the inside of the ceiling light fixture, though he risks serious injury when he climbs on a chair that he has balanced on top of another piece of furniture. The bottle now safely tucked away, he is content: one bottle cleverly hidden from his brother's nosy intervention and the other next to him as he eases himself into a chair. There is something immensely sensual in Milland's subsequent actions in this scene. A close-up reveals him removing his jacket and loosening his tie as, with a climactic sigh and a self-satisfied smile, he settles back for an evening of pleasure. And the evening, of course, turns into the lost weekend.

Since the film version of *The Lost Weekend* lacks the limited, third person point of view and the reminiscences of Don Birnam that Charles Jackson handles so skillfully in the novel, the movie's narrative is propelled instead through a series of flashbacks: stories that Milland relates to the cynical bartender as he offers an apologia for his misspent years. Whereas the novel's Don Birnam is described in the third person and talks to himself throughout in the second person, the movie's Don Birnam must necessarily be seen interacting with the people who inhabit and inhibit the drunken boundaries of his life. For instance, the woman in whom he professes some romantic interest is given a much more prominent role than she is allowed in the novel, where she is merely a shadowy figure, one whom neither Birnam nor the reader takes too seriously. But the earnest cinematic figure of Jane Wyman has trouble coping with the sneaky Milland.

From the first meeting between Don and Helen, Don begins the sly, furtive, deceptive behavior that will underscore his subsequent relationship with her. When she sees a bottle accidentally slip out of his coat and break on the sidewalk, he implausibly excuses its presence by saying that he was taking its contents to a sick friend. The "sick friend" is forgotten, however, when Don seizes the moment and accepts Helen's offer to accompany her to a cocktail party. So all is not lost: liquor is still on the horizon. That Helen is only too anxious to accept Don's story is symptomatic of her continued willful determination not to see what is only too evident about this very disarming man. Moreover, her blindness is abetted by Don's determination to remain sober all the while he is courting her. Initially, she does not suspect that she is walking into muddy waters and that she will nearly be dragged down into the mire that Don has made of his life.

What precipitates her unsought revelation about Birnam's alcoholism is a conversation that Don overhears between Helen's visiting parents as the two sit in a hotel lobby, waiting to meet the man with whom Helen has fallen in love. This overheard dialogue, which involves their misgivings about the worthiness of this stranger—a writer who appears to have few prospects— propels the already nervous Birnam to hastily exit the hotel and to embark on a bender that once and for all leaves the infatuated Helen with no doubt about the truth of Birnam's addiction.

And what contributes to the heartrending quality of this addiction is Birnam's willingness to at last confess everything to Helen, albeit his confession is couched in terms suggesting that his alcoholism is the result of the horrible blows dealt him by the world's cruelties. His speech to her following the aborted meeting with her parents is a paradigm of self-mockery, self-flagellation, and self-defense. When Helen patiently and helpfully suggests that there must be a reason that Don drinks, his reply is bitter and revealing:

I know the reason. The reason is me. What I am. Or, rather, what I'm not.... You see, in college I passed for a genius. They couldn't get out the college magazine without one of my stories. Boy, was I hot. Hemingway stuff.... Sold a piece to the Atlantic Monthly. It was reprinted in the Readers' Digest. Who wants to stay in college when he's Hemingway? My mother bought me a brand new typewriter, and I moved right in on New York. Well, the first thing I wrote, that didn't quite come off. And the second I dropped. The public wasn't ready for that one. I started a third, a fourth, only about then somebody began to look over my shoulder and whisper ... Don Birnam, he'd whisper, it's not good enough.... How about a couple of drinks just to put it on its feet? So I had a couple.[25]

Don laments the fact that he reached his peak as a writer when he was nineteen and that he has been unable to sell anything since. He also ruefully concedes that he has been living off the largesse of his brother, who is depicted as a true codependent. Thus Helen is allowed to draw the inevitable conclusion: Don drinks because he has convinced himself that he is a failure, both professionally and personally. Birnam's creator, Charles Jackson, knew a good deal about the rationalizations that accompany the alcoholic writer's need to explain his failures, for Jackson had long identified himself with the gifted and perceptive but sadly tormented F. Scott Fitzgerald, an alcoholic who poured much of his talent into a liquor bottle and subsequently drowned his sense of self.

Following this tell-all scene, we once again witness the range of Milland's acting ability. Back in the present, Birnam is alone in his apartment with the awful prospect of being without a full liquor bottle. He has a fuzzy recollection of hiding one somewhere, but he cannot remember where. Forgetting that help is at hand, tucked away in the ceiling light fixture, he frantically dismantles the apartment, tearing down the bedding, tossing clothes from the closet, spreading disarray everywhere. Had law enforcement authorities ripped apart his belongings as they searched for drugs, they could not have done a more thorough job than does Birnam in his frenzied search for his priceless whiskey.

Giving up for the moment, he crashes into a chair, an empty bottle and equally empty shot glass in the foreground, framing his frustrated expression, his glance focusing on a matchbook cover from a local nightspot. *The Lost Weekend* contains many remarkable point of view shots, many done through the utilization of effective close-ups, and this vision of the bottle, shot glass, and matchbook cover represents some of the more provocative uses by cinematographer John F. Seitz. Aha! thinks Birnam, looking thirstily at the matchbook, and recalling a place where he can at last find liquor.

So, though the hidden bottle has been lost, the evening has not. Cut to the smoky interior of the nightclub, where it becomes clear that Birnam has already found a good deal of solace in many cocktails. But when he finishes drinking, he also finds that he does not have enough money to pay the check. What to do now?

In a scene that parallels one in the original novel, Birnam decides upon theft as the most convenient solution. In his increasingly intoxicated state, Birnam is sure that he can use his abundant store of savoir-faire to pull off the theft smoothly. Once again, cinematographer Seitz utilizes close-ups to reveal the tempting nearness of a lady's purse, at present unobserved by its owner, who is snuggling with her date at the next table. Birnam is cool as he inches the purse toward him and eases it under his jacket. Like a shoplifter making his way out of a store, Birnam heads toward the men's room where he surreptitiously removes a ten dollar bill from the purse, replaces it under his jacket, and confidently goes back to his table — where he finds many of the nightclub's visitors and its employees awaiting his return.[26] He gives up the purse easily, returns the ten dollars to the irate lady, who declines to press charges, and is unceremoniously ejected from the club, to the accompaniment of raucous, mocking shouts of the crowd and the pianist. It is a chilling moment, made all the more so because of the incongruity between Birnam's pathetic attempt to act like a genial bon vivant and the reality of his stupefied drunken state.

But help is at hand. Stumbling back to his disaster-strewn apartment, Birnam collapses on his daybed. Another memorable close-up reveals Birnam's unkempt appearance — a decided change from his smooth-shaven, rather elegant, formal attire earlier that day when he had been sober, but hungry for the means to buy some liquor. Now he is a desperate man: beard unshaven, clothes disheveled, eyes glazed. And these eyes at last mingle with his fuzzy brain cells to remember where that elusive bottle can be found. In a reprise of the earlier scene where he had hidden the bottle, he grabs the chair, balances it precariously on the table, and rescues the bottle from the light fixture. No longer concerned with the niceties of social drinking, he drinks his find straight from the bottle, his behavior resembling that of an infant who cannot wait for its pacifier. Milland shows us a man who has been reduced to his most primal state.

Nor is his state any more civilized the following day. The next scene begins with a disconcerting close-up of Birnam's eyeball, which gradually moves around in its socket as though trying to find its way out of the dark woods inside of Birnam's brain. Simultaneously, we hear the dissonant sound of a phone ringing. It is the only sound we hear, and it is thereby magnified. For a man with a hangover, the sound is like the pounding of a jackhammer by construction workers. Birnam is still dressed, still befuddled, and still craving the bottle — and he obviously ignores the phone, which in his present state he considers insistently obscene. And the full bottle from the night before is empty — now he has two empty bottles to contend with. Never one to give up, however, he grabs one in each hand and simultaneously pours their nonexistent contents into the shot glass. For all of his heroic efforts, he ekes out one drop, which he hastily drinks. The scene symbolizes the futility of Birnam's struggle with life. Because his addiction *is* his life, this tiny taste of alcohol represents the minutiae of his being: the reduction of the days, the hours, the minutes, and the seconds into one droplet of existence. Nothing remains of Birnam but a tiny speck, returning to its infantile origins in the womb and simultaneously, paradoxically, hastening toward its death.

Once more, Birnam's need for alcohol outweighs any other consideration, including any and all physical challenges. So, having for the moment abandoned the book he had promised himself that he would write — a book appropriately entitled *The Bottle*— Birnam decides upon a more constructive use for his typewriter; it will become a source of revenue for more booze. Determined to pawn it, he sets out one Saturday morning upon a long walk up Third Avenue, dragging himself along from 55th Street to 110th Street. In their screenplay directions, writers Brackett and Wilder call Third Avenue Birnam's "Via Dolorosa."[27] Tracking shots and montage allow us to see the sad, lengthy journey Birnam undertakes in his futile quest to find an open pawnshop. That this sequence looks so remarkably realistic is a tribute to the unflagging efforts of Milland, director Wilder, and the camera crew. Milland's long walk was filmed in a single day on location, with Milland actually walking up Third Avenue while the camera, which was hidden in a bakery truck, followed him.[28] In addition, the action was photographed on a Sunday, when the pawnbrokers' establishments were actually closed, and the pedestrians were taking a leisurely Sunday morning outing. We see block after block punctuated by the three hanging globes: endless signposts signaling the pawnbroker. These dangling circles are a reminder of the 'O' of the window shade cord as well as the interlocking rings left by the shot glasses on the bar. Likewise, Birnam's trip up and down Third Avenue is a circular one: he finishes where he has begun, for, although in the world of the film it is Saturday, Birnam had been unaware that all of the shops are closed due to Yom Kippur. Furthermore, as Birnam nears the end of his completed circle, it becomes increasingly evident that the typewriter is becoming heavier and heavier: excessive luggage to a man with a terrible hangover.

Finally returning to Nat's bar, he stumbles in and drops his burden on the bar, begging that Nat give him just one free drink. When the cynical bartender obliges him, he props the glass on top of his typewriter, barely able to hold it in his shaking hands, and finishes it in one gulp. Here are the conjoined symbols of his futile artistic endeavors and of his uncontrollable addiction: typewriter and booze adhere in a precarious union.

Nowhere is the precariousness of his existence more evident than in his subsequent calamities. Following a fall down the stairs of an apartment building, he awakens to true horror in an alcoholic ward, complete with barred windows, screams from a patient in a nearby bed as he beats off imagined insects, and a nurse from hell (Frank Faylen) who takes a twisted pleasure in the knowledge that the inmates who survive after their return to the streets will soon be back inside the ward. Shadows from the bars on the windows fall across Birnam's terrified face, bleak reminders of his imprisoned status.

But he doesn't stay imprisoned for long. As daylight comes, he escapes from the chaos of this asylum, still dressed in his pajamas and robe.[29] After grabbing a quart of rye from a dumbfounded liquor store proprietor, who has just opened for the day's business, he returns to his apartment, which is still in a shambles. So once more he settles, stolen rye bottle in hand, into his chair — one of the few objects in his living space that is still intact. But this time, his alcoholic refuge is not so relaxing. Superb use of sound and picture come together to reveal a man on the verge of imploding solely from the sensation of physical overload. The phone jars him with its nerve-shattering, high-pitched ring: its sound a cacophonous counterpoint to the whirring, haunting melody — this tune an aural correlative to what Jack London has described as the White Logic accompanying a drunk's darkest moments: "John Barleycorn sends his White Logic, the argent messenger of truth beyond truth, the antithesis of life, cruel and bleak as interstellar space, pulseless and frozen as absolute zero, dazzling with the frost of irrefragable logic and unforgettable fact."[30] This musical background motif, a cold, screeching white noise inseparable from this White Logic, underscores Birnam's most desperate moments throughout the film, for by this point he has indeed reached absolute zero.

And now, providing an eerie background accompaniment to the jarring, whirring sounds reverberating in Birnam's skull, the squeaking noise of a mouse can be heard on the soundtrack. Immediately following, we see through a unique close-up a vision of what Birnam only *thinks* he sees: a little gray field mouse squeezing through a crack in the wall plaster. Birnam gazes quizzically at the rodent, its eyes seemingly fastened on its human companion, its vocalizing similar to and as innocuous as a canary's chirp; Birnam even appears somewhat amused by the unexpected sight. Not so humorous to Birnam, however, is his subsequent hallucination: a bat that dives at him from varying angles. The sight is a horrific one — made even

Ray Milland as Don Birnam has reached bottom in this unsettling scene from *The Lost Weekend* (Paramount, 1945). The flying bat tormenting Milland is only one in a series of terrifying hallucinations that he will experience before his lost weekend is over (Photofest).

more so by the spectacle of Birnam's terror. If the mouse represents the physically annoying but minor inconveniences attendant upon an occasional hangover, the plunging bat, aiming at the horizon of Birnam's bloated brain, is the last frayed remnant of the alcoholic's tattered life. Then bat and mouse merge, as the bat flings itself against the wall, grabbing its victim, even as the rodent tries to squeeze back into the security of its hole in the plaster. But too late: Birnam's last glimpse of both creatures is of the bat devouring the mouse, leaving only a thin trail of blood oozing down the wall, the superb black-and-white cinematography emphasizing the *blackness* of the blood. In this daring scene, Birnam's scream at this fantastic illusion takes the viewer beyond anguish; here is the White Logic magnified, depicted in a way that had never previously been done on the screen.

Having now reached the nadir of his life, Birnam resolves that he has no option remaining except suicide. Revolver in hand, he composes a farewell note. But this final way out is aborted by a visit from Helen. When she sees the reflection of Birnam's revolver in the bathroom mirror, she devises a peculiar plan to save his life by attempting to coax him into having a drink. Finally admitting that she has spotted the gun, she declares that she would rather see him drunk than dead — an improbable, illogical conclusion, the irony of which is not lost on Birnam as he smiles sardonically, declines the drink, and tries to push her out of his apartment. Once again, the character of Helen is seen as one who, although she is in many respects an intelligent professional — in fact, a writer for *Time* magazine — she is nonetheless incapable of understanding, much less solving, the dilemma of the alcoholic.

Nevertheless, in spite of Helen's dimness with respect to Don's serious addiction, the scriptwriters devise a fitting deus ex machina for the film. Helen gives a speech about how Don's life is worth saving because he has real talent, that he can contribute a genuine legacy if only he does not give up. Then suddenly, apropos of nothing, Nat appears at Don's door; he is carrying Don's beat up typewriter, which he has apparently found floating somewhere nearby.

Now all of the plot strands can be tidily put together, as Helen declares that the resurfacing of the typewriter is a good omen. His suicide attempt all but forgotten, Don agrees that his new mission will be to finish his aborted novel, which so far consists of only a title — *The Bottle*. In accomplishing this artistic feat, Don is convinced that he will speak for and give comfort to all of those alcoholics buried out there in the city under the impersonal surfaces of concrete. So the movie ends as it has begun: with a panning shot of the New York City skyline as we fade out with an upbeat note, far different from Charles Jackson's original, grittier, more realistic ending.

In fact, the last chapter of the novel is entitled "The End," which has final, terminal implications, for here Charles Jackson prophesizes the end of Don Birnam. Curiously and significantly, the novel concludes as the movie had begun: with Don Birnam tying a pint of liquor to a string, attaching this string to a part of the window awning, and lowering the bottle so that it dangles outside the window. He repeats the process so that a second bottle hangs from the other side of the window. Moreover, the ever-resourceful Birnam has tucked a third pint relatively neatly, if somewhat inappropriately, inside the toilet's water tank. Not satisfied with these three pints, Birnam has two more in reserve — one he has put in a bookcase where he knows that his sanctimonious brother Wick will find it. Content with his stash, Birnam settles down to savor the fifth pint, which he does without ceremony, quickly drinking two glasses. Unlike the cinema's Don Birnam, this Don has no hint of any messianic fervor about him. His passion involves getting plastered, even though he is all too aware that he has only about thirty dollars left in the world and that this fairly insubstantial sum will not be enough to sustain his addiction for very long. His final act in the novel involves his neat, artful arranging of this money, as he carefully stacks the coins to make a centerpiece and fans the bills around the silver, being certain that each of the bills can be seen. He appears to be erecting an altar to the dead, an altar composed of his dissolving resources, which are all too emblematic of the dissolution of his life.

After creating this macabre centerpiece, Don returns to the security of his room, where he "poured another drink, drank it, and crawled in, feeling like a million dollars." What follows this pessimistic observation is the novel's last paragraph, which narrates a chilling reminder that Don Birnam's life has circled back to where it had been when Jackson first described him, only now Birnam is not temporarily sober but definitely drunk, and pitifully doomed to stay that way.

> He hurried back to his room. He poured another drink, drank it, and crawled in, feeling like a million dollars. He lay listening now for Wick. Let him come any time now. The thing was over. He himself was back home God knows why or how but he had come through one more. No telling what might happen the next time but why worry about that? This one was over and nothing had happened at all. Why did they make such a fuss?[31]

A comparison between this paragraph and the final dialogue in the movie reveals that screenwriters Charles Brackett and Billy Wilder had clearly succumbed to the studio pressures and allowed an unrealistically optimistic ending to their picture. At the conclusion of the movie, Brackett and Wilder allow some cozy, comforting dialogue between Helen and Don. His recent thoughts of suicide nearly forgotten, Don swears that he will write the story of his weekend. He even confesses to Helen his fantasy of seeing his book in print, with his brother all admiration for the prodigal's accomplishments: "Imagine Wick standing in front of a book store. A great big pyramid of my books. A novel by Don Birnam. 'That's my brother, you know.'" Helen, in turn, replies in her best cheerleading manner: "That's by my fellow. Didn't I always tell you?"[32] Nonetheless, despite this dishonest conclusion, with Don vowing to the ever-patient Helen that he is going to write about his weekend and thereby forever exorcise his own demons of White Logic, the film remains a stunning achievement, a credit to the skill of Wilder, Brackett, cinematographer John Seitz, Ray Milland, and a talented supporting cast.

Limelight: *Chaplin's Farewell to All That*

The slapstick comedy of the early films of Charlie Chaplin — the Chaplin of Keystone, Essanay, and Mutual — the Chaplin whose inebriated pranks coupled with his graceful encounters with people and objects provided moviegoers of the 1910s with much laughter — would eventually fade and merge with the more serious, mature Chaplin of *Limelight* (1952). In this, Chaplin's last film made in America, we see more than just a sentimental story of a music hall comedian who drinks too much because he remembers all too well, more than a tale of a washed-up entertainer's final days. It is Chaplin's poignant, albeit occasionally overwrought, farewell to the country where he had spent forty-one years and where he had made his reputation as one of the best-known celebrities in the world.

By the end of 1951, however, Chaplin was beset with a number of major crises. Among them were his alleged underreporting of income tax and his suspected ties to the Communist party. Harassed by the U. S. government, he was nonetheless afraid to leave the United States lest he not be allowed to return. In fact, Chaplin's fears were realized, for by the time *Limelight* was released in the latter part of 1952, Chaplin's reentry permit into this country had already been revoked.[33] Against this background, one that doubtless prompted him to question his long years of creativity in the United States, Chaplin called forth memories of his hardscrabble London childhood in order to create Calvero. This character is Chaplin himself: an aging, self-deprecating music hall entertainer questioning his life as a clown. He is a man so full of pain that his every gesture is a defensive one, and a man so longing for his past successes that he risks everything in a vain attempt to rejoin a world that he realizes no longer has room for him. In essence, then, despite all of Charles Chaplin's worldwide fame, Calvero is the summation of Chaplin's fears; he is Chaplin unbound.

Limelight is thus Chaplin's farewell to many things; in Calvero the clown Chaplin probes his lifelong ambivalence toward the public, toward women, toward money, and toward the nature of humor itself. And, in an unChaplinesque touch, he resolves these many feelings of ambivalence by allowing the death of Calvero at the end of the film. But this death comes as no surprise, for Chaplin's Calvero is an old man who lives in 1918 London: a veteran music hall performer with a regretful and self-destructive bent to his personality. He is a comic who understands that being funny is a serious undertaking and that, when audiences stop laughing, a comic dies.

So Calvero drinks. When we first see him, he is drunk, stumbling up the front stairs to the outer door of his London flat. Unlike his portrayals of the cheerfully confused drunks of the early silent films, however, Chaplin's method of depicting the inebriated Calvero is far more realistic. As a matter of fact, Chaplin shows us a man who is behaving as most intoxicated people are wont to do; he is trying very hard to walk normally and to pronounce his words without slurring every syllable. In short, Calvero is behaving exactly as one would expect a man with a befogged brain to behave if he were pretending to be indisputably sober. Here is a man convinced of the elusive, illusory white logic of alcohol. Gone are the frantic gestures of *The Rounders* and *A Night Out*: the exaggerated swaggers and the clumsy collisions with furniture. Instead, we have a man who is trying desperately to maintain his composure while simultaneously striving to remain upright.

Indeed, the most effective scenes in the movie are the ones in which Chaplin's Calvero is either drunk, or, if not intoxicated, both sober and rueful about his prior drinking escapades. It is in these two types of episodes where Chaplin reveals his ability to underplay, to work within the intimate framework created by the camera. And he is genuinely touching without being cloying. Perhaps because Chaplin is recalling his squalid, precarious childhood and his mother's fragile mental balance — probably the result of her addiction to adulterated alcohol that was readily available in the London slums— he treats Calvero's alcoholism with a gentle tolerance.[34] But when Chaplin turns to one of his favorite techniques: overly distraught preaching; when he resorts to wide, expansive gestures and to shouted, hyperbolic speeches— the former, more appropriate to silent films, and the latter, to live theater —*Limelight* loses its emotional resonance. Had Chaplin not engaged in self-indulgent histrionics, had he not encouraged his costar Claire Bloom to play many of her scenes in the same overwrought manner, *Limelight* would have been a stunning, nostalgic masterpiece.

A few film historians/analysts would disagree that Chaplin's Calvero is overblown and preachy. It has been suggested by some — notably Julian Smith in *Chaplin*— that the Chaplin of *Limelight* seems leery of even the spoken word, that most of his exhortations to the character of Terry (Claire Bloom) are life affirming and tinged with irony.[35] In short, then, according to this analysis, it is Calvero speaking, not Chaplin himself. It is Calvero who pretends to be all knowing and wise.

Even with all of its flaws, however, *Limelight* is a fitting climax to Chaplin's long, unparalleled American career, for the film contains many scenes that work quite effectively on a visceral level. Chaplin in his sixties can convey the same poignant despair that characterized the best work of Chaplin in his thirties (in *The Gold Rush*, for instance). The liquid eyes still have the power to haunt, and the slender, nimble hands still convey an expressive desire to be heeded.

Because of this lasting ability to evoke an emotional response in his audience, Chaplin allows us to sympathize with the alcoholic Calvero. Moreover, Chaplin ultimately makes us aware that Calvero's death from heart disease is the direct consequence of Calvero's many years of drinking: an addiction born out of his lifelong fear of failing in front of musical hall audiences. Yet, for all that, there is a dignity that Chaplin gives to Calvero. Such dignity can be seen from the opening scene, for although at first sight Calvero is drunk, he is not homeless drunk, not gutter drunk. Instead, he looks quite respectable, dressed in a light-colored, perfectly tailored suit, and wearing a stylish hat.

Chaplin's actions in this opening scene, however, are inconsistent with his distinguished apparel. For one, he finds that using a key to open the outer doors of his flat represents an almost insurmountable challenge. He wants to appear in complete control, yet he is thwarted by a distinct lack of coordination and visual acuity. After inaccurately aiming his key several times in the general direction of the lock and after knocking in vain for the landlady, he finally points his key at the correct spot and opens the door.

As he enters, he is cognizant enough to realize that something is amiss, that there is a peculiar and unpleasant odor coming from some as yet unidentified location. Here, Chaplin introduces a nice, subtle comic touch as he checks the bottoms of his shoes. This is the sort of response that Chaplin would have used so effectively in his early silent comedies. Then, finding nothing suspicious on his soles, he finally manages to focus his blurry vision on the source of the odor: an adjacent flat. Still unsteady, he breaks down the door and finds a beautiful girl unconscious on the bed. As he picks her up, throws her over his shoulder, and totes her out of her flat, Chaplin demonstrates that he is still an agile master of pantomime; he is able to maneuver her out into the hall and fling her onto the steps while simultaneously staggering drunkenly. Walking as though he were on the deck of a gently rolling ship, Chaplin next totters across the street and summons a doctor, who is played by Chaplin's younger half-brother, Wheeler Dryden. Upon their arrival at the flat, the doctor clearly assesses the situation better than the inebriated rescuer of the still unconscious lady. Their conversation is brief, to the point, and understated. Chaplin is at his best in the following dialogue, for he says little but communicates much about his level of understanding:

DOCTOR: Did you turn off the gas?

CALVERO: (*Solemn, trying to maintain his composure, but clearly puzzled*): What gas?

In due course, the gas having been turned off and the windows aired in the girl's flat, Chaplin's Calvero and the doctor awkwardly lug the unfortunate would-be suicide up the stairs to Calvero's own flat. After the doctor has treated the girl and departed, Calvero is left on his own to take care of her. Much of the following business involving his well-meaning but drunken efforts to provide help for his new acquaintance has comic overtones; for instance, Chaplin returns from the greengrocer's carrying a sack full of food, but the labors involved in taking both himself and the sack up two flights of stairs prove fraught with complications. Oranges roll out of the sack and bounce rhythmically on the stairs like so many softballs, though in his semi-aware state Calvero heeds neither the noise nor the potential hazard they offer. Likewise, upon being told by his disapproving landlady, the cantankerous, termagant Mrs. Alsop (Marjorie Bennett), that the girl has been sick since she rented the flat, Chaplin takes numerous precautions not to come in very close contact with the personal possessions of the girl who is now sleeping in his bed.

When Calvero sobers up and the girl, Terry Ambrose, wakes up, his questions to her are often gentle and probing, as he tries to elicit some facts about the nature of Terry's illness. He implies that there are modern cures for diseases that strike young girls who are "alone in the world." When he discovers to his relief that she is a dancer, and not a prostitute as he had initially feared, he confesses that he is an entertainer as well, though the word *former* is now an appropriate prefix to the name of his profession. In fact, he admits that his drinking began when his career began: a career that was always accompanied by the terrors of facing an audience while trying to be funny.

Chaplin is at his best in the scenes where he looks at himself and his failings honestly. For instance, shortly after rescuing Terry, he regretfully muses about his past, admitting that he is all washed up as a comedian. Attempting to explain his predicament, he offers the following: "Perhaps I drank too much." The subsequent dialogue hits the right note, with Claire Bloom as Terry now offering him her support:

TERRY: There's usually a reason for drinking.

CALVERO (*wryly, quietly*): Oh, yes.

TERRY: Unhappiness, I suppose.

CALVERO (*firm, resigned*): No, I'm used to that. It was more complicated. You know, as a man gets on in years, he wants to live deeply A feeling of sad dignity comes on him, and that's fatal for a comic. It affected my work.

As he talks with Terry, Chaplin paces around the room, sits on the bed where Terry has remained since her attempted suicide, gets up and paces some more. He is clearly uncomfortable with his confession, yet he has made himself vulnerable to this young girl, as she has to him. He is lonely, alone, and needs someone. And so he makes himself even more vulnerable by revealing his fears. He reminds her that being funny is a treacherous business and that, when he was unable to "warm up" to an audience, he started drinking. He had to have the liquor before he went on, couldn't be funny without it. Chaplin makes Calvero a man who, for all of his weaknesses, is at least unafraid to face himself with some honesty. Like Jack London, the world-weary Calvero understands the irrational nature of the white logic of alcohol. And thus Calvero sums up his impasse: "The more I drank ... it became a vicious circle." Yet Terry is concerned; she wants to learn more: "What happened?" Once again, the ensuing dialogue is understated and effective, with a melancholy undertone:

CALVERO: A heart attack. I almost died.

TERRY: And you're *still* drinking?

CALVERO: Occasionally, when I think of things.

One of the dreaded things that Calvero thinks of is the possibility that he will never be able to return to the stage. Chaplin's screenplay makes clear that Calvero's name is "poison" throughout the music hall world, that he is truly washed up as a performer. So when an old acquaintance and agent Redfern (Barry Bernard) persuades the managers at a dingy small time theater, the Middlesex, to allow Calvero to appear — albeit way down on the bill — Calvero is both happy and apprehensive. We later learn that the Middlesex is a theater catering to third-rate entertainers and down-at-the heels audiences, the English equivalent of the third-string American vaudeville circuits at this time. And it is there that Calvero will face one of the worst humiliations of his life, all the more devastating because he knows that the audience is less than discriminating, that the dissipated characters who show up to berate him are themselves squalid losers and that, most important, his chances to regain his sense of self are inexorably diminishing.

But before his evening of misadventure, Calvero tries to remain positive and confident. And he shares these feelings with Terry. With her, he has found a nonjudgmental confidante, one who will listen to his frequent bouts of lecturing. Chaplin himself had no illusions about this tendency to preach, his most obvious artistic weakness as an actor. Next, Calvero tells Terry that "since I've been preaching and moralizing to you, it's really affected me. I'm beginning to believe it myself. Do you realize I haven't taken a drink since I've known you? And I'm not going to, even on the opening night."

This noble decision, however, is one that Calvero will come to regret, for his attempts at humoring the Middlesex audience are pitiful, the jokes forced, his efforts to be funny unnatural, born out of desperation and the

desire to be noticed once more. He leaves the stage defeated. The scene perhaps reflects Chaplin's lifelong nightmarish dread of returning to the stage,
where it was impossible to achieve perfection because of the uncertainty
that naturally accompanies live theater. Once Chaplin was given the chance
to make motion pictures, he preferred the fluidity of the movie medium —
and the opportunity it afforded him to do multiple retakes. So in many
ways, *Limelight* is Chaplin's farewell to his hardscrabble beginnings in
England.

Following his disgraceful, embarrassing exit from the Middlesex theater stage, to the accompaniment of hollers and catcalls, Calvero wanders
the streets till early morning, dreading his return to Terry, whom he has
continued to shelter. But, anticipating his distress, although still unaware
that he has actually made his debut at the Middlesex that evening, she has
been unable to sleep and is waiting for him to return. His defeat is immediately obvious as he confesses that he has just made his first and final
appearance at the Middlesex. The initial part of the exchange between Terry
and Calvero is poignant and understated; he tells her that he was hooted
off the stage, a humiliation that he had not suffered since he was a beginner. But he hastily diagnoses what has gone wrong. There is a wry regret in
his painful confession: "I wasn't funny. The trouble is, I was sober. I should
have been drunk before going on."

Defeated, despairing, and disillusioned, Calvero is about to confront
once and for all the terrors that have been lurking just beyond his sober consciousness. As he stumbles and hesitates throughout his next bit of dialogue, he protests that his life has come full circle; in being taunted until
he retreated off the stage, he has reverted to his early days as a novice, that
he has been treated as a "beginner." While he is reluctantly telling her this,
he desperately clasps and unclasps his hand, all the while groping into the
air for some unseen relief, his fingers exclamation points of pain. Finally,
he weeps, thus allowing Terry to enter for the first time his own private
nightmares. In addition, his crying is all the more poignant because Calvero
is sober at this point: his tears are not the result of drunken self-pity.

Just for this one night, he has again faced the dreaded enemy and it
has won; he knows that he will never be allowed to return to the site of his
defeat, the Middlesex. He is convinced that his days as a clown are finally
over. And from this point on, Calvero's drinking begins anew.

The renewed drinking is precipitated by Calvero's inadequate feelings
about the vagaries of life. Contributing to these feelings of frustration is
the fact that Terry now has a job dancing at a first-rate theater and can
therefore afford to support them. As a consequence, Calvero's self-esteem
has sunk considerably since he first rescued Terry from her own demons.

The body language of Charlie Chaplin as Calvero in *Limelight* (United Artists, 1952) reveals his insecurities. Here is the aging musical hall entertainer, often drunk, terrified of failure, yet afraid that he cannot ever again face an audience unless he has been drinking. Pictured with him is Claire Bloom as Terry Ambrose, his young protégée whom he has saved from suicide and who, in turn, tries to give him the self-confidence he needs in order to stop drinking and return to the stage.

So he drinks. One evening, Terry returns late from performing and finds Calvero with three old cronies from his music hall days. They are playing a sort of concert in Calvero's living room, which is stocked with liquor bottles—all of them empty. They have even invited the long-suffering landlady, Mrs. Alsop (Marjorie Bennett) to the impromptu party, and she is as plastered and as contented as any of the men. Chaplin gives to this scene a humorous touch as the five inebriates confront a major crisis: they have run out of beer. Terry takes advantage of the dry spell to remind the guests that it is quite late. So Mrs. Alsop leads the revelers on a stumbling trip out of the door and down the stairs, presumably in search of more booze. Their ungraceful exit leaves Calvero and Terry alone; now, together, they must face Calvero's terrors.

But the ever patient Terry maintains a strong respect for Calvero and his manifold kindness as well as his weaknesses. Nowhere are these two paradoxical traits more evident than in the ensuing scene where Terry undresses the wobbly Calvero and prepares him for bed. All the while he is allowing her to treat him as one would a toddler, he is trying to offer a sort of apology for his behavior:

CALVERO: I'm sorry, my dear. I'm drunk.

TERRY: It's your health I'm worried about. You know what the doctor said.

CALVERO: Yes, it's bad for the heart. What about the mind? Suppose that be clear and alert so that I can contemplate the future. The prospect of joining those gray-haired nymphs that sleep on the Thames embankment at night. (*Here Calvero suddenly recalls the duties of the present, as he ruefully chastises himself.*) Oh, but I forgot to get your supper. I'm no good.

The allusion to *food* reminds Calvero that he does, after all, prefer drinking to eating because "a man's true character comes out when he's drunk. Me — I'm funnier. It's too bad I didn't drink at the Middlesex."

Now that he has begun drinking again, Calvero naturally finds it difficult to stay sober. Gone is the earlier resolve that he had boasted about to Terry; gone is his resolve to follow abstinence from this point on. Further, as Terry's dancing career resumes and she becomes more and more successful — eventually becoming the featured ballerina at the Empire Theatre — Calvero's days as an entertainer seem more and more ended. One evening, after he has watched Terry's stunning performance on the Empire stage, Calvero decides that he can no longer be the invisible partner, so he escapes from the theater and retreats to a local pub. Here he engages in some drunken banter with the men who inhabit the bar. One of these local habitués recognizes Calvero from his stage appearances in the late 1800s, a fact that pleases the despondent former comedian. But there is little to make him happy; in fact, when a messenger sent by Terry invites him to have dinner with her and her theater friends, Calvero declines, saying that Terry should be informed that he has gone home to bed.

But Terry is not the sort of woman who gloats over her success. Indeed, she is one of those young, innocent, naïve, saintly women whom Chaplin had so eloquently depicted in many of his silent movies. She even intercedes to get Calvero a job as a clown in the show in which she is the featured dancer, an action for which Calvero — whose pride is daily diminishing — is grateful.

But Calvero's stage comeback is, once again, short-lived. Shortly after he has opened in a legitimate musical, he encounters on the street a fellow performer whom he had known years before. In the course of their conversation, Calvero's old acquaintance unwittingly reveals a sad truth: that Calvero has been simply tolerated in Terry's show, patronized solely because of the popularity and persuasive powers of Terry herself. Now Calvero realizes even more poignantly that he owes his job to Terry's largesse and to her increasing renown as a dancer. What is now revealed to Calvero is that his old associate is on his way to try out for the role of the clown in this particular production because the management is unhappy with its current clown, Calvero himself. As he has done in a number of previous scenes, Chaplin underplays this exchange that is nonetheless clearly hurting him deeply. As his expression registers anguish at the knowledge that he is still unwanted in the business, he politely, formally wishes his friend good luck.

Once again the crushed entertainer, Calvero decides to leave Terry. Unable to face her with his decision to clear out — a decision that obviously hurts him deeply — he vanishes from their rooms without a warning and with only a note, the contents of which we never learn. She returns that same evening to find that he has disappeared, taking with him every trace of his existence, including all of the mementos of his early musical hall days. Forsaking the security which she can now give him; and, feeling more than ever vulnerable to his advancing years, to his ill health, to his fondness for alcohol during tough times, and — most important — to his love for her, he retreats to the relative security of the pubs. Here he can perform for passersby and for the customers inside. Here he no longer has to fear rejection by the only slightly more discriminating music hall crowd. So, together with his pals from those fuzzy late evening concerts in Mrs. Alsop's rented flat, he becomes a sidewalk musician, working outside the many pubs found in London's theater district. When he has garnered enough coins to fill his outstretched hat, he hastens into the pub to exchange money for liquor.

But Terry has heard where he is working, drives by in a cab, sees him on the street, and follows him into the pub. When he recognizes her, his face registers surprise, delight, and considerable awkwardness. She begs him to come back to her, but he replies that he cannot, that he must go forward. When she pleads that she still loves him and that she would do anything in the world for him, he breaks down, admitting that her offer "hurts." When she tells him that his old friend Postant has plans to put him back on the stage — not out of charity but out of a desire to see him work again — he relents. He confesses that he has in mind an act that he has wanted to do with a fellow comic from the old days.

And so Calvero returns to his roots, still recalling his last, most recent disgrace before an audience. Here Chaplin appears onscreen for the first time with Buster Keaton — a reminder to 1952 viewers of a time when movies needed no words to convey joy or pain. As these two silent screen giants prepare backstage, the character played by Keaton reveals his own uncertainties as he insists that he is tired of hearing their visitors remark that all of this seems "like old times." Nor is Calvero at all confident with respect to what is about to happen. After the impresario Postant has reminded Calvero that he should feel secure because he is no longer an amateur, Calvero apologetically replies: "That's all any of us are — amateurs. We don't live long enough to be anything else."

When Terry comes backstage a few minutes later to wish him luck, he seems especially frail and frightened, a prey to all of the insecurities that have forever haunted him. When she tries to reassure him by reminding him that he loves the theater, his reply is both resigned and paradoxical: "I hate the theater ... I hate the sight of blood, but it is in my veins." He might very well have added that Calvero/Chaplin has always hated the sight of audience bloodlust.

However, when Calvero faces the audience, he and his partner (Keaton) are greeted by a wildly excited crowd. Although Terry has planted people in the audience who have been instructed to laugh on cue ("plants" which do not fool Calvero), these individuals clearly are not needed. But Calvero has little time to relish his triumph, for at the conclusion of the act amid audience cheers, he smashes into a drum in the orchestra pit, the victim of a final heart attack. Appropriately and paradoxically, the audience at first thinks that Calvero's collapse is a part of the act, for he is still clowning by taking pratfalls. He appears, then, to conclude the act by falling into this drum. Carried offstage, still seated uncomfortably in the drum, he tells the doctor, "I believe I'm dying ... but I've died so many times." Ironically, Calvero is sober at last, but his sobriety comes too late. Years of hard drinking and frustrated living have at last taken their revenge.

Ultimately, then, Chaplin allows the death of Calvero: the hero of his last American film. And with Calvero die some very important parts of Chaplin's life: his painful recollections of his own mother and his subsequent understanding of what alcohol could do to a person's mind and body; his youthful days in the music halls; his complex relationships with women; his ambivalence toward wealth; and his conviction that humor and sadness are one. Although Chaplin, the actor, would star in only one more film, the cynical, heavy-handed, overblown satire *A King in New York* (1957), he would never again try to recreate the past as he does in *Limelight*. The past was too painful; he was finally through with all that.[36]

7

Three Stars Are Born

Ascent was on a ladder with many broken rungs.

— Peter Gay, *Schnitzler's Century*, 2002

Lowell Sherman Sets the Standard

What Price Hollywood? (1932), though a largely neglected film today, has nonetheless sometimes been cited by film historians as the cinema prototype for the story of the alcoholic motion picture veteran who destroys himself even as his young feminine protégée becomes an almost instant star in Hollywood. The three later manifestations of this plot, all of which appeared under the title *A Star Is Born*, were filmed in 1937, 1954, and 1976; all of them are better known than the 1932 film. However, *What Price Hollywood?* is a fine movie in its own right, though it differs in a number of important respects from the 1937 and 1954 versions. For one, in this early talking picture, the starlet does not marry the drunken roué but instead finds a more conservative, stable man to wed, one with no ties to the motion picture business. In addition, the character of the cynical, wise cracking journalist/press agent does not appear in *What Price Hollywood?* As portrayed by two excellent character actors in the first two versions of *A Star Is Born* — Lionel Stander in 1937 and Jack Carson in 1954 — this is a newshound who needles the Hollywood veteran with constant jibes, which subsequently become an endless source of grief to the actor. On the other hand, the alcoholic himself in *What Price Hollywood?*, played by the multi-talented Lowell Sherman, is the sharp tongued, world-weary skeptic who disparages everything that the ordinary person might value. In short, he is a true devotee of Jack London's White Logic.

A further distinction between the two pictures of the 1930s and the film made two decades later may be found in the technological advances of the postwar period. While *What Price Hollywood?* and the 1937 *A Star Is Born* are set in the radio age, which offered no discernible competition to motion pictures, the 1954 *A Star Is Born* is firmly planted in the television era, which, by the mid–1950s, was a decided threat to the movies. For instance, when Janet Gaynor as Vicki Lester wins a Best Actress award for her role in a motion picture, she makes her acceptance speech at a relatively intimate dinner held for members of the motion picture industry. We cannot tell if the proceedings are broadcast on radio. On the other hand, when Judy Garland as Vicki Lester appears before a large audience to accept her Best Actress Academy Award, we see that the ceremony is being televised. Garland is photographed in Technicolor in a long shot to the left of center, while on the right is a large television screen that projects an identical Garland in black and white — but pictured much larger than she is in life. Director George Cukor frames the shot so that we are reminded of the omnipresence of television and its intrusion into the world of motion pictures.

A final contrast between *What Price Hollywood?* and the 1937 and 1954 versions of *A Star Is Born* involves the age difference between the Hollywood veteran and the young hopeful. Unlike Fredric March paired with Janet Gaynor and James Mason with Judy Garland in the 1937 and 1954 versions, respectively, Lowell Sherman is much older than his costar; in fact, he does not even approximate the age of his "discovery," Mary Evans (Constance Bennett, who looks as sophisticated here as a waitress as she does as a high society lady in the two later films, *After Office Hours* and *Topper*.) Moreover, Sherman's appearance and his manner are similar to John Barrymore's demeanor in *Dinner at Eight*, which was made the following year. It is perhaps no coincidence that George Cukor directed both Sherman and Barrymore in these two outstanding pictures. Cukor's astute guidance and his control of mise-en-scène for maximum emotional effects enabled both actors to give performances that reveal their keen awareness of the bitter absurdities surrounding their long but self-abused lives.

Nor do their similarities end with appearances. Sherman's Maximillan "Max" Carey and Barrymore's Larry Renault are well past middle age and have long ago paid for their years of drinking, both internally and externally. Both are adored by young women, though Barrymore's character has been married multiple times and is married at the time he is being pursued by a very young Paula Jordan (Madge Evans). On the other hand, Max Carey is on his own; we know nothing about his past relationships with women, though we might assume that his iconoclastic lifestyle has discouraged women from seeking him out. Furthermore, although Mary Evans clearly idolizes the director who gives her a start in films, there is no suggestion that they are in love or that they are even physically attracted to one another. So too, although both Max Carey and Larry Renault are agonizingly aware that the world is one great cosmic joke, Carey is wittier, more in control of the well-timed riposte, the bon mot, and the absurdly meaningless gesture.

For instance, early in the picture we see Carey as he enters the Brown Derby restaurant, perennial symbol of Hollywood's discovery of previously unheralded talent. He is slightly tipsy but elegantly dressed in tie and tails. His air of insouciance manifests itself as he delivers clusters of flowers to all he sees in the Brown Derby. These are mementos that he has just graciously bought from an old lady at the entrance; he has purchased every flower in her possession. Following this sweeping gesture of generous goodwill, he has further demonstrated his commitment to noblesse oblige by sending the flower seller home in his car. It is in the Brown Derby that he meets Mary Evans, who is dying for a chance to be in movies and who has arranged to wait on his table. Because she compliments him and flatters his already huge ego, he returns her flattery: "You're the smartest girl I've met here tonight." In short, he is so taken with her that he escorts her out of the Derby and impulsively pays fifty dollars for a car parked just outside: a shabby vehicle that had refused to start, despite its owner's repeated efforts to crank it up. The car engine turned over at last, Carey drives his new admirer in his new, used car to the premiere of his latest movie.

By the time they reach the theater, the radiator is boiling over, to the vast amusement of both Carey and the fans lining the sidewalk in front of the theater. Now more intoxicated than ever, Carey maintains his air of damn-the-consequences as he goes to the ubiquitous microphone, forever a staple of movie premieres in those radio days, and demonstrates his contempt for the pretentious proceedings by giving the listening audience a raspberry. When the studio boss Julius Saxe (Gregory Ratoff) admonishes him for excessive drinking, telling Carey, one of his best directors, that whiskey is a problem that is ruining his career, Carey adopts his world-weary sophisticate pose as he replies: "You're right. What the picture business needs is light wines and beer."

Later, after Bennett becomes a star with Carey's encouragement and guidance, she goes to Carey to announce her engagement to Lonny Borden (Neil Hamilton). Carey — at this point completely sober — tries to camouflage his hurt pride with a wisecrack. When Bennett asks, "Aren't you going to congratulate me?" Carey's retort is both cynical and cruel: "What for? It'll never last." To this, Hamilton replies, "What won't last?" Carey's rejoinder is self-deprecating and painful: "My liver and a movie star's marriage." Despite Carey's efforts to discourage the marriage, Mary and Lonny are wed, but Carey tries everything he can to get revenge. His motives for such actions are complicated; he is possibly jealous that a young, attractive woman should turn her attentions to another man. It is also possible that, in his loneliness, he has found her nonjudgmental companionship and sympathy desirable and even somewhat comforting. One evening, shortly after the Bennett/Hamilton marriage, Carey keeps Bennett working very late on the set, knowing that her husband is watching and waiting for her to finish. Carey finds fault with everything she does and insults Hamilton by calling him "*Mr.* Evans."

Yet there are a number of comic touches that occur in the first part of the movie. Furthermore, as with everything associated with Lowell Sherman's Max Carey, these lighter moments also have a bittersweet tinge to them. For instance, Carey's butler, played by Eddie "Rochester" Anderson, is the keeper of Carey's liquor supply. When Carey returns home following one of his typical nights on the town and wants a generous nightcap to finish off the evening, Anderson hands him the bottle and watches as Carey empties some of its contents, and then uses a pencil to mark the level at which he has left the liquid. Then, when he is out of Carey's sight, Anderson takes the bottle, drinks some of the remainder himself, erases the mark, and replaces it with his own. Carey is probably all too aware of Anderson's tampering with the vital alcohol supply, but, in his usual bemused manner, he lets it go, probably finding Anderson's efforts at deception amusing.

Other slight gestures on Carey's part show that Lowell Sherman is as adept at body language as he is at appropriate word choice in order to reveal his disdain. To illustrate, early in the film, following a showing of Bennett's successful screen test, he sits in the screening room, his crossed feet propped up on the seat in front, and listens to a conversation between Bennett's Mary Evans and the studio head Julius Saxe. Saxe is offering Mary the standard seven-year contract, which will lock her in to a fairly small salary and which will give her no way out if she decides that she wants to quit the studio. In short, she is being purchased by the studio as a commodity to be used in any way that the studio bosses see fit. However, the young and naïve Mary does not understand the ramifications of what she is being offered, and she eagerly accepts. Carey's reaction is wordless but says wonders, for the only thing that the camera discloses is a shot of Carey's propped up feet; as Carey listens to Mary's glee at Saxe's offer, he guides his feet in doing a graceful, sitting entrechat.

Yet for all of his derision of the system that has obviously made him famous and rich, the sober Carey can be utterly charming and completely serious when he is directing a picture or when he is watching the dailies. Unlike the decrepit actor played by Barrymore in *Dinner at Eight*, Sherman's Max Carey is seen actually working for a living — and doing a sober, professional job. We see Carey directing Bennett in a screen test, in which she initially gives an execrable performance. We watch him as he shows a mixture of exasperation and patience, even as he allows her to retake the scene. We see him on the set of a film in progress, giving orders and showing mastery of his craft. In point of fact, Lowell Sherman himself was a creative director who worked with Katherine Hepburn in her Academy Award winning performance in *Morning Glory* (1933) and with Mae West and Cary Grant in *She Done Him Wrong* (1933). In both pictures, his ability to deal with bizarre personality types and to take the edge off their extremes comes through.

Perhaps his experience in working both sides of the camera gave Lowell Sherman the added insight into what inner demons would drive a man such as Max Carey. And the demons are many and tragic. By the last third of the picture, Carey no longer has any masks left to wear. What little remains of his savoir faire has been peeled away by the poison of alcohol. One evening, Carey arrives at the Bennett/Hamilton home. He is drunk as usual and, when they refuse to acknowledge him, he retaliates by trying to set fire to their house. Dismissed from his last picture for going on a one-week binge and no longer amusing, he nonetheless finally gets their attention through his pyrotechnics. After the small fire is put out, Bennett persuades her husband to let him in. Yet if Carey's intention all along has been to break up the marriage, he has finally succeeded; that night a disgusted Hamilton walks out on Bennett, declaring that he can no longer live with her and put up with the Hollywood lifestyle. So she is left alone with the completely soused director, to whom she will remain intensely loyal for what little time is left of his shattered life.

Indeed, Carey has few opportunities remaining to ponder his mistakes. About two years pass; one evening Bennett is summoned to get Carey out of jail. He has given a bad check, which Bennett makes good before she rescues the hollowed-out director. No longer the insouciant man-about-town, Carey looks like a bum; he is unshaven, his tie askew. He is a worn out shell, a man exhausted and used up. It does not take him long to pick through and sign for the handful of belongings kept in a small envelope that the jailer returns to him. These represent the detritus of his existence. Filled with love, pity, guilt, and regret, Bennett takes him home with her. Yet Carey is not comforted. Having reached the nadir of his life, he too is filled with conflicting emotions: gratitude, shame, embarrassment, and terror. He tries to hide his feelings with weak jokes. Finding himself in Bennett's home, clad in pajamas and propped up in bed, he self-mockingly addresses Bennett's butler, "Martin, thank you for the nightie." But then, when Bennett offers him help and sympathy, Carey turns to self-pity, "I feel as though I oughta say thank you. You should have left me where I was." He continues in this vein when he assures her that he didn't at all mind being in jail, for he doesn't really exist anymore, that he's all burned out. "Don't you see," he nearly pleads for her understanding, "I'm dead inside. I should feel ashamed, degraded. I just can't feel anything."

When Bennett refuses to listen to this self-annihilation, insisting that Carey is going back to work, Carey's reply is both honest and self-defeating. He knows that he's washed up in pictures, that he can no longer kid himself: "Work and I haven't been on speaking terms for quite some time." Then, thinking to assuage her hurt feelings, he adds, "Now that you're top of the heap, I'm happy." When she replies by attempting a pep talk, assuring him that from that night onward he will go dry, his answer is deliberately ambiguous and tragically prescient, "From now on, I won't cause you any more trouble." Although he does not have a clear plan in mind for ending these troubles, Carey does realize that he has nothing more to look forward to on this earth. So after Bennett turns out the light, Carey gets out of bed and begins his search for the end. The first thing he locates is a bottle hidden in one of her cabinets; after taking a drink, he looks for a match to light his cigarette. Instead, he hits upon a bit of good luck: he finds a revolver in one of the drawers.

The ensuing scene will be echoed in the suicidal actions of John Barrymore's Larry Renault the following year in George Cukor's *Dinner at Eight*. In both films, night contributes to the melancholy, deadly effect of the drama. Additionally, light from the street causes shadows to be filtered through the windows, making the room in which Carey will spend his final moments look as though it has bars streaked across it. Like Larry Renault, Max Carey goes to a mirror and is terrified by the hideous image that he sees reflected back. As Carey lights his cigarette, his face is illuminated from below, causing shadows to fall on it and highlighting the dissipation of the grotesque visage. A similar reaction will occur with Larry Renault when he sees what he has become. At this point, however, Carey is even more forcefully reminded of past days when he looks at a photo of himself that Bennett has placed beneath the mirror. The photo had been taken some years earlier and shows a dapper, well-groomed man. But this Dr. Jekyll has turned into Mr. Hyde and, like Stevenson's famous split personality character, can no longer return of his own volition to the sober, rational, good-hearted Dr. Jekyll. When it dawns on Carey that Mr. Hyde has at last taken over completely, the cigarette drops from his mouth and he pushes aside the photo of his former identity in order to take a perverse pleasure in looking at his current self. And what he sees is indeed monstrous: the eyes are wide, staring; the mouth set in a determined, clenched-jaw expression. Through the use of a montage superposed over this reflection, we see his thoughts: he is a much younger, more attractive man, partying and drinking. Then there follows a panning shot of his most recent memory: the prison bars.

No longer able to stomach the vision, he puts his hands over his face, but he cannot efface the gelatinous images. He uncovers his face to the accompaniment of a grating soundtrack noise, a sound calculated to cause impalpable pain, similar to the feeling caused in some individuals when chalk is scraped across a chalkboard. Only this particular sound resembles the noise of a pneumatic drill being used underwater. The drilling reverberation is emphasized through the superposition of a dizzying montage of swirling liquid. Here is the aural and visual embodiment of the White Logic, come to take away its next victim. Nearly overtaken by the force of this White Logic, Carey remembers the revolver, which he now grabs from the drawer, places against his chest, and fires. Unlike Barrymore's Larry Renault, who assumes a more dramatic air as he poses, his best profile forward, while waiting for the gas to work, Carey chooses a messier way, a quicker way to get rid of the buzzing in his head.[1] And so he falls forward, leaving others to clean up the mess that he has made: both in his life and in his death.

It is important to note that, unlike Max Carey, the real-life Lowell Sherman was both a disciplined actor and director, but one who nonetheless displayed a few touches of the bizarre behavior demonstrated by Carey. For instance, Anthony Slide has commented on some of Sherman's odd directorial methods. Sherman's last completed film was *Night Life of the Gods* (1935), released after his death in 1934. Declaring that it was too hot to work efficiently while properly attired, Sherman directed this picture clad only in his underwear. Significantly, Sherman died of pneumonia only twenty-four days into the shooting of his next picture, *Becky Sharp* (1935). Slide questions whether there might have been a causal relationship between Sherman's state of undress on *Night Life of the Gods* and his subsequent death from pneumonia.[2] Perhaps. But what is more, Max Carey would have probably delighted in the cosmic absurdity of such a connection.

Fredric March and the Gentleman as Drunk

The first movie with the title *A Star Is Born* was made in 1937. It was supposedly based in part on the life of John Gilbert, an exceedingly handsome, popular silent star who failed to make the transition to sound pictures. While Gilbert was at the peak of his popularity, he had married the promising young actress Virginia Bruce, who indeed would achieve a certain amount of fame, even as Gilbert was declining both personally and professionally.[3] In this particular incarnation of the story of the young woman mentored by the older and declining show business veteran, Janet Gaynor is the stars-in-her-eyes woman with the dreadful name of Esther Blodgett, which sounds like a name W. C. Fields would delight in giving to one of his characters. Esther travels from the staid stability of the rural Middle West to the alluring fakery of Hollywood. In fact, it is her salt-of-the-earth, no-nonsense grandma (May Robson) who gives her the money to get away. From the outset, Gaynor appears more countrified than her predecessor, Constance Bennett. Even as a waitress, Bennett is glamorous, displaying her angular thin body with fashion-model aplomb. Gaynor, on the other hand, even after she has attained stardom in her first picture, looks like a Kodak advertisement featuring a woman who is enjoying a picnic in a bucolic Technicolor setting. She never looks sophisticated enough to pose in the rotogravure section of the newspaper. In fact, with fifteen years shaved off her age, she might have played Dorothy in *The Wizard of Oz*.

Yet, like Bennett, she speedily becomes famous through the help of a movie veteran. This time, however, it is popular actor Norman Maine (Fredric March) rather than a well-known director who pulls her from obscurity. Furthermore, March does not dominate his scenes in the hard, commanding way that Lowell Sherman does. Though March's Norman Maine is also an alcoholic, he is a far more gentlemanly alcoholic. Even at his most inebriated, he never displays the ragged edges of Sherman's Max Carey. Perhaps one reason that March seems to have a much smoother style is that March is younger and handsomer than Sherman. With his comparative youth and good looks, he resembles Ray Milland in *The Lost Weekend*. Norman Maine also has a brooding intensity that the witty Max Carey lacks.

Yet with Esther's first glimpse of Norman Maine in *A Star Is Born*, we realize that here is a man who is not at all embarrassed by his own public displays of drunkenness. But when the idealistic Esther sees him noisily stumble to his seat at a concert at the Hollywood Bowl, all she can see is that here is one of her idols, in person. She turns to her escort, neighbor Daniel "Danny" McGuire (Andy Devine) and whispers, awestruck, "That's *Norman Maine*." Danny replies with some amusement, "He seems to have had that one extra cocktail." Since he is so soused, Maine does not seem worthy of anyone's admiration at this point. Though he is formally dressed, his behavior is boorish. When the audience applauds as he is taking his seat, he thinks that the applause is for him so he begins bowing and clasping his hands over his head, raising his arms in a prizefighter's salute. The sophisticated lady accompanying him is annoyed and chastises him: "Sit down, you dope. That's for the orchestra leader." But her admonishment for more civilized behavior is in vain; before the concert begins, Norman brawls with a photographer who has the temerity to try to take his picture. Esther, however, is still enchanted with this appearance of one of her favorite movie stars, so her loyal friend Danny arranges for her to serve as a waitress at a fancy Hollywood dinner party to which he knows that Norman has been invited. The relationship between Esther and Danny is worthy of examination. As played by the likable, rotund character actor Andy Devine, Danny is a decent fellow who lives in the same hotel as Esther and who befriends her when she first arrives in Hollywood with very little money and even fewer chances of becoming a star. Danny would have been a good husband for Esther — dependable, caring, sober — a far better choice than the good-looking but self-destructive Norman. Yet Esther has her own streak of self-annihilation — she is a far softer character than the one played by Constance Bennett — so she chooses instead to marry the larger-than-life actor.

And interestingly, it is Danny who is the instrument of their meeting. Just as Danny had predicted, Esther encounters Norman at the party. He is, of course, drunk, but he is taken by her wistful quality so he gallantly offers to help her put dishes away. His slightly off center unsteadiness causes him to break more crockery than he places on the shelf. When his jealous lady-of-the-moment enters and finds him with a menial but attractive servant, she grabs a serving tray, conks him over the head, and leaves in a snit, but not before she has succeeding in flattening him onto the floor, where he lies—conscious but somewhat nonplussed at his undignified position. "Help me up," he ruefully asks Esther. Esther, concerned, obliges, asking, "Are you hurt?" Norman's reply is forthright, "No more than usual." Furthermore, Norman knows a good opportunity when he sees one; therefore, he insists that the two of them escape the kitchen, proclaiming, "The wolves are on us." In a final gesture of perverted obligation, he deliberately smashes a few more plates as they exit, announcing that the dishes are done. It is a deliciously anti-social gesture that Max Carey would have also been proud to make.

And so Norman takes Esther home, just as Max Carey had drunkenly escorted Mary Evans home from the movie premiere in *What Price Hollywood?* However, unlike Carey's paternal interest in Mary Evans, Norman's interest in Esther is less than fatherly. After parking in front of her hotel, he tries out a couple of propositions on her. First, he invites her to his place. Good girl that she is, Esther refuses. Knowing that he has received a setback in that department, he walks her to the door. Turning her face upward, he looks longingly at her and next tries an old line: "Has anyone ever told you that you're lovely?"

Though Esther obviously rebuffs Norman's advances (with a name like *Esther Blodgett* a girl would have to stay innocent), Norman is still smitten enough by her unique beauty and her unpretentiousness that the next day he calls the studio boss Oliver Niles (Adolph Menjou) and arranges to do a screen test with Esther. When the test proves successful, Niles signs her to a contract and, like Mary Evans in *What Price Hollywood?* she becomes studio property. Wise guy press agent Matt Libby (Lionel Stander) concocts a background for her, and she is transformed from Esther Blodgett into Vicki Lester. At first, she is given only a bit part in a movie, a one-liner for which most actors receive no credit. But while she is rehearsing her line in the studio commissary, she is spotted by Norman Maine — who (surprise! surprise!) just happens to be in search of a new leading lady for his latest picture. He is, as usual, hung over, but he is sentient enough to realize that Esther/Vicki is the ideal physical type for the role. And, of course, she gets the part and is a big hit at the movie preview, her reviews better than his.

But Norman Maine, like Max Carey, is never presented as mean-spirited. Neither one of these artists is really jealous of the success of the star that each has helped to create. Following the successful preview of the picture in which Esther/Vicki makes her astonishing debut, Norman stands with her on the balcony of his apartment and discusses the future. Hers is a promising one; his no longer exists. Yet he can still feel with some poignancy the missed chances, the hollow words of the celluloid world around which he has centered his life, the alcohol that has made this world a little more bearable. As they listen to the song "Dancing in the Dark" playing in the background, he opens up to reveal to her just how melancholy he is:

NORMAN: You have everything in the world you want. I hope it'll make you happy.

ESTHER: Doesn't it you?

NORMAN (emphatically shaking his head): That was one thing I never had. Lots of times I told myself I had it, but I always knew I was lying. Still, I never stopped looking for it.

ESTHER: Maybe it'll come.

NORMAN: Oh, I think it has come, Esther. I only wish it weren't too late.

Yet Norman does try for happiness by marrying Esther, hoping that a little of her health, vitality, optimism, and all-round can-do attitude will rub off on him. At this point, it might be appropriate to comment on the curious fact that Gaynor's voice in this film sounds much like Jeanette Mac-

Donald's. Some of her gestures and expressions even resemble the coy arch-ness of MacDonald: a defect that characterized the singer's movies from the late 1930s onward.

Despite Esther's occasionally cloying personality, the Esther/Norman union works—briefly. Leaving behind the artificiality of Hollywood, they travel through the west by car; what is more, in order to emphasize the new pastoral life they have chosen, they are pulling a camper equipped with a kitchen and bathroom. These homey refinements, although prehistoric according to the standards expected by today's RV trekkers, were doubtless considered the latest in modern "roughing it" equipment in 1937. Deter-mined to redefine himself by getting away from it all with his bride and by enjoying some primitive living conditions to which he is obviously unac-customed, Norman stays sober, at least for a while.

But the honeymoon does not last long. Like Max Carey in *What Price Hollywood?* Norman is dismissed from the studio because of his unreliabil-ity. While Esther continues to work as a successful actress, he tries his best to be a proper househusband, even preparing dinner to serve her when she returns from a hard day at the studio. Though he seems outwardly calm and tries to stay sober, he broods about his self-inflicted idle state. This brooding comes to a head one night at an Academy Awards dinner. As Esther/Vicki is making a winsomely modest acceptance speech for her Best Actress award, Norman, clearly drunk, makes a boisterous entrance and grabs center stage from his wife, proclaiming that he had won such an award and that the prize is meaningless. Then he taunts both the hoi polloi gath-ered for the festivities as well as his own empty existence when he challenges all present to award him a statue for the three worst performances of the year: "Do I get 'em?" he exhorts, "Answer *yes* or *no!*"

While Norman is giving his worst performance number four, Esther/Vicki is on her way to rescue him from a display that is equally embarrass-ing to both of them. As she maneuvers her way to come up behind him, he gestures wildly, punctuating his diatribe but also slapping her in the face as he does so. His reaction to this inadvertent violence reveals that he is aston-ished yet horrified at what he has done. Gaynor's character dons her usual patient and forgiving expression as she leads him back to her table.

Following this boorish and all-too-public exhibition, Norman lands in a sanitarium, but his drying out there is only a temporary bandage to cover a deep wound for which there is no healing. And one factor that pre-vents such recovery is his knowledge that he has damned himself within the movie business. In a scene reminiscent of the one between Lee Tracy and John Barrymore in *Dinner at Eight*, Oliver Niles visits Norman in this temporary prison and offers Norman a very minor part in a film. Like

Barrymore when Tracy suggests that there might be a small role for him in a picture, Norman rejects anything that does not reflect his former title of Leading Man. So much for Norman's comeback. Nor can he come back on the terms that he had enjoyed with others in his social set when he was on top in Hollywood. When he is finally dismissed from the sanitarium, his skin is sallow, his nerves are frayed, and his sobriety is tenuous. All of his former acquaintances shun him.

The beginning of his final decline occurs at the bar at the Santa Anita racetrack, which Norman visits shortly after his sanitarium stay. After ordering ginger ale and trying to maintain some sense of decorum, Norman makes the mistake of trying to be cordial to press agent Matt Libby. As played by Lionel Stander, Libby is crafty, serpentine, amoral, crude, and completely disgusting. He picks away at Norman's insecurities, especially those involving Esther's role as the breadwinner and those relating to Norman's inability to do any sort of work. Norman is not steady enough to land an accurate punch on Libby, so Libby knocks him to the floor. When Norman is finally able to pull himself upright and sit at the bar once again, he orders a double scotch and asks the waiter to leave the bottle with him. Soon, in typical alcoholic fashion, he follows the dictates of the White Logic and disappears for several days. When he resurfaces, he is facing jail time for being drunk and disorderly.

At this point, we may have begun to wonder just why Esther does not dump Norman. He no longer has the good looks that had made him such a popular screen favorite; so too, though he keeps insisting that he loves her, his actions belie his words. He cannot stay sober. Yet poor Esther remains a disgustingly dutiful wife. When she hears of his arrest, she and the ever patient Oliver Niles go to Night Court where they see Norman led in for sentencing along with other down-and-out denizens of the Los Angeles streets. The Night Court judge, played by Jonathan Hale — an excellent character actor with a beautifully cadenced voice — at first sentences Norman to ninety days in jail. But hearing Esther's pleas to allow Norman into her custody, the judge relents and the increasingly humiliated Norman goes back home. However, he finds no comfort or security there. Lying in bed and listening to the conversation between Esther and Oliver in the next room, he is appalled at what Esther is saying. She tells Oliver that she is through with motion pictures, that she is going away with Norman. Oliver naturally protests: "It's your *life* you're giving up, Vicki." Yet the forever self-sacrificing, simpering Esther replies adamantly, "There'll be no more Vicki Lester." Here her voice breaks, so that we know that her resolve is not quite as solid as she pretends.

This scene between Esther and Oliver is crosscut with a shot of Norman in bed, taking in every word. The camera focuses only on Norman's eyes, which are highlighted by bright lights. The rest of the frame is dark. And the eyes convey his understanding of what his drinking has cost. Thus, after Oliver leaves, he comes out of the bedroom and tells Esther that he is going for a swim but that they will have supper when he returns. Poor Esther. She is obviously too dim to understand just what Norman has planned. But Norman knows just what to do. He turns toward the west, where a beautiful Technicolor sunset is floating just over the horizon. Leaving his robe and slippers behind for the waves to wash over them in a nice symbolic touch, Norman walks into the water for his last swim. The superb underplaying of Fredric March keeps the scene from being maudlin and melodramatic. Not so with the next few scenes where Esther is determined to give up all and return to her rural roots. Fortunately, Granny (May Robson) comes from somewhere in the hinterlands and, in her best the-show-must-go-on rhetoric, persuades Esther to carry on. Perhaps now Esther will renounce her dippy ways and have the good sense to marry Andy Devine, who remains devoted and at her side at Norman's funeral as well as at the premiere of her next picture. While he is not handsome, he has a cuddly winsome quality to him, and he does stay sober.

In many respects, the earlier *What Price Hollywood?* is a better movie than this version of *A Star Is Born*. While both Lowell Sherman and Fredric March were fine, versatile actors, Sherman has better lines and is thereby able to create a more complex character in Max Carey than March is allowed with Norman Maine. Norman goes from drunkenness to a remorseful sobriety, then back to drunkenness and thence to another remorseful sobriety. The pattern continues until the remorseful sobriety wins the day and ends Norman's life. March has little else to do except follow the pattern. Nonetheless, March was a skilled actor and makes the most of what he is given to do. A contemporary reviewer for the National Board of Review of Motion Pictures summarized quite well the Norman Maine role and March's excellent portrayal as "a grim picture of disintegration":

> A charming and generous, even an intelligent man he is, but a screen idol whose day is done, contemptuous of the public adoration that raised him so high, but with the adoration gone unable to find a foothold to stop his downward plunge, finding in drink the only thing that keeps reality from being unendurable. And finally even drink cannot keep life endurable. It is a tragic part ... splendidly written and magnificently acted. Fredric March has never had a better chance to show what a fine and honest actor he can be.[4]

In addition to March's characterization as the doomed Norman, the movie also has some affecting moments and good performances by a number of the supporting players, specifically Lionel Stander and Adolph Menjou. One could wish for just a little less sentimentality and more of the hard-edged wit and cynicism displayed by all of the major characters in *What Price Hollywood?* Even the studio head Niles in *A Star Is Born* is a much kinder, gentler person than the acerbic Julius Saxe as played by Gregory Ratoff in the earlier film.

Finally, mention should be made concerning the ironic circumstances of the two leading players of *A Star Is Born*. By 1937, Janet Gaynor, who had been a popular silent star, was less well known than Fredric March, who would continue to have a long and distinguished motion picture career.

Judy Garland: Saved from the Abyss

Constance Bennett and Janet Gaynor were popular stars of the 1930s who aged relatively gracefully; in the 1950s and 1960s, each appeared in one more movie, playing a mature, but not matronly, lady: Gaynor in *Bernadine* in 1957 and Bennett in *Madame X*, released in 1966 after Bennett's death in 1965. But neither actress ever approached the iconic, megastar status of Judy Garland, the second Esther Blodgett in *A Star Is Born* (1954). By 1954, the talented but fragile Garland had been appearing in major motion pictures for eighteen years. In 1936, in her first feature-length movie, *Pigskin Parade*, she was miscast as the hillbilly sister of the equally miscast hillbilly Stuart Erwin, although she was given a few songs to sing. But by 1939, the industry was attempting to publicize her as a femme fatale; she was already featured in glamorous, full-page photos in major fan magazines, accompanied by rhapsodic, hyperbolic captions that stretched credulity. For instance, a 1939 *Photoplay* displays Garland in three quarter profile, looking seductively over her shoulder. The copy underneath the picture tells us about this young star:

> Sixteen! The transformation of Baby Frances Gumm of Grand Rapids into starlet Judy Garland of Hollywood is complete. But two things have never changed — her desire to sing, which she satisfies in "Babes in Arms" — and her desire to be a doctor, which she satisfies with ambitious plans to build a hospital for children.[5]

Yet by the mid–1950s, all medical aspirations forgotten, Garland had earned a reputation for irresponsibility and undependability. In the late 1940s, she had been fired from a number of important pictures because of her inability to arrive on time for filming or because of her refusal to show up at all. MGM finally lost patience with her mood swings and fired her in 1950. By the time she began work on *A Star Is Born*, she had endured two failed marriages, had undergone an abortion, and had made at least one suicide attempt. But Warner Bros. took a chance on the brittle star, promoting its expensive production with the exclamation: "$6,000,000 and 2½ years to make it!"[6] What this ecstatic advertisement fails to mention, however, is that Garland's perennial instability, including long periods of sulking and her general temperamental behavior on the set, caused the film to run way over budget. It ultimately cost more than twice its original estimate.[7]

Despite the bloated cost, Warner's gamble on Garland in this particular instance succeeded. Though *A Star Is Born* was to be her last musical and her last truly good picture, Garland's return to films was dazzling. In an interesting coincidence, this version of *A Star Is Born* was directed by George Cukor, who had also directed *What Price Hollywood?* twenty-two years earlier. It was Cukor's first musical, but he brings to it the same ironic sensibility that he had expressed so well in his depiction of Hollywood in 1932. By the same token, Cukor coaxes a superb performance from Garland, softening some of the more frenetic edges of her personality.

Yet her stunning performance is two-sided, for even under Cukor's guidance, Garland casts a large shadow over her fellow actors; in all of her films, Garland's autobiographical presence suggests a roller coaster passenger who is about to undo her safety strap before the ride's final plunge. Richard Schickel has aptly summarized the force of Judy Garland's personality. His analysis here is especially apropos to Garland's performance in *A Star Is Born*:

> In general, good performances, especially on film, seem to result from an inner tension, the tension created by raw energy and the performer's control of that energy. At her finest, Miss Garland, especially in her maturity, seems always about to be destroyed by her own inner forces. It puts a quiver of passion in her voice and a chill in the listener's spine. At every moment of a Garland performance you feel that you stand with the star on the brink of disaster, and a hundred times a night she saves herself—and her sympathetic admirers—from the abyss.[8]

Because these hyperactive, on-the-brink-of-disaster performances always demand the audience's full attention, James Mason's tormented alcoholic, Norman Maine, is less central to *A Star Is Born* than the character would have been had a minor star played Esther. Yet Mason manages to hold his own against Garland's persistent agitation and delivers a memorable portrayal as the ill-fated actor overshadowed by his larger-than-life wife. In fact, Mason's Norman Maine has more style and polish than Sherman's Max Carey and more depth than March's Norman Maine. In addition, Mason brings to his scenes with Garland a true feeling for his discovery's talent and a genuine concern and affection for her. Such obvious manifestation of love and adoration is absent from the characterizations of both Sherman and March in the earlier films.

Interestingly, George Cukor's first choice to play Norman Maine was Cary Grant. Cukor was convinced that the role of the aging alcoholic was a part perfectly suited to Grant's personality. But after Grant read the screenplay, he turned down the part for that very reason.[9] Grant knew that Norman Maine's weaknesses—his manifest character flaws—cut too close to the bone. He quite astutely saw too many aspects of himself in the character; the very private, self-conscious Grant, who had his own off-screen battles with alcohol, did not want to expose his nerve endings in such a public manner. One can only speculate as to what sort of performance Grant would have given, but had he given free rein to the darker side of his personality—as he did when he worked with Hitchcock, for instance—he would have doubtless provided an effective foil to the hyper-charged Garland.

Yet though James Mason was not Cukor's first choice, his performance as Norman Maine was one of the best of the year, earning him an Academy Award nomination. Furthermore, because Judy Garland was far more talented than either Constance Bennett or Janet Gaynor, Mason's awe at her gifts is all the more believable. In fact, Garland's Esther Blodgett is already an established performer—albeit a minor one—when superstar James Mason meets her. Moreover, from the outset he has reason to be grateful to Garland, who rescues the drunken Norman Maine from excruciating embarrassment when he stumbles onto the stage where she is performing in a Hollywood benefit. She grabs him, holds him up, and makes him a part of the act, even pushing him off the stage with her at the conclusion of her song. Thus, as with Lowell Sherman and Fredric March, from the beginning of the narrative Mason is established as an unreliable, frequently violent, but somewhat charming drunk. But he is not so drunk that he fails to see Garland's charm, and he manages to find where she works—a small club that he subsequently visits. It is here that he listens to her as she sings "The Man That Got Away."

Once again, the difference between this version of A Star Is Born and the two earlier pictures is clearly the result of Garland's immense gifts. Whereas Constance Bennett and Janet Gaynor are somewhat credible as young women with a modicum of talent, their less-than-spectacular abilities fail to convince us of the speed with which they so rapidly become superstars. Both have certain appealing qualities. Bennett is attractive, lean, hard-edged, and rather amusing. She holds her own against the Hollywood establishment with a certain wry humor. On the other hand, Gaynor is winsome in an offbeat way, but her simpering fidelity to the loutish though unquestionably handsome March wears thin quite early in the film. However, with Judy Garland, it is easy to see why she quickly mesmerizes Mason. Like his earlier counterparts, he has some moments of insight and sobriety. It is during one of these moments that he first hears her sing, and his efforts to communicate to her the way she has made him feel are shy, hesitant, and touching. Assuring her that he will arrange a screen test for her, he persuades her to stay in Hollywood rather than to go back on tour with her small group of musicians.

But Norman Maine goes home that evening, gets drunk, and stays drunk. The next day, all promises forgotten, he leaves to go on location for his next movie; still in a drunken stupor, he must be hauled away by the studio bosses for the filming. Meanwhile, having given up on Norman Maine, Esther Blodgett remains in Hollywood, still patiently hoping for a chance to prove her worth. And she gets this chance when Norman returns and finally succeeds in locating her. Though we don't see the test, we know that Garland must have been stunning because now she becomes studio property. As a part of this appropriation of her being, the studio must alter Esther's very identity, beginning with the way she looks. The developing relationship between Esther — who is about to be transformed into Vicki Lester — and Norman Maine is reinforced when Maine sees what the makeup department has done to Esther's appearance. Film critic/historian Gerald Mast has referred to those who run Hollywood studio publicity departments as "cops." These "cops," according to Mast, "who believe in graven images, attempt to convert Esther Blodgett into an image named Vicki Lester — a photograph, a singing marionette, a face in a mirror, a painted doll in makeup."[10]

Indeed, when Mason sees Garland — the painted doll with a blonde wig, blatantly red cheeks, and clad in a dress that makes her look like a character in a Victor Herbert operetta — he takes charge and immediately removes the wig and gently scrubs her face. Once again, the sober Norman is genuinely worried about Esther herself; he does not want her to be a graven image to be carved up by studio publicity demons. He is concerned with Esther as Esther. Such personal apprehension had not been shown by either Lowell Sherman or Fredric March toward their discoveries. But this Norman Maine — who is on his final, inebriated descent into the arms of the irrefutable White Logic — lacks the hubris of both Sherman's Max Carey and March's Norman Maine. Though he can be cruel and devious when he is drunk, he is also more giving, far less narcissistic than his predecessors. As a consequence, his death will seem more deserving of our pity though, to his credit, Mason never asks for sympathy for Norman.

In fact, this Norman Maine is so taken with Esther Blodgett/Vicki Lester that his every gesture toward her is filled with a self-sacrificial longing for her success. For instance, as he drives her to the preview of her first starring film, he coaches her on how to behave. Moreover, when they arrive at the theater, he notes with delight that the feature attraction is one of his own movies—a picture that Maine cheerfully refers to as a "stinker." Her musical film debut, he assures her, will be a hit: since his movie is so awful, the newly created Vicki Lester will benefit from the comparison. As in other scenes in which he encourages Garland to continue hoping for success, Mason's character is sober and consequently supportive of the woman with whom he has become both awestruck and infatuated.

Later, at a party held to celebrate Garland's achievement on screen, Garland and Mason show their love for each other in a scene that is far more subtly acted and consequently more affecting than any of the love scenes between March and Gaynor in the 1937 version. Garland is both shy and frantic as she declares that she loves him. For his part, Mason, who is clearly touched by her declaration, protests, "I destroy everything I touch. I always have. Forget me. You've come too late." But for all his cynicism, there is still a longing for what might have been and for what might yet be as he tells her that he wants to believe. Mason's performance here is outstanding, especially in the way that he responds to Garland's vulnerability. He shows us a man who is in genuine agony over his feelings.

At this point, it is useful to contrast the Garland/Mason rapport with parallel scenes between Gaynor/March in the earlier *A Star Is Born*. Though Fredric March was a splendid actor — his is arguably the best Willy Loman ever performed on stage or screen — in this film he appears wooden, not truly convincing either as a drunk or as a man deeply in love with the rising star. By the same token, Garland is far more credible than Gaynor as a woman in love with a has-been alcoholic. Gaynor is too perfect, too coy, too saccharine in her unswerving devotion to her man; contrarily, Garland is as insecure in her own way as her husband. Her love scenes with Mason ring true because both characters convey within their respective weaknesses the depth of their need to be wanted and loved. And each character appreciates the strengths of the other. Garland loves Mason for his gentleness, his good manners, and his good humor, all of which he amply demonstrates when he is sober. By the same token, Mason loves Garland for her altruism, for her practicality coupled with her fragile sense of self, and above all, for her ability to grab his emotions when she sings. One has only to look at Mason watching Garland interpret a song to see his wistful, caring expression and consequently to understand why he is in such awe of her.

And so they are married. But the setting for their marriage does not bode well for their future. Seeking to avoid publicity, they elope to a small California town and are married by a Justice of the Peace; as they exchange wedding vows, they stand just a few yards away from prison bars, while among their witnesses are curious, bemused inmates of the county jail. Nor is the atmosphere of their honeymoon site any more auspicious. They spend their wedding night in a rundown motel, though neither seems at all disconcerted by their seedy surroundings. Yet even in such a dreary, inappropriate atmosphere, Garland takes the spotlight when she sings the love song "A New World" to her new husband. As she kneels at his feet, she is brightly lit by white light that accentuates the bright red in her clothing, while the colorless Mason is photographed in the shadows in three quarter profile. Both the setting and director Cukor's control of mise-en-scène contribute to the claustrophobic foreshadowing of doom: an ominous premonition that is not present in the 1937 version directed by William Wellman. Whereas Wellman emphasizes the healing power of nature in the Norman Maine/Esther Blodgett honeymoon, Cukor focuses on the ironic contrast between Garland's hopeful singing of a new beginning with the reality of their squalid surroundings—an environment that the illusory world of Hollywood glamour can never fully eradicate.

Such reality hits Vicki Lester a short while after she marries Norman; though they have been married only a brief time, Norman has quickly tired of always coming in second to his wife. He has been fired from the studio because of his drinking and consequent undependability and has become increasingly restive at home, somewhat jealous of Vicki's success. All of these depressing circumstances come to a head one night at the Academy Awards ceremony where Vicki wins a Best Actress award. In a scene that in many ways parallels the one in the 1937 version where Vicki Lester wins a Best Actress award, Norman Maine drunkenly interrupts Garland's graciously modest acceptance speech. He is, of course, exceedingly tight as he stumbles forward to the stage. Unlike Fredric March, however, Mason can be seen by millions of people across the country via television. He is, therefore, a much greater embarrassment to Garland than March was to the whimpering Gaynor. So too, his speech is much longer than March's. We can see more clearly in this version the many self-indulgent reasons for Norman Maine's bitterness. It is a fine piece of acting, made even more so by the fact that Mason must share the stage with Garland's awe-inspiring presence.

He begins his tirade by approaching the stage: "Congratulations, my dear. I made it just in time, didn't I?" He follows this boorish opening remark by accosting the flustered Garland and kissing her. Next, because he finds it difficult to maintain an upright position, he sits on the risers directly in front of Garland and addresses various horrified audience members who he thinks have not treated him fairly: "I know most of you sit-

James Mason as a very drunk Norman Maine strikes Judy Garland as Vicki Lester, deliberately interrupting her Academy Award acceptance speech, in *A Star Is Born* (Warner Bros., 1954). Maine is belligerent, angry, defensive, and jealous as he proceeds to deliver his own speech about the unforgiving nature of the Hollywood elite (Photofest).

ting out there by your first names, don't I?" Then he becomes more belligerent as he pulls himself up and stumbles from one side of the stage to the other, drunkenly demanding of them: "I need a job now — that's it, that's the speech. I need a *job*." Then, as in the 1937 version, he gestures expansively with both arms outstretched and hits Garland. Once again, this Norman Maine shows remorse and dismay as he embraces her and allows her to help him off the stage. In the meantime, we know that his public humiliation is being shown live to a television audience across the country.

The denouement of the 1954 *A Star Is Born* follows much the same plot structure as the 1937 version. However, one can see a number of revealing differences between the two. First, in the scene in which Mason's Norman Maine leaves the sanitarium and visits the racetrack, most of the men are dressed in the iconic symbol of the 1950s: the colorless, featureless grey flannel suit. Sloan Wilson's popular novel, *The Man in the Grey Flannel Suit*, was not published until 1956, and many of the main characters in that work are alcoholics. Thus, there is something vaguely prophetic about the clothing worn in this particular shot of the racetrack bar. One notable exception to this greyness is Jack Carson, excellent as the taunting, twisted Libby, who is appropriately wearing black.

A second difference occurs when Garland and Charles Bickford's Oliver Niles retrieve Mason from his jail stint in night court; here we see that it is the Christmas season, perhaps a reminder of the home, hearth, and happiness: all of those things that have eluded Garland and Mason. Third, while Garland is telling Niles that she will give up her career in order to go away with Norman, the eavesdropping Mason is clearly more distraught than March had been, even weeping as he listens to Niles declare that Norman is not worth the sacrifice, that he is just a shell, that "twenty years of quiet and steady drinking do something to a man." Finally, there is the contrast between Janet Gaynor and Judy Garland. Where Gaynor is patient, steady, and long-suffering, Garland is either crying or on the verge of crying: her desperation so palpable that we feel she is in constant need of protecting and consoling.

Such consolation comes ironically from Mason in his final scene with her. After Niles leaves, having failed to persuade Garland not to relinquish her career, Mason emerges from the bedroom, dressed in a white robe. Once again, Cukor creates a symbolic mise-en-scène in his use of light and color to frame Mason as he first appears to Garland. He is seen against a background of glass doors that reflect in two directions: behind the doors is the ocean surf; in front of the glass is the white radiance from the fading day. This beam accentuates Mason's white robe by spreading a hazy fog around it. A supernatural, prescient atmosphere pervades this scene, with Mason, the angel, preparing to redeem himself from his wasted life. Mason's face in close-up reveals the agony behind his decision to forgo once and for all the allure of the White Logic. On the one hand, he shows his determination to give himself up to the surf; on the other, he demonstrates his resolve to appear cheerful in front of Garland, even as he is planning his finale. It is a subtle, understated piece of acting.

After telling her that he has decided to make a new beginning by promoting a sound body with a sound mind, he announces that he going for a swim. He asks her to sing for him as he leaves the house. So Garland reprises "A New World" while this Norman Maine again walks away into the sunset. His figure as he moves toward the beach is at first photographed as a reflection in the glass; we do not see him directly until he is actually at the water's edge. Throughout these last few scenes, the use of glass as a reflector of Norman Maine's image serves as a reminder of the illusory world that Norman has inhabited for most of his life, both on and off the screen. So too, the reflective power of glass to swallow the person who stands before it will be echoed in the power of the ocean to obliterate Norman Maine.

Mason's subtle performance as the alcoholic is one of the best of 1954, yet from the outset, he sensed that there would be many problems associated with the project. At first, he was unreceptive to the idea of even making the movie, largely because Garland's husband, Sid Luft, was scheduled to be the producer. Mason knew that Luft had no experience in overseeing such an ambitious venture. Nor was Mason pleased with the outcome, specifically with the way in which the film was finally edited. The original version ran three hours, a length that proved unpopular with audiences at the initial screenings. So twenty-seven minutes were cut: an editing decision that, Mason later claimed, resulted in the deletion of some of his best dramatic scenes. He also resented the long musical numbers, which he thought were a liability. As he told an interviewer: "I think Wellman's *A Star Is Born* is a much better picture because it tells the story more simply and correctly, because really the emphasis should be on the man rather than the girl. It's more his story and to tell it correctly the balance should be in his favor, and that's the way it was in the original film."[11] In short, James Mason was much less enthusiastic about Judy Garland's musical talents and much less self-sacrificing than his movie counterpart was.

A Final Comparison

My favorite among the three movies just discussed is *What Price Hollywood?* And my favorite among the three Hollywood has-beens is Lowell Sherman. Though all three actors did outstanding work in films, I think that Sherman is the most fun to watch among the leading men in this trio of pictures. His Max Carey is witty without being overblown; sympathetic without being cloying; sad without being maudlin. With both the Fredric March and James Mason interpretations of Norman Maine, we are relieved when the desperate character takes that final swim: not so with Lowell Sherman. Because Sherman has created a character with few traces of self-pity, he makes us truly sorry when he decides to kill himself; we want to stop him, to give him another chance. But Sherman makes us realize that Max Carey is far too savvy, much too self-aware to believe in second acts. Carey knows that his chances have run out, and so we are content with his decision to die.

8

The Alcoholic Reporter

You pay and you pay and you pay. You never stop paying for the
bottle.

— James Cagney, *Come Fill the Cup* (1951)

Beyond Stereotype

The stereotype of the alcoholic reporter is one of the most commonly
found in motion pictures. Yet the newspaper film genre contains some fine
pictures that transcend any and all stereotyping. Among these are *The Front
Page* (1931), *Five Star Final* (1931), *Platinum Blonde* (1931), *Okay, America!*
(1932), *Blessed Event* (1932), *Hi, Nellie!* (1934), *Libeled Lady* (1936), *His Girl
Friday* (1940), and *Come Fill the Cup* (1951).

In the talking era, one of the earliest of these drunken reporter films
is *Big News* (1929). In it, the gruff, no-nonsense, handsome character actor
Robert Armstrong plays a dissolute reporter named Steve Banks, whose
excessive drinking irritates both his editor Addison (Charles Sellon) as well
as his wife (Carole Lombard), a Jazz Age flapper who just happens to be a
reporter for a competing newspaper. By the final reel, however, Banks turns
out to be nothing more than a non-serious, casual drunk, so he eventually
becomes a teetotaler and redeems himself by exposing a drug-peddling ring
and solving a murder.

But before such transformation can occur, Banks must first be
reformed. His self-indulgent character is established at the outset when one
of his newsroom colleagues Hansel (Louis Payne) finds him in the editor's
office early one morning, sleeping off a hard night's work in a speakeasy.

He is uncomfortably dozing under a pile of newspapers and groans when his colleague disturbs him: "What a way to start a day," he grumbles. Still woozy, he complains, "If you don't have some blankets and a pillow put in this office, I'm going to quit working here." Retorts his disgusted colleague: "Same thing after every payday. Drunk and disorderly." Equally disgusted is his wife, who wants a divorce. She confesses to him her admiration for his talent, but offers this caveat: "You'd be the best newspaperman in this town, if only you'd quit drinking." Lombard's Mrs. Banks is obviously not a flapper in the mold of Anita Page or Joan Crawford. She would never be caught recklessly indulging in spirits or sharing the secrets of the pillow with anyone but her husband. Even his editor Addison decides that Banks can no longer be trusted to do his job, so he fires Banks after hearing complaints about Banks's behavior the previous evening: "Set out on an assignment. And what happens? Drunk and disorderly in a cheap speakeasy."

Since he is now without any occupational duties to distract him, Banks returns to the notorious speakeasy, run by a disreputable, officious man named Reno, played by the droll, cynical, Sam Hardy. The purpose of this visit is to confirm Banks's suspicion that Reno is not only bootlegging but also peddling drugs. In due course, Banks, still the muckraking reporter at heart, proves that Reno is both a drug pusher and the murderer of Addison, who had been getting too close to getting the goods on Reno. All ends happily for Banks and his wife, as they reconcile, Banks's promising that he will stick to tea drinking from this time forward.

Howard Good has suggested that *Big News* projects ambivalence about those who drink alcohol to excess. On the one hand, Robert Armstrong's Banks is a lush; on the other, he is a charming fellow: "His fondness for the bottle may be a flaw, but it is a glamorous flaw, a mark of his freedom from the gray and narrow confines of the Protestant work ethic."[1] By the same token, the script suggests that, although alcohol is addictive, Banks could stop his overindulgence whenever he chooses.[2] And so Banks chooses to be a good guy after all; by the final scene, he opts for the comforts of tea and the return to hearth and home as symbolized by his ever-patient wife.

Unlike the largely unknown *Big News, The Front Page* (1931) is one of the best-remembered films of the newspaper genre, in part because it has been successfully remade at least five times. It is a cynical picture, with a witty script and a fast pace; in addition, alcohol as metaphor is used to good effect in one of the opening scenes. A jailer has just emerged from the death house, where he has been supervising some tests on the strength of rope being prepared for use in an upcoming hanging. As he walks down the street, his attention is diverted by a liquor bottle, which has just been tossed from an upper story window, shattering at his feet. The culprit with the throwing arm is a reporter who is known to the jailer. Showing a distinct lack of remorse for the vandalism and holding a small, liquor-filled cup, the newspaperman shouts down at his target: "Quit playing with those gallows. How do you expect us to do any work?" Then, demonstrating a fairly good aim and a lack of good manners, he leans out the window and spits booze upon the face of the jailer. Here, the reporter's cavalier, boorish behavior with the liquor becomes the representation of a major motif of the film: throughout the movie, a reporter is seen as an opportunistic life form with no conscience whatsoever.

One such life form is editor Walter Burns (Adolph Menjou), who is upset that his ace reporter Hildy Johnson (Pat O'Brien) has quit the paper in order to get married. The character of Walter Burns was said to have been based on a Chicago city editor named Walter Howie, whom screenwriter Ben Hecht had known in his newspaper days. It was well known that Howie had a glass eye; Hecht was often heard to say that one could easily identify which was the glass eye — it was the warmer one.[3] Nor is Menjou's Walter Burns a particularly warm character; rather he is sly, conniving, and rational. Thinking that he can entice Hildy back through some well-chosen words and some efficiently poured drinks, Burns lures Hildy into a speakeasy. Initially, Hildy refuses the offer of a drink, but in the following conversation, Burns pours shot after shot of liquor, which Hildy appears to be downing quite unconsciously.

BURNS: So you're leaving me for marriage? Why?

HILDY (*angrily*): None of your business.

BURNS: How'd it happen?

HILDY: There was a moon.

Yet Burns's efforts to soften Hildy do not pay off. Even as he is protesting how hurt he is by Hildy's ungrateful behavior and as he is offering to throw Hildy a farewell party, Hildy manages to slide away from the bar, escape out a window, and get away from further alcoholic lures that Burns is prepared to offer. Nor is it only the reporters who drink. Toward the end of the film, a falsely condemned killer named Earl Williams (George E. Stone) is saved with the governor's reprieve, which is delivered by a very drunk Irving Pincus (Slim Summerville). Pincus haltingly reports that he has been bribed by both the sheriff, Peter B. "Pinky" Hartman (the oily Clarence Wilson) and Fred, the mayor, (James Gordon) not to deliver the reprieve. Both of these politicians are as cynical as the reporters with whom they are frequently in competition, and both would have preferred to have Williams hanged rather than risk losing votes in the next election. Once Hildy Johnson has seen this particular cliff-hanging story through to its conclusion with the freeing of Earl Williams, he vows that he will at long last marry his fiancée Peggy Grant (Mary Brian); moreover, he promises her that he will cut out "drinking and swearing and everything connected with the newspaper business." Yet Walter Burns has other plans; as a wedding present, he graciously gives Hildy a watch that Burns says was given to him and has much sentimental value. Then, after Hildy leaves to catch a train, Burns arranges to have Hildy arrested on one of the train stops. The charge? Stealing Burns's watch. The ending is far more cynical than that of *Big News*. Unlike Steve Banks, who has presumably sworn off the booze forever, Hildy Johnson will be returned to Walter Burns and will subsequently give up neither reporting nor drinking.

Beware the Platinum Blonde

One of the great joys of Frank Capra's 1931 film *Platinum Blonde* is watching the talented, charismatic Robert Williams as reporter Stew Smith. Despite the presence of the very photogenic and obviously braless Jean Harlow as his love interest, it is Williams who is the focus of every scene in which he appears. He is gently humorous in an ironic way, yet he is also sexually attractive. When he glances at a woman, he calmly eyes her carefully up and down, much as his contemporary James Cagney did. In fact, Williams strikes the viewer as a combination of Lee Tracy minus the on-the-edge hysteria and James Cagney minus the pugnacious, frenetic ebullience. Unfortunately, Williams's promising cinematic career ended shortly after the release of *Platinum Blonde*: he was thirty-four when he died in November 1931 from peritonitis as a result of a burst appendix. In *Platinum Blonde*, Williams demonstrates an immense talent sadly aborted.

Though Williams's Stew Smith drinks a good deal of bootleg liquor in the course of the narrative, he never really appears drunk; he always seems to have his active wits about him. However, from our initial glimpse of him, we are reminded that drinking is very much a part of his life. When we first see him in the newspaper office, he is hiding behind a screen with fellow reporter Gallagher (Loretta Young). They are intent on playing with one of those handheld toys, the purpose of which is to roll a number of silver balls into the corresponding number of holes. Stew is having such a hard time coordinating his eye and hand movements that Gallagher comments, "Your hands are shaking. You've been drinking again." Somewhat later, Smith introduces himself to heiress Anne Schuyler (Jean Harlow) by boasting, "Name is Stewart Smith. My friends all call me Stew, which is an injustice too because I hold my liquor all right."

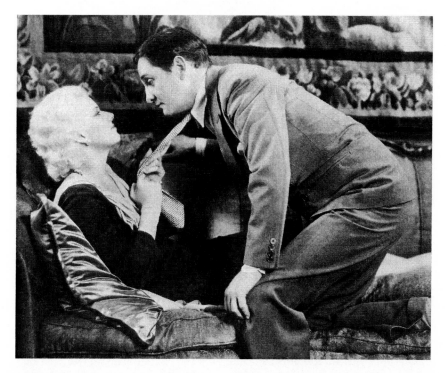

Jean Harlow is heiress Anne Schuyler in *Platinum Blonde* (Columbia, 1931). With her is the intense, compelling Robert Williams, who plays Stew Smith, the ace reporter. Whether he is going after a story or pursuing the wealthy, spoiled Schuyler, the hard-drinking Smith always seems a little off balance, often on the verge of dozing off. Here, his equilibrium is compromised not only by alcohol but also by the seductive Schuyler, whom he makes the mistake of marrying.

And the place where all the reporters in *Platinum Blonde* feel the most comfortable holding their liquor is a popular, raucous, but friendly speakeasy called Joe's. It is at Joe's that his reporter buddies offer to help Stew celebrate after he has married Anne Schuyler, an event that soon proves to have been an error. Yet when Stew first meets Jean Harlow's Anne, he deliberately ignores her more obvious limitations; she is wealthy, sexy, available, and controlling. Their pre-nuptial love scenes make it clear that sex is the only reason for their mutual attraction. However, after Stew marries her, he discovers that sex is a poor substitute for mutual consideration. Anne becomes even more controlling. Her behavior soon wears so thin that Stew tells Gallagher he will not live off his wife's millions, that he will not become a "speakeasy rat." Yet his marriage prompts him to drink even more heavily. Late one morning, he awakens in a luxurious bed, dressed in fancy silk pajamas. Hovering over him is a valet named Dawson (Claud Allister), eager to begin his job as personal attendant to the rich newlywed. Stew, however, is not impressed, though he is curious enough about this strange man's presence to ask, "Was I very drunk last night? I must have been plastered if I hired a valet." Informed by Dawson that Mrs. Smith had done the hiring, Stew begins to recognize that even alcohol cannot obliterate the mistake that Anne represents.

The final breakup of the Schuylers is precipitated by an impromptu drunken party held by Stew at the Schuyler mansion while his wife, his mother-in-law (Louise Closser Hale) and a family friend Dexter (Reginald Owen) are away for the evening. The comic tone of the party is established as one after another of Stew's newspaper colleagues come through the door: "kinda thirsty," as one reporter describes the mood. Following the arrival of about thirty guests pushing their way through the entrance, another friend reassures Stew, "The rest of the gang had to get out the morning edition, but they'll be down later." The festivities are so engaging that even Smythe the butler (Halliwell Hobbes) gets pleasantly plastered on the Schuylers's liquor. And what a silly bunch the drunken reporters become. By the time the indignantly surprised Schuylers return, the party has reached the limits of foolishness. Someone is playing a discordant tune on the piano, many of the guests are giving an off-key accompaniment to the piano, one man is sprawled on the floor, a few are happily skipping along like elementary school children, and one giddy individual is sliding down the banister.

Meanwhile, Stew is not at his own party but is in one of the many upstairs rooms with his old pal Gallagher, a woman whom he has heretofore inexplicably refused to acknowledge as being of the opposite sex; they are working on a play that Stew has been trying for many months to write. Anne naturally finds them together; she and Stew have the inevitable showdown as she reminds him that he and his inebriated friends are in *her* house. The reminder is too much for him; consequently, he finally asserts his independence. Refusing to be her gigolo any longer, he moves out that evening, divorces her, and finally declares his love for Gallagher, who has been waiting for a long time for Stew to recognize that she is indeed a female. We may safely assume that, had it not been for the reporters' penchant for alcoholic revelry in the sumptuous rooms of the Schuyler home, Stew and Gallagher (she who has no first name) would have failed to get together in such a timely fashion.

Platinum Blonde has some fine supporting performances, chiefly from Louise Closser Hale who, as Jean Harlow's stuffy mother, looks as though she has a clothespin attached to her nose. So too, veteran character actor Halliwell Hobbes as Smythe, the butler, dutifully endures the daily drivel of the simpering Schuylers. Hobbes continues his servile duties until he realizes that he is a prisoner in a gilt-edged box and cuts his way out by getting potted along with the rest of Stew's reporter pals. On the other hand, Loretta Young looks too attractive, too fragile, too genteel to be a tough-talking big city reporter. Her soft, delicate appearance belies the ho-hum attitude that Stew assumes toward her — at least until the fade-out when his eyesight clears and he at last sees a woman.

However, no one would ever deny the feminine attractions of Jean Harlow. She is fairly effective here as the femme fatale who pulls Stew up from his stable, working class roots, only to leave him suspended with no clear values to grasp. Moreover, Harlow gives a more natural, much less stilted performance here than she does in another 1931 movie, *The Public Enemy*. In this famous gangster picture, she is embarrassingly stiff and awkward as one of Jimmy Cagney's flings. Yet under the direction of Frank Capra, in *Platinum Blonde* she begins to demonstrate a talent for comedy. She refined her comic ability in later pictures such as *Dinner at Eight* (1933), and *Libeled Lady* (1936). Like Robert Williams, Harlow would die young, at twenty-six, and never get the opportunity to realize her full acting potential. But it is Robert Williams who carries the picture. Subtle, witty, crafty, romantic, caring, and intelligent, he gives a superb performance, one of the best of the decade.

The Drunken Ex-Reporter

In Woody Allen's 1985 film *The Purple Rose of Cairo*, which is set in the early 1930s, Mia Farrow plays Cecilia, a star struck girl who spends most of her spare time going to the movies. In one of the opening scenes, she discusses with her sister (played by Mia's real-life sister Stephanie Farrow) a movie that she has seen the previous night. She rhapsodizes over the picture, *Okay America!*, specifically sighing over the extremely handsome Lew Ayres. Her dreamy-eyed commentary is really an inside joke, one which most moviegoers of 1985 would have missed. The joke involves Mia Farrow's allusion to *Okay America!*, a 1932 movie that happens to feature Farrow's mother, Maureen O'Sullivan. In fact, O'Sullivan has a large role in the film, costarring with Lew Ayres as his secretary, Sheila Barton. The adoring Sheila assiduously pursues scandal sheet reporter Larry "Ego" Wayne (Ayres) throughout the picture. That *Okay America!* is hardly a title on anyone's list of the one thousand greatest movies of all time does not diminish its importance as an entertaining newspaper picture. Moreover, in its portrayal of down-and-out ex-reporter Joe Morton (Rollo Lloyd), it depicts the dire consequences of alcoholism. Throughout the movie, the desperate Morton feeds Larry Wayne allegedly hot tips that Morton makes up. Wayne, however, is not fooled, although for this bogus information, Wayne gives Morton the charitable sum of two dollars per day. Thus both men perpetuate the lie that Morton is still a useful, productive seeker of news.

Larry Wayne's generosity is born out of a curious combination of altruism and cynicism. As a scandal sheet reporter, he destroys lives and damages reputations. An opening shot of the movie shows a man committing suicide over an item Wayne has written for the newspaper. People who don't want to become victims of his vitriolic newspaper columns duck under tables when he enters his favorite speakeasy. Especially sensitive to being seen are cheating husbands and wives. Yet Wayne also knows that a reporter's life is hard and often dangerous. When Maureen O'Sullivan as Sheila Barton asks Wayne why he continues to support a wino like Joe Morton, Wayne replies: "Oh, he used to be a great reporter. Poor guy; he's cracked, thinks he's working for me." Wayne concludes that the money Morton receives protects Morton's pride and keeps him alive. But often the two dollars is not enough.

At one point, there is a fairly humorous dialogue between Wayne and Morton; their conversation takes place on the street where Morton accosts Wayne and, soused as usual, haltingly begs for an advance on his next day's "salary." Feeling that he must give an explanation for his dearth of immediate cash, Morton offers a number of plausible reasons. First, he says, he gave one dollar to his "poor old mother" because, as he offers with irrefutable logic, "your mother is your mother." Next, continues Morton, he split one dollar between four down-and-out buddies. Finally, forgetting his elementary math, he adds, "And then I gave another dollar to the Salvation Army," for their great service to the nation during the Great War. To this curious, creative bit of addition, Wayne responds incredulously, "You mean you did all this with the two dollars I gave you this afternoon?" Yet even as Wayne asks this, he gives Morton another couple of dollars. Here poor Morton is so grateful at Wayne's generosity that he lets go of some blubbery sobs, claiming that he is nothing more than a bum who has been "costing you for a long time." Furthermore, he even admits that his "tips" have consisted of his scribbling on scraps of paper whatever has popped into his head in order to get the dough. Then he adds an astonishing piece of information — news that will serve to propel the narrative forward: "But I sort of squared things with the story I gave you today, didn't I?"

Since Wayne always tears up Morton's daily scribbled scraps shortly after Morton has staggered away, he naturally knows nothing of the scoop Morton has earlier handed him. Morton, however, fills him in when he suggests that the news involved the name of the kidnapper of a famous heiress, a woman who has been anxiously sought by many interested parties for the past several days. When Wayne learns from Morton that the guilty man is Mileaway Russell (the smooth Louis Calhern), a wealthy bootlegger and gang boss, he finds himself in a position that is filled with both possibility and danger. And ironically, it is the totally besotted ex-reporter who has put Wayne in such a position. When Wayne confronts Mileaway, the bootlegger admits that he had snatched the girl Ruth Drake (Margaret Lindsay) because, while cruising on her boat, she had spotted Mileaway in his own boat — running liquor. In the spirit of fun, she had posed as a government agent and forced Mileaway to dump $100,000 worth of uncut stuff — all honest-to-God good liquor — into the water. When he discovered that a mere girl had duped him, he grabbed her and is holding her in order to get from her rich old man "every cent I lost."

Now Wayne has a definite scoop for his paper: as yet, no one else knows the identity of Ruth Drake's kidnapper. But he is also in a precarious situation, which is exacerbated by the duplicitous nature of Mileaway and his thugs. Offering to act as a go-between and to deliver the ransom in exchange for Ruth, Wayne is double-crossed when Ruth is not delivered. But the intrepid Wayne gets another chance to cut a deal. This opportunity comes from Mileaway's boss Duke Morgan (Edward Arnold), an unscrupulous character with a large number of government indictments pending against him. He is not pleased to have so much baggage, so he has arbitrarily decided that he would like to do a maximum of two years in federal prison. In order to get such a reduced sentence, however, Morgan needs to negotiate with none other than the President of the United States. The exchange is simple: Ruth Drake's life for a little less jail time. Furthermore, in a nice coincidental plot twist, Ruth Drake's father is a friend of the President's. So once again, Larry Wayne is set up to deliver the goods. This time he is accompanied by Mr. and Mrs. Drake; all three visit the Chief Executive at the White House and present Morgan's generous offer of an exchange: one daughter for one crook. But the morally upright Mr. Herbert Hoover will have none of that. No deal.

But, since Larry Wayne is played by clean-cut Lew Ayres, Larry turns out to be a brave, noble, good guy after all. He returns to Duke Morgan with a lie, telling this villain that the President is willing to make a deal because Duke is such a powerful figure. Though such a falsehood stretches credulity, the worldly Duke is nonetheless only too happy to believe Wayne and releases the girl. Once Wayne knows that the girl is safe, he tells Duke the truth and summarily executes him with several bullets to the stomach. With Duke out of the way, Wayne makes a fatalistic final appearance on his radio program, where, as he begins his nightly broadcast of gossip, he is melodramatically shot on the air by a member of Duke's mob. So Maureen O'Sullivan will not get her man; and ex-reporter Morton, the drunk who provided the fatally important tip, will no longer get handouts from Larry Wayne.

   Okay, America! is an unique film for the time in that its protagonist/ hero dies in the end. Though Larry Wayne is presented at the outset as one who will do anything to get and publish the dirt on the private lives of anyone with a recognizable name, he reveals his more compassionate side in his generosity to the alcoholic Morton. Perhaps because he realizes the sadness of the lonely, alienated lives led by most reporters, he can become one with Morton's self-annihilating suffering and, in Morton, see himself some fifteen or twenty years hence. But Wayne does not have fifteen or twenty years remaining; the film's narrative contains some unusual plot twists not ordinarily found in the newspaper genre, specifically in the brutal, naturalistic conclusion to this picture. And twenty-two-year-old Lew Ayres carries the picture quite well: his intense, brash impetuousness coupled with his fresh, idealistic naïveté work effectively to maintain the overall bittersweet tone of the movie.

   Contemporary reviewers took note of the movie's strengths. In a brief overview of Ayres's career to that point, one writer offered the following opinion:

> The nation hummed with excited interest when Lew Ayres appeared in his unforgettable characterization of Paul Baumer in *All Quiet on the Western Front* but he had established a standard of achievement that would be difficult for any man to live up to. His succeeding roles naturally suffered through comparison but in *Okay, America!* as the wise-cracking columnist of the Winchell type, Lew again came into his own. Given equal opportunity, he will indisputably register again.[4]

The Curious Case of Johnny Sykes

   One illustration of the alcoholic reporter that is hard to interpret occurs in *Viva Villa!* (1934) in which Stuart Erwin plays newspaper reporter Johnny Sykes, who has been assigned to cover the nefarious activities of the bandit Pancho Villa (Wallace Beery). At one point, Erwin is so drunk that he writes an incredibly erroneous story about Villa winning a battle and capturing a city. However, we never actually see him fabricating the story while in this drunken condition. We do witness Villa as he asks the obviously inebriated reporter where he got his information. Erwin confesses that the scoop came from "a bartender."

Yet the tone of this scene is hard to grasp, an ambivalence symptomatic of a failing of the entire movie. In fact, Erwin's reporter, Johnny Sykes, drunkenly persuades Villa to attack this town anyway, lest he suffer public humiliation for writing a false story, one that has made the front page of the newspaper, no less. Trying to save his reputation, which he has already pumped to about four times its actual size, Erwin adopts a tone that is both pleading and placating as he tells Villa: "I'd do the same for you." Beery's Villa, who is fifty percent preschool childish and fifty percent cutthroat murderous, obliges Erwin, and the result is an enormous loss of life. The scene between Stuart Erwin as Sykes and Wallace Beery as Pancho Villa where Sykes persuades Villa to legitimize a false story is emotionally difficult to read, largely because the screenplay asks the two actors to play their parts for laughs, even though the result of their shenanigans is overwhelmingly destructive. The darkly comic tone of the movie is hard to reconcile with the underlying horror of what Villa is perpetrating on his enemies.

Perhaps one reason for the erratic narrative lies in the fact that Stuart Erwin was not the original choice for the drunken reporter Johnny Sykes. Much of the script had to be altered to fit Erwin's acting style when he replaced Lee Tracy, a highly excitable actor who had been removed from the picture by M-G-M chief Louis Mayer. (For the details of Tracy's misadventure, see Note 9, Chapter Six.) Whatever the reason for the inability of the script to sustain a coherent tone, the result is an ultimately disappointing movie.

James Cagney: The Price of Alcohol

James Cagney's father was an alcoholic. For awhile in the early 1900s, the elder Cagney, James Francis Cagney Sr., worked in a saloon on New York's Lower East Side. Later, for one year, he actually owned a saloon in the Yorkville area between 80th and 81st streets on First Avenue.[5] However, his venture into tavern ownership was relatively brief because he was an improvident, inept businessman who drank away most of his profits. Yet he was also an easy-going, genial man; according to some accounts, he had more friends than a Tammany district leader. His four sons would later recall that, whenever he sent the boys off on errands, he would call out to them a reminder: "Tell 'im Jimmy Cagney sent you." In addition, he disliked arguments; he would do anything to avoid confrontational problems. He found it much easier to give someone a dollar than to make excuses as to why he couldn't hand it over.[6]

But the drinking had inevitably dire consequences. By the time his son was a small boy, around 1905, Cagney Sr. had already destroyed much of his brain. Some of the actor's earliest, most terrifying memories involved watching his father at the dining table as the elder Cagney let out agonizing moans and shrieks, the result of brain-piercing headaches brought on by his alcohol addiction. To the relief of his children seated around the table, the ever-understanding and patient Mrs. Cagney usually came to her husband's rescue by vigorously massaging his forehead and neck. All of the Cagney children would come to refer to their father's frightening outbursts as "Dad's fits."[7]

When Cagney Sr.'s "fits" started to come with frighteningly increasing frequency, Mrs. Cagney knew that she had to take drastic action, so she obtained a court order of involuntary commitment. This order sentenced her husband to sixty days in the prison on Blackwell's Island. Young Jimmy Cagney was given the dreadful task of personally delivering the order to his father, who had temporarily moved into a room near the family's apartment. The elder Cagney hoped that such a move, with time to himself, would effect a sort of "cure." It did not, nor did the stay on Blackwell's Island. In his autobiography, Cagney describes his father as a charming ne'er-do-well who always thought that he was doing the best for his family, even though his habits of drinking and playing the horses forced the Cagneys to live precariously.

In spite of Cagney Sr.'s inability to stay sober for more than one or two weeks at a time, and in spite of the hardships that this mind-numbing addiction forced upon the family, Jimmy Cagney loved his father — a man who was, from all accounts, a genial individual whose own inner, conscience-driven demons constantly tormented him. In a 1937 interview, Cagney recalled his father's charm: a man with a "heart of gold that passed out many a free beer to those who were down on their luck."[8] Although fan magazine interviews are often suspect, not necessarily noted for being factual, the following account given by Cagney in 1937 is probably accurate, as it is in keeping with many of his later reminiscences about his father:

> Father was a star in his own right.... His world was his public, too. His homecomings were always events to us kids. I can remember him, swaggering in, hat a little cocked over one eye, especially if he had a beer or so in him, fending us off as we hurled ourselves against him, saying gruffly, "If I thought you meant it, I'd let you have it," giving us a light upper cut to the chin with one flat, then swallowing us up in bear hugs and kisses as tender as our mother's.[9]

Some thirty-nine years later, Jimmy Cagney would still write affectionately of his father: "He was irrepressible. He sailed happily through life, charming everyone, and all the time belting down the sauce that I suppose helped to sustain both his charm and his improvidence. When the flu epidemic of

1918 came along, the inroads of all that booze made him an easy victim. Dead in two, swift terrible days. My mother loved him deeply, and his going was an agony for her."[10] Likewise, in a 1956 interview with Pete Martin, Cagney gives the following account of his father:

> By the end of a day he'd downed quite a lot of booze. But he was kind; he had a host of friends and he was good-natured — too good-natured. As soon as he got his mitts on anything, he spent it. If anybody bought him a drink, he'd buy two back. He was called Two-for-One Bar-tender, and there's no future in that.
>
> Because my father ran a saloon, my whole family had a fix against booze. Booze was the heavy in our house — the evil that lived with us. To this day, my brothers Harry and Eddie, and my sister, Jeanne, have never taken a drink, and I disliked saloons so much that I was never in a night club until I was twenty-nine. In 1947 I did the first national broadcast ever put on by Alcoholics Anonymous.
>
> Near the end of his life, alcohol made pop so sick they'd wheel an ambulance up to the door and take him away to a hospital. It was rough to see that, if you loved him as we did.[11]

It is evident, then, that throughout Cagney Sr.'s brief, anxiety-filled life, the suffering was not any less for the entire Cagney family, especially for his desperate wife, who continued to love her increasingly debilitated husband. At one point later in her life, when referring to her decision to have her husband committed, she pleaded with her famous son, "But will someone please tell me in God's good name what else I could have done?"[12]

The answer was, of course, nothing, for James Cagney Sr. remained close to the bottle until is death in 1918. He was forty-three when he died, leaving a pregnant wife and four children. And his son and namesake never forgot the torments, the efforts to quit, the toll on the family. Nor did he ever forget the awful hurt he had suffered when, as a young boy, he had wept as he took his father that commitment order to Blackwell's Island.

Moreover, the father's influence was far-reaching: there is a good deal of the character of Cagney Sr. in most of Jimmy Cagney's portrayals. For instance, we can see the elder Cagney's frequent "fits" in the searing headaches of the psychopathic Cody Jarrett in *White Heat* (1949). And in *Come Fill the Cup* (1951) Cagney, in his portrayal of Lew Marsh, the world weary, savvy newspaper reporter cum reformed alcoholic, draws heavily on memories of his father's futile battles with alcohol. Although the movie is fairly faithful to the Harlan Ware novel on which it is based, the filmmakers capitalize on Cagney's energy, wit, intelligence, and wryly sardonic humor. As a result, the character of Lew Marsh in the movie is far more dynamic than he appears in the novel. Likewise, since the movie eliminates most of the novel's subplots, many of which do not center around Marsh's character, Cagney dominates almost every scene. Even in the episodes in which he appears with thirty-eight-year-old Gig Young as the apparently happy drunk whom Lew Marsh has been ordered to reform, Cagney is the one that we watch. In fact, Cagney's own observation about what it takes to communicate effectively to an audience is a fine illustration of his own special gift, one that is especially evident in this film: "A good actor is one who makes the longest scenes seem like the shortest."[13] Thus, even though Young has a showier role, one for which he received a Best Supporting Actor Academy Award nomination, our attention still centers around Cagney.

And this focus on Cagney remains throughout the film in spite of the fact that, during the filming, Cagney himself provided much-needed emotional support to a nervous, intimidated Young. Young had idolized Cagney from the time that he had had a minor part in Cagney's *Captains of the Clouds* (1941) and had carefully watched and admired Cagney's approach to the acting craft.[14] As a result, Young was particularly anxious about performing well with the actor for whom he had so much respect. Young's anxiety only increased when, early in the shooting schedule, he heard rumors that executives at the Warner Brothers front office were dissatisfied with the daily screenings and that they wanted Young off the picture. But Cagney also heard the rumors and told producer Henry Blanke that if Young were removed from the picture, the studio would need to replace two actors: Young and Cagney himself. Not wanting to lose their star, the studio heads decided to keep Young, but his confidence had nonetheless been shaken, and the veteran actor had to remind his costar that, when the two of them had a scene together and Young was set to be the central focus, he had better try to grab the frame or Cagney would wipe him away. Bolstered by this challenge, Young managed to at least hold his own against Cagney's dominating presence.[15]

What is more, it is a presence that is felt from the beginning. The opening shot of *Come Fill the Cup* sets the tone for the movie's moral center. The camera focuses on a blinking sign proclaiming the enticing allure of 7 Dwarfs Bourbon, with the seven little elves lined in ascending order like innocuous lightning bugs, all of them moving upward, doubtless seeking a drink of their favorite beverage. The fairy tale allusion is appropriate, for one of the film's central motifs is the ineffable fact of liquor's hold on those for whom there is no reality except that which can be seen through a bottle. And Cagney's portrayal of Lew Marsh is hard-edged and unrelenting in its demonstration of those demons lurking at the bottom of the bottle. We initially witness these demons at the beginning of *Come Fill the Cup* when we first see Lew Marsh, the lush: the chronic drinker before he resolves to quit drinking.

Here again there is a difference between novel and film. From the outset of the Harlan Ware narrative, Lew Marsh is sober — already a reformed, productive citizen. Nor do we ever see him succumb again to alcohol. Various characters tell tales of his past and his attendant irresponsible, boorish behavior; in fact, he recalls a few of these stories himself, but author Ware, who was a personal friend of Cagney's, never allows Lew Marsh to drink in the present time of the novel's narrative. On the other hand, in the movie version, the earliest glimpse we have of Cagney's Lew Marsh as he enters the newsroom following a five-day debauch reveals a man barely able to hold himself together. Indeed, though Cagney vainly tries to assume the jaunty strut that we always associate with his onscreen persona, the actor still makes it clear that the halting stride which he gives to Lew Marsh is all bravado, born out of a desperate attempt to try for normality.

After making his accustomed, joking pass at the switchboard operator, he carefully points himself in the direction of his desk and, unaware that it has already been cleaned out, begins typing the lead to a story. When his boss Julian Cuscaden (Larry Keating) reminds him that the story is already five days old, he is confused — but not really surprised. Nor is he surprised when Cuscaden informs him that he no longer has a job. Resigned to his unemployed status, Lew Marsh makes his unsteady way out of the newsroom and heads for his favorite nesting place — the bar across the street.

It is in these early scenes that Cagney demonstrates his inimitable ability to get inside his characters and expose their pain: a lifelong talent that would forever set him apart from lesser screen actors. Here he probes the soul of a man tortured by the creeping White Logic of alcohol addiction. He turns away his girlfriend and coworker Paula (Phyllis Thaxter), who has come into the bar to offer unasked for and unwanted sympathy. He reluctantly rebuffs her by admitting that he would cut his right arm off for her but that he cannot stop drinking. As he tells her this, Cagney — age fifty-two at the time of filming — looks and acts more like Paula's uncle than like an old flame. His Lew Marsh appears about twenty years older than he is portrayed in the novel; Cagney makes his alcoholic more like an older mentor than like the novel's young man, a character who is still struggling against addiction and still interested in finding a wife.

Despite this age discrepancy between the two stars, Cagney makes his character convincing; moreover, it is particularly in these early scenes where we see Cagney's subtle ability to convey the various stages of an alcoholic's deterioration. When he first enters the bar following his ejection from the newsroom, Cagney's Lew Marsh is hung over but tentatively sober. Yet in a subsequent scene occurring the following day, Marsh is unkempt, unshaven, shaking for want of another drink as he desperately waits for the bar to open for the day. Even his voice has changed; when he begs the bartender for a second drink, even though he has just spent his last quarter on the first one, the vocal timbre is much different from the calm, well-modulated sounds he had used in his farewell to Paula. The voice is pitched lower, coming from deep in the throat, the pronunciation less sure. His efforts to control his cravings echo those portrayed by Ray Milland in *The Lost Weekend* (1945), but Cagney's character is more practical, less smooth and polished than Milland's. Lew Marsh has a harder, earthier edge than Don Birnam. But like Birnam, Lew Marsh sinks to the bottom of the bottle and winds up screaming in an alcoholic ward.

When he is released, he is befriended by recovering alcoholic Charley Dolan (James Gleason), from whom he had borrowed a quarter a few days earlier when his cravings had reached their nadir. It is significant to note that in the Harlen Ware novel, Charley is not only a recovering alcoholic but also a black man. In fact, Ware's inclusion of Charley Donahue, a "Negro," avoids the stereotypical picture of the Uncle Tom. In addition, the fictional Charley always speaks clear, standard English. Though he has had a tough life on the streets and has done jail time, he nonetheless becomes a true helpmate to Lew. Ware's only concession to racial distinction lies in the fact that Charley is less educated than Lew, and that he acts as Lew's combination cook/butler — a "gentleman's gentleman"[16] — the phrase Lew had earlier suggested when he first mentioned that they might live together. As Ware describes Charley: "He was a light-skinned colored man, with a pencil scar from a knife-cut on his right cheek, remnant of a bloody argument with a lifer in the exercise yard at Joliet. Tonight he also wore his serving jacket, Lew's old linen evening coat. Proud of himself. Felt good."[17]

Despite the novel's fairly liberal depiction of the light-skinned Charley, the black man must perforce lighten up for the movie version. One Cagney biographer has explained that the original screenplay, by Ivan Goff and Ben Roberts, did specify that the role of Charley should be played by a black man. But, as Goff later told the story, Jack Warner objected to Charley's color, protesting, "You think Cagney's gonna be under the same roof as a nigger?"[18] Thus, the cinematic change from black to white was necessitated by the racial strictures of the early 1950s, as interpreted by studio boss Warner. As in the novel, Charley and Lew move in together, with Charley subsequently becoming a kindly father figure to the younger man, but this time Charley is the white actor James Gleason. Warner was probably incorrect in his boorish and insensitive remark; the majority of 1951 audiences might very well have accepted the racial equality implied in the original story: two alcoholics of different races living together for mutual help and support. However, in the transformation from novel to motion picture, Warner prevailed, and Charley becomes white.

James Cagney (left) is newspaperman Lew Marsh and James Gleason is Charley
Dolan; they are recovering alcoholics as well as roommates in *Come Fill the Cup*
(Warner Bros., 1951). Here, Dolan offers Marsh emotional support after Marsh
learns that his girl has married someone else. Both Marsh and Dolan know that,
at any time and under any circumstances, an alcoholic can easily be pushed over
the edge and go on another binge.

After Lew and Charley become housemates, Charley does the cooking
and housekeeping while serving as a moral ballast to Lew, who is always
aware that it would not take much effort for him to topple back into the
alcoholic abyss. Several years pass; with Charley as a stabilizing force, Lew
gets a job back on the paper, gets promoted, and one day is asked by Cuscaden to do a favor for his publisher, John Ives (Raymond Massey). Ives's
nephew, Boyd Copeland, is a drunk who needs rehabilitation. Complicating Lew's decision to take on such a nearly impossible task are two factors:
first, Ives will not take a negative response since Lew owes him a favor for
reinstating him on the paper when Lew badly needed to return to work;
second, Boyd is married to Paula, Lew's former flame from the bad old days
when he could not resist a drink. So Lew agrees, knowing all the while that
he has no chance of success with a man who, by all accounts, is quite content to be perpetually drunk.

Gig Young as Boyd is remarkably well cast, with just the right mixture
of confusion, bravado, fear, shyness, self-abasement, and self-destruction:

all qualities that Young possessed abundantly — and tragically — in real life. His scenes with Cagney are effective because the actors play off well against each other. Where Lew Marsh is sharp, quick-witted, and edgy, Boyd Copeland is soft, sly, and laid back. Yet both have an ironic sense of humor and ultimately come to respect one another because they share a belief in fair play and justice.

Yet Marsh's introduction to Copeland is not an auspicious one. Having been given a room in the house where Copeland and his mother are living with John Ives, Marsh is awakened from sleep by Copeland's piano playing. In his first confrontation with the man whom Marsh has been ordered to "cure," Marsh treats Copeland with a wry detachment; the reporter makes it clear to the talented but drunk composer that he is there only on orders from Copeland's uncle who, it seems, has the crazy idea that Marsh can sober up Copeland. Cagney is at his subtle best in this initial scene with Young; he taunts Copeland with his raised eyebrows and sardonic, I-know-more-than-you-do grin, which convey his grimly realistic conviction that no one can help a drunk unless he wants help himself. When Copeland inquires why Marsh is the one to sober him up, Marsh coolly, matter-of-factly replies "Because I'm a drunk."

Now Copeland is intrigued: although he is definitely inebriated, he still manages a few probing questions. He eases himself around Marsh's shoulder, so that he is peering over him, as though he were about to whisper in the older man's ear:

COPELAND: Drunk now?

MARSH: No.

COPELAND: Yesterday?

MARSH: No.

COPELAND: Lately?

MARSH: No.

COPELAND (*looking woebegone, sympathetically patting Marsh on the shoulder*): Oh — retired.

Here Copeland walks away, as though he wants to allow Marsh's confession to soak in. Then, another thought occurs to his fuzzy brain, so he asks: "When do we start sobering me up?" Marsh's reply is abrupt and straightforward: "We don't — can't be done." Now Copeland is truly curious, for he has been accustomed to nagging from his family, all of whom have attempted the usual, but ineffective, persuasive techniques to try to keep him from drinking. His mother is a whining ninny (Selena Royle) who calls her son *Boydie* and thinks she can control him by pushing him back into infancy. One of Marsh's first official acts is to order John Ives to send his sister packing. In addition to mother's interference, Copeland has had to listen to various other family members describe cirrhosis of the liver, brain damage, and the general havoc that his drinking is wreaking upon loved ones. Marsh knows better than to use any of these techniques, for he knows that the only one who can stop a drunk from drinking is the drunk himself. As recovering alcoholics, Marsh and Charley Dolan have agreed that what makes a person quit once and for all is fear of death, which is heralded by the whirring sound of a phenomenon that they have named Angel Feathers. Boyd Copeland will finally hear the sound, but only after death has paused briefly — and horrifyingly — in order to touch him.

This death comes around the midpoint of the movie, and it comes to Charley Dolan. In a most indirect way, Charley is a victim of Boyd Copeland's alcoholism. One evening, after retrieving Copeland from a local nightspot, Charley reluctantly gets into Copeland's car and, equally reluctantly, allows the clearly intoxicated Boyd to drive. Boyd's driving is erratic and far too fast; in addition, when a large truck pulls in front of them on a rain-soaked highway, Boyd is unable to stop because the brakes do not work. And so Charley dies in the crash. Lew Marsh, desperate for news about his friend, arrives as the wreckage is being cleaned off the highway. The subsequent scene between Cagney and Young is one of the most memorable film moments of 1951. Cagney has just talked to James Gleason's Charley, who has been trapped in the crushed metal of the car. He has also just witnessed Charley's death. Now Boyd Copeland approaches him fearfully and tentatively. Copeland is shaken but not really hurt, so when Cagney sees Young standing beside the highway, anxious for information about Charley and apparently physically untouched by the wreck that has just killed Cagney's best friend, Cagney lets loose with all of his bitterness, perhaps in part the result of his real-life memories of watching his alcoholic father destroy all that he loved.

The effective use of mise en scène heightens the tension of the moment. Cagney is pictured in three quarter profile, standing somewhat behind Young, who is shown in a foreground shot, also in three quarter profile. At this point, neither wants to look directly at the other. In fact, Cagney looks like an old warrior who is warily taking the measure of his opponent. So, when Young insists that he'll do anything to make right the wrong that he has done to Charley, Cagney is more than prepared to do battle. He begins by retorting that Copeland has always paid his way out of everything. Then he delivers a hard slap across Copeland's face. Throughout the ensuing lambast, Cagney continues to slap Copeland, all the while weeping over his lost friend, over all the lives lost from alcoholism. Meanwhile, Copeland allows himself to be subjected to Cagney's attack; he listens remorsefully while Cagney thrusts the following knife-like accusations: "But you can't buy your way out of this, Boydie. You can't bury your head in Mama's lap and forget it. Not this time, Boydie. Charley's there and you're here, and it oughta be the other way around." Here he knocks Copeland to the ground and walks away, still weeping.

Although Jimmy Cagney is often remembered primarily for his gangster roles, he also had the ability to convey genuine warmth and depth of feeling and to weep unashamedly when the part called for it. In such movies as *Taxi* (1932), *Each Dawn I Die* (1939), *Strawberry Blonde* (1941), and *Yankee Doodle Dandy* (1942), he cries believably — not from self-pity but from genuine feelings born out of a sense of loss: of both the opportunities as well as of the people that have passed him by. And in *Come Fill the Cup*, he plays this highly charged scene with Gig Young with the same sensation of unabashed grief.

In addition, he continues his downward spin in the next scene as he initially approaches the Sun Herald building, presumably to return to his office. He hesitates only a moment, turns, and hastens across the street to the bar, nearly being hit by oncoming traffic in his desperation to once again find solace in the bottle. Though it has been many years since Lew Marsh has had a drink, Cagney depicts quite well the recovering alcoholic's omnipresent fear: that the temptation of alcohol will prove to be too much when a person has decided once again to take that first drink.

Like Ray Milland in *The Lost Weekend*, Cagney looks apprehensively at the recently poured shot glass on the bar; he is indecisive, fidgety, so he hesitates, toys with it, and raises the glass. He has made the decision to drink. But Cagney is the hero of this movie, so he is saved from falling into another terrifying slide to nowhere when one of his newspaper colleagues runs up to the bar with the news that the brakes on Copeland's car had been tampered with, that Copeland could not have stopped had he wanted to. This information revitalizes Cagney, so much so that he replaces the full glass on the bar and hastens out in pursuit of Charley's real killers, who turn out to be gangsters. Like the novel itself, the remainder of the movie is less about alcoholism than about revenge, with Cagney for the most part reverting to his familiar hoodlum type. All ends happily, with Gig Young staying forever sober, reclaiming wife Phyllis Thaxter, and Cagney happily at work in his newsroom office, still sober.

One other scene stands out as a reminder of what alcohol can do to the mind and body. Shortly after Charley's death, Copeland has reached down so far that he has only two alternatives: death or rehabilitation. He has gone to Cagney's apartment and is suffering from the excruciating effects of withdrawal, convinced, as he tells Cagney, that he is unable "to stand it anymore." Cagney tries the tactic of offering him a drink, "for medicinal purposes," but Young pushes the glass aside. Cagney now believes that perhaps Young really means it this time, that his resolution to quit represents more than just cotton candy promises. Both actors give convincing performances here, especially when Cagney briefly walks from the room, thus allowing Young to grab a revolver with which he intends to terminate his mental and physical anguish. But Cagney sees him in time to rush back in, grab it, and chastise him by declaring, "Nobody wins that way, kid," as he removes the bullets. Young's action parallels Milland's suicidal determination at the conclusion of *The Lost Weekend*; in this earlier film, it is the woman who saves Don Birnam from death by revolver. However, the scene between Young and Cagney is also an eerie foreshadowing of Gig Young's own death twenty-seven years later, when the sixty-four-year-old actor shot and killed his young bride of three weeks and then placed the gun into his mouth and fired. Unhappily, Gig Young shared many of Boyd Copeland's inner demons, including insecurity over career failures as well as alcohol addiction. But in the cinematic world of 1951, all ends for the best.

And yet it is Cagney who has the final word. One of the most touching lines in the picture comes at the end when John Ives (Raymond Massey) congratulates Marsh on the good job he has done with Copeland. Marsh is seated at his desk and Ives offers to drive him home. But Marsh replies with a self-assuredness that comes when one is finally at peace with oneself: "Don't you see," he informs Ives, "I *am* home." And we believe him, because Cagney projects an honesty that comes through in all his pictures.

Kenneth Tynan has written at length of the Cagney persona, a description that could apply quite well to his Lew Marsh in *Come Fill the Cup*:

> He was never a romantic figure himself — at his height you can't be — nor was he sentimental — Cheshire cats never are — but he possessed, possibly in greater abundance than any other name star of the time, irresistible charm. It was a cocky, picaresque charm, the charm of pert urchins, the *gaminerie* of unlicked juvenile delinquents.[19]

In a parting comment, John Ives tells Marsh that Marsh will be a world beater when he grows up, and that he should make it soon. In reply, Cagney gives him that Cheshire cat smile and replies, "Meet a kid of seventeen." Juvenile delinquent he may be, but Cagney's recovering alcoholic — wry, modest, and yes, even cocky — continues to be "unlicked."

Richard Schickel has argued that in *Come Fill the Cup* Cagney reprises the scenes of his drunken downfall in *The Roaring Twenties*.[20] However, the focus in the later film is on the alcoholic himself whereas the spotlight in the earlier picture is on the illegal alcohol. Nonetheless, both films superbly illustrate James Cagney's ability to find the emotional center of his character and to hold fast to it. He asks no sympathy. He simply plays the role as he sees it and that, as audiences throughout the decades have always understood, is enough.

9

The Alcoholic Marriage: The 1950s and Beyond

Mr. Odets's drama is a searching and pitiless thing. It cuts to the hearts of three people without mercy or concern for their deep shame.

— Bosley Crowther in his review of *The Country Girl*, *The New York Times*, December 16, 1954

The 1950s was a decade of discovery, change, and uncertainty. It was the decade when the United States tested the world's first hydrogen bomb, when World War II GI's returned to college in unprecedented numbers, when Joseph McCarthy hunted for Communists everywhere, and when racial segregation in schools and neighborhoods was the norm. It was also the decade of television, the long-playing phonograph record, the dishwasher, and home air conditioning. It was the decade that saw the discovery of the polio vaccine, that first described DNA, and that touted advances in treatment for heart disease. But it was also a time for fear of things not understood. Schoolchildren in the early part of the decade participated in atomic bomb drills in which they were told to go to their school's basement, to crouch on the floor, and to put their coats over their heads in preparation for the great flash of light to come.

Despite the omnipresent threat of global annihilation, it was also a decade that cheerily glorified the family. *Togetherness* and *cookout* became favorite catchwords of the time. Magazine advertisements showed couples enjoying their new car, their favorite brand of cigarette, and their latest home entertainment center featuring a radio, television, and phonograph, all combined into one attractive cabinet. Even ads for alcohol showed pleasant gatherings of family and friends, basking in the warm glow of companionship while grilling steaks on the patio and enjoying beer, wine, or whiskey.

Just as significant as these advertisements promoting alcohol as the drink of choice for the average American was the increasing number of pills being consumed as the decade advanced. "By 1956, 80 percent of drugs being prescribed had reached the market in the previous fifteen years. These included tranquilizers such as Milltown ('don't give a damn pills,' *Time* called them), which were first introduced in the mid–1950s."[1] On the surface, then, although the 1950s appears to have been a decade of relative peace and stability for Americans, there was a dark side to this good life. The feelings of apathy and ennui felt by the prospering blue collar and middle class whites were often exacerbated by their reliance on mind-numbing tranquilizers and alcohol. And motion pictures were gradually reflecting this superficially stable but ultimately uncertain time. A number of important movies of the 1950s and early 1960s depict the despair at the heart of the American Dream of success.

The Volatile Mixture of Alcohol and Marriage

However, by 1952, one illustration of the good life led by the middle class was the growing ownership of television sets. In that year, there were 15.3 million televisions in the United States.[2] As more people opted for *togetherness* by gathering in their homes to watch their favorite comedies, plays, and sports events, movie theater attendance dropped; indeed, many small town movie houses closed for good. Because the motion picture industry had to find some way to compete with the small screen black-and-white images, many cinematic advances in technology were evident in the 1950s. Improvements were made in sound; color cinematography was more widespread than it had been in the 1940s; screen size became more all encompassing with such innovations as Cinemascope, VistaVision, Todd-AO, and Cinerama. In addition, 3-D offered some novelty for a while, although the 3-D glasses given to the movie patrons were awkward, and the industry's efforts to make use of this special effect soon wore thin. Although filmmakers strained to make 3-D interesting, audiences soon tired of looking at actors dangling on wires above the theater aisles or at cattle coming at them from just off the screen. Consequently, many movies that were originally shot in 3-D were released in flat versions, notably Hitchcock's *Dial "M" for Murder* (1954) and the Cole Porter musical *Kiss Me Kate* (1953).

In fact, some of the best movies from the 1950s and early 1960s eschewed special effects and "glorious Technicolor" and instead concentrated on superb acting, well-written screenplays, realistic settings, and excellent black-and-white cinematography. Among these are *All About Eve* (1950), *Sunset Boulevard* (1950), *A Streetcar Named Desire* (1951), *Come Back, Little Sheba* (1952), *The Country Girl* (1954), *On the Waterfront* (1954), *Marty* (1955), *Written on the Wind* (1956), *The Apartment* (1960), and *Days of Wine and Roses* (1962). Three of these—*Come Back, Little Sheba, The Country Girl*, and *Days of Wine and Roses*— are graphic, realistic depictions of alcohol and its effects on a marriage. Among the most memorable films of the mid-twentieth century, these three are unsentimental and unsparing in their portrayal of family life gone wrong.

Waiting for Sheba

The alcoholic in *Come Back, Little Sheba* (1952) is an individual whom we know only as "Doc" Delaney. As portrayed by Burt Lancaster, Doc is a defeated but resigned character, one who has tried, often without success, to do the right thing. But, in spite of Lancaster's disciplined, understated portrayal of a recovering alcoholic struggling to stay sober, *Come Back, Little Sheba* really belongs to a veteran stage star, fifty-four-year-old Shirley Booth, a fine actress who was making her movie debut. As Doc's wife, she repeats her 1950 stage role, for which she won the Best Actress Tony Award. In the film version, for which she won the Best Actress Academy Award, she gives one of the most riveting performances of the decade as a lost, lonely woman in search of someone to love.

It is a testament to Booth's acting skill that, long after we have seen the movie, we can still recall scenes that demonstrate her haunting portrayal. We remember her descending the stairs at the film's opening — dressed in a tattered bathrobe, her hair uncombed, her expression pathetically eager as she goes to answer the doorbell. Another actress would have looked slatternly, but Booth simply looks sad and rejected. We remember her fleeting look of pain and then acceptance as Doc announces that he has rented her sewing room to a local college girl (Terry Moore). "It is my house," he had told the student when she had asked if Mrs. Delaney would mind giving up the room. We remember her inviting the postman into the house and offering him a glass of water but apologizing to him for fear that the glass might still contain a taste of cantaloupe. When he leaves, she offers him a toy from a cereal box, telling him that it is for his grandchildren. Here is a woman who has received no mail for two weeks, a fact that the grateful postman, touched by her kindness, alludes to as he leaves: "I'm gonna see that you get a letter if I have to write it myself." We recall her child-like delight in having an attractive and on-the-make young girl board with them. We remember her wistful reminiscences to her husband about why she had been forced to marry him some twenty years earlier when she discovered that she was pregnant. And again and again we hear her voice — part plead-ing, part terrified, part despairing — as she reminds Doc of their baby's death and asks him if he regrets going through with the marriage, once he no longer had a reason for doing so.

We recall the scene where she stands by herself and calls plaintively for Little Sheba, the dog that had wandered off months before, never to come back. As she does so, she slowly, tenderly rubs her abdomen, and through this subtle movement, she reminds us of the baby she had lost and of the children she will never have. We watch again as she does an energetic Charleston while Doc happily claps his hands in time to the music played on the radio. Their carefree behavior provides one of the rare, light-hearted moments in the movie. Finally, we see again her surprise, disbelief, confu-sion, fear, and frenzy when she goes to the kitchen cupboard and discov-ers that a liquor bottle, which Doc had kept on the top shelf through his past year of sobriety, is no longer there.

Providing capable support to Shirley Booth's outstanding performance are Burt Lancaster as the alcoholic Doc, the chiropractor who is not a "real" doctor because he never finished college; Terry Moore as Marie Buckholder, the Delaneys' sexy, teasing boarder who nearly destroys Doc's hard-won year of sobriety; Richard Jaeckel as Turk, the equally sexy, on-the-make college athlete whom Marie tantalizes and who wants nothing more from Marie than a night of hot sex, which she ultimately refuses to give him. It is the triangle that develops around these three characters that ultimately sends Doc back to the bottle.

Not always noted for the subtlety of his acting, Lancaster here gives a beautifully understated portrayal as the weak, subdued failure: a man who tries hard not to look back on his past for fear that he will be forced to face his character flaws in the present. Though some critics thought that Lan-caster was miscast, that he was too young and that his acting range was too limited for the role, he nonetheless gives the audience a realistic glimpse of a defeated man. Moreover, Lancaster later told an interviewer how much he had wanted the part: "I guess I wanted to play [the role] more than any other I ever got close to. Doc Delaney is the most human, if imperfect, kind of guy ever written into a play or script. I purposely didn't see the play, because I had my own ideas of how Doc should be portrayed."[3]

One such idea that Lancaster conveys about Delaney is the character's sense of failure and a feeling of "What if?" That is, Doc is a man who is not at peace with himself because he knows that he has allowed himself to be carried along by circumstances and that he has made many wrong choices, so he always wonders about alternatives—"What if I had done this?" or "What if I had not done that?" "Might I have been more successful had I made different choices?" But Doc has made his unfortunate choices many years earlier and, as a result of his early and seemingly directionless drifting, Lancaster's character has no identity. We never learn his true first name. Even the two "names" given him in the movie and in the original play by William Inge are not names at all: his wife calls him either "Doc" or "Daddy." The fact that he is neither a doctor nor a daddy is significant; neither name truly identifies him because he has everlastingly lost the chance to be either one. Because of his drinking, he had to quit medical school before he finished his medical degree. And he never became a father because Lola lost the child that had been conceived before their marriage, and she was subsequently unable to have any more children. Moreover, at one point, Lola suggests that adoption was never possible because Doc was unable to take on the responsibility: he was always drunk.

Yet *Come Back, Little Sheba* is more than just a narrative of what-might-have-been. It is also a story about sex: frustrated sex, forbidden sex, secret sex, denied sex. In all four of the major characters, we can see manifestations of each of these types. Late one night, Turk tries to lure Marie into her room at the Delaney house so that she can put forth those comforts that her provocative manner has seemed to promise. Yet Turk finally leaves with his urges unsatisfied: disgusted and frustrated by Marie's ultimate denial. With Doc and Lola, the sexual dilemma is more complicated. Whereas Lola is charmed and excited in a romantic, school girlish way when she sees Turk and Marie together, Doc is both jealous of Turk's sexual advances toward Marie and repulsed by the thought of their actually enjoying a night of sex in his house. In fact, having seen Turk go into Marie's room one night and having watched under her door as her light went out, Doc assumes that Turk and Marie are spending the night together; he does not realize that Turk had left minutes earlier, escaping out the window. Disappointed in the girl who, he has always told himself, is sweet and innocent, and feeling guilty over his own lustful feelings toward her, he slowly climbs the stairs to the bedroom, which he shares with Lola in a platonic manner. The next morning in the kitchen, he gazes lovingly but tentatively at Marie. After she leaves the room, he puts on his suit jacket, hesitates, carefully closes the kitchen door, and goes to the cabinet, taking the liquor bottle from the kitchen shelf and hiding it in the pocket of his raincoat, which he casually drapes over his arm as he leaves for work. As he is walking out, he rejects Marie's offer to walk with him to the corner, saying abruptly, "I'm late," as he hastily exits. For Doc, sex is both alluring and dangerous. After all, it was sex that forced him into marrying Lola. But Lola at this point is thinking only about Doc's odd behavior as he leaves that morning. In an ironic foreshadowing of the next forty-eight hours, Lola wonders aloud why Doc took his raincoat, "It's a beautiful day. There isn't a cloud in sight."

But the clouds have been building for many years in the Delaney marriage, exacerbated by Lola's continually reminding Doc of the past. Her references serve two purposes: first, they provide important information for our understanding of the tragedies that underlie the Delaney relationship; next, they add insight into Lola's character, helping us to see her insecurities and her attendant need for reassurance. At one point early in the film, she asks Doc:

LOLA: Are you sorry you *had* to marry me?

DOC: We were never going to talk about that, baby. If the baby had lived, everyone would have known.

LOLA: My losing her like that — the way it turned out — you wouldn't have had to marry me.

DOC: Honey, what's done is done.

LOLA: But it must make you feel bad sometimes to think you had to give up your studies to support a wife. If the baby had lived, she'd be just like Marie.

DOC: Lola, people have gotta forget the past and live for the present. We all make mistakes.

At this point, it is instructive to note that the screenplay, coauthored by Ketti Frings and William Inge, differs somewhat from the original script as written for the stage by William Inge. In the stage production, Lola and Doc also discuss their lost child, but their dialogue is more specific; we learn in more detail just why the Delaneys lost the baby. Moreover, the stage version reinforces our understanding of Doc's need to drink. On stage, Lola begins the conversation by referring to the secret of her long ago pregnancy:

LOLA: I don't think anyone knows about it except my folks. Do you?

DOC: Of course not, Baby.

LOLA: I wish the baby had lived, Doc. I don't think that woman knew her business, do you, Doc?

DOC: I guess not.

LOLA: If we'd gone to a doctor, she would have lived, don't you think?

DOC: Perhaps.

LOLA: A doctor wouldn't have known we'd just got married, would he? Why were we so afraid?

DOC: We were just kids. Kids don't know how to look after things.[4]

Although Inge's play is still somewhat circumspect, the text does impart some important information lacking in the screenplay: that someone other than a doctor — a midwife, perhaps — attended the birth of the Delaney child, a girl. Likewise, the preceding dialogue implies that the Delaneys never consulted a doctor at any time during Lola's pregnancy. It also suggests that the Delaneys waited until almost the end of Lola's pregnancy before they married. These facts are significant, for they suggest that the Delaneys' reluctance to marry until the last moment was finally overcome by their shame at having a baby out of wedlock and, more important, that their refusal to see a doctor contributed to their newborn infant's death.

The film version omits these subtleties that might have reinforced viewers' appreciation of Doc's frustration and despair, his heightened sense of "What if?" and his subsequent attachment to the bottle. Nevertheless, the character of Doc as presented on both stage and screen offers a rueful, honest bit of self-revelation. In the film version, Doc reminds Lola that, years before, when his family died and left him a good deal of money, he could have used that income to return to school and finish his degree; instead, he had wasted his inheritance by "drinking it all up." This is a self-assessment that does nothing to assuage Lola's guilt, however: guilt gnawing at her since that moment when both knew that he would "have" to marry her. In addition, such guilt is compounded in Lola's mind over the years by the omnipresent terror associated with Doc's constant drinking. Though Doc has been sober for one year, and though Lola tries to convince both of them that his bad old days of drinking are behind them, both know that it would be very easy for him to start again at any time.

And so he does. The day on which Doc leaves the house with the bottle hidden in his raincoat pocket is the day on which Lola spends hours cleaning house and preparing a romantic dinner for Marie and her fiancé Bruce. Deciding to fix a cocktail for her recently arrived guests, Lola discovers the empty space in the cabinet. At first she is confused, thinking and hoping that she has looked on the wrong shelf. But after opening door after door, she realizes with horror that the bottle is indeed gone and that Doc will not be coming home that night. Trying to put the best face on her despair, she instructs Marie and Bruce not to wait for Doc. Nor does she eat either; she is too distraught, edgy, apprehensive. She is all too aware of what will follow Doc's night of drinking.

And what actually happens when Doc returns early that morning is even worse than what she had anticipated. He eases himself into the house, walking gingerly and carefully, as though he were dizzy. He is carrying a full bottle, which he carefully replaces on the shelf. Here, Doc exemplifies the typical alcoholic's fuzzy thinking; he illogically hopes that, if he brings back an unopened bottle to replace a partially opened one, no one will know that he has taken it. In this action, Doc resembles those seasoned drinkers who persist in adding water to the liquor bottle in the hope that no one in the household will know that they have been imbibing.

Yet all of Doc's plans for secrecy are forgotten when he confronts Lola, who has been sleeping fitfully on the living room sofa, still dressed in neatly tailored outfit from the previous evening, though now it is wrinkled and disheveled. Lola's efforts to be solicitous and forgiving only intensify his anger and increase his desire for more booze. However, before he takes that next drink, he turns on her and unleashes all of his heretofore repressed disgust at the events of the recent past:

"You and Marie are both a couple of sluts," he announces hatefully. Referring to Marie's dinner guest of the previous evening — a man to whom she has been "sort of" engaged for some time — he turns on Lola by telling her that Bruce probably has to marry Marie, "just like I had to marry you." He continues his bitter harangue: "What are you good for? You can't even sweep the floors till some bozo comes along and makes love to Marie. You can't even get up in the mornings and fix my breakfast." Here he looks at the fancy china still on the table from dinner the previous night and, even more enraged than ever, knocks it off onto the floor. "My mother didn't buy these dishes for *sluts*," he reminds her.

By now, he has become so frenzied that he cannot allow the newly settled bottle to stay long on the shelf; however, he is thwarted in his efforts to open it by ordinary means. Desperate for more alcohol, he breaks the neck of the bottle by smashing it against the sink and pours a glassful, obviously risking a cut mouth as he takes a much-needed drink from the glass.[5] Meanwhile, a terrified Lola calls one of Doc's friends from Alcoholics Anonymous, an action that angers Doc even more. He stalks her with a kitchen knife, accusing of her knowing what went on between Marie and Turk two nights before, irrationally adding that these sorts of things must have been occurring since they were married, with Lola continually running a lonely hearts club. But Lola is saved by Doc's drunken exhaustion; he collapses as he is about to strangle her. Two of Doc's fellow AA members arrive and haul him off to the city hospital for a brief drying out period.

The movie denouement is less than exciting. As he does in the play, a chastened Doc returns from the hospital, promising to make a new start and reassuring Lola that he couldn't make it without her. For her part, the

Lola of both stage and screen resigns herself to the irrefutable fact that their little dog Sheba is never going to come back.

Despite this less-than-credible cheerful ending, *Come Back, Little Sheba* is an excellent picture. Contributing to its realistic tone is the fine black-and-white cinematography by James Wong Howe, the superb set design by Sam Comer and Ross Dowd, and capable art decoration by Henry Bumstead and Hal Pereira. In addition, costumes by Edith Head add to the ominous feeling of lurking disaster, notably in the tight-fitting, breast-enhancing clothes she has designed for Terry Moore and in the loose-fitting, any-which-way garments she has created for Shirley Booth. Specifically, Head's costumes for the character of Lola include a dress with a slight, nearly imperceptible tear along the side. So too, even one of Lola's "better" outfits allows us to see an inch or two of her slip showing. Additionally, Edith Head has designed slip-on, wrap-around dresses for Lola, ones that she can easily move in and out of as she goes from her bathrobe to house-dress to more formal attire for the fancy dinner she has lovingly planned for Marie and Bruce. Interestingly enough, these dresses are not unattractive, but Head has fashioned them so that they accentuate Shirley Booth's short stature. Though Booth's figure is fairly good, Head designs the dresses so as to make the diminutive actress appear dumpy; they are deliberately unflattering. Such subtle costuming touches thus reveal the character of a woman who has given up on her appearance because she has given up on any expectations of a better life. The world she sees — a world circumscribed by the scruffy house she lives in — is all the world there is.

The set design of *Come Back, Little Sheba* also reminds us of the shabbiness of the Delaney life. The Delaneys live in a blue collar, lower middle class neighborhood. The steps leading to their front porch are cracked; the interior of their house looks respectable and somewhat comfortable, but barren. Their furniture is worn; their appliances are old — even for 1952. For instance, their kitchen contains an old-fashioned icebox; their stove has gas burners that require lighting with a match. For entertainment, they do have a radio, which Lola is constantly turning on in order to hear music and to listen to a favorite fantasy program, but there is no phonograph in sight. They have just one bathroom — not unusual in those days— but it is on the second floor, where there are two bedrooms. Lola has a sewing room — evidence that she makes her own clothes— but she is forced to give up even the luxury of that extra space when Doc cavalierly rents the room to Marie. (Doc's arbitrary rental of this particular room is not in the play. As the play opens, Marie has already rented an available spare room.)

The cinematography of James Wong Howe expertly complements the set design. Especially noteworthy is Howe's use of close-ups to delineate character. Particularly effective are his close-ups of Shirley Booth and Terry Moore. He brilliantly captures Marie's sly, coy, conniving, flirtatious nature in his framing of Terry Moore's face in the opening scene where she is already thinking about the possibility of snatching Lola's sewing room for herself. Howe's photography also reveals Marie's come-hither, teasing personality as she flirts, in turn, with Doc, Turk, and Bruce. Howe also utilizes his close-ups for maximum effect as he helps us to see Lola's desperation. Booth's remarkable acting combines with Howe's skill to expose Lola's frantic desire to rid herself of the darkness that always lurks on the edge of her consciousness. For instance, as Lola pleads for Doc's reassurance that he has no regrets about marrying her, we see her agonizing desire for acceptance. Likewise, when she first realizes that Doc has taken the bottle from the cabinet and then subsequently calls Doc's friend at the AA, she is shown in close-up: her face a study in anguish. Later, after Doc has been taken to the hospital following his brutal attack on her, Lola calls her parents. Once more, her face betrays her tentative struggle for family acceptance as, with both fear and hopelessness in her voice, she asks her mother if she might stay with them for a few days. What she wants is security and comfort, but it is clear from her end of the conversation that neither of her parents wants her to come there to see them. Like her little dog Sheba, Lola is forever lost, unlikely to return to a place of safety. But, thankfully, Shirley Booth is forever captured in this role: her sublime Lola a timeless reminder of her gifted portrayal.

A Stylish Country Girl

One of the hardest challenges that an actor faces is the task of taking a relatively unsympathetic character and making that individual at least understandable, if not entirely likable. In *The Country Girl* (1954,) Bing Crosby confronts just such a challenge in his portrayal of Frank Elgin, an unemployed, down-on-his luck, alcoholic musical comedy star who is afraid of living because he is afraid of failing. As expertly depicted by Crosby, Elgin is by turns charming, glib, duplicitous, pathetic, grasping, obsequious, and terrified. Crosby is ably supported by Grace Kelly, cast against type as his long-suffering, overly protective wife Georgie; and by William Holden as the brash young director who insists on taking a chance on the once-popular recording star. *The Country Girl* contains the sort of plot that might have descended into sticky sentimentality, but for the most part, its depiction of the plight of the alcoholic and of the alcoholic marriage remains both objective and brutal. In a review of the movie, Bosley Crowther offers the following observation about one of the few times that the script allows Crosby to play on audience emotions: "But the more sentimental obtrusion is a ballad, 'The Search Is Through,' which is wrapped up with misty recollections of happier days and a little son who was killed. Naturally, Mr. Crosby tugs when the strings are in his hands."[6]

This sentimental song is reprised throughout, recurring from time to time to remind us of the tragic accident that killed Elgin's toddler son (Jon Provost). It is an accident for which Elgin continues to blame himself. Yet Crosby handles even this "sentimental obtrusion" with a good deal of professional aplomb; his famous laid-back style and his casual laissez faire approach to life serve him well, especially in those scenes that might otherwise have descended into melodramatic excess.

It is significant to note here that the film version of *The Country Girl* was perforce tailored to Crosby's musical talents. Clifford Odets's original play starred Paul Kelly as Frank Elgin. Kelly, a wry, tough-talking performer, was strictly a non-musical, dramatic actor; therefore, his abilities were perfectly suited to the part as originally written. In the play, Frank Elgin tries out for and is subsequently cast in a dramatic role. Moreover, there are only a couple of references to the Elgin child — this one, a daughter. Whereas the movie contains a number of sentimental flashbacks in which we see the Elgin son and learn just how he died, the original play simply mentions the dead child. Early in the stage play, Frank is speaking to Bernie about the past, trying to convince the director that he is able to stay sober when he is working:

FRANK. (*Sullenly.*) I don't drink on a show.

BERNIE. (*Sharply.*) Not according to Gilbert. I checked with him — you worked with him in '44? What happened? (*Frank looks at Georgie before answering.*)

FRANK. We lost our little daughter ... that year.[7]

On the other hand, in the film version, much is made of the death of Elgin's son. In fact, we are led to believe that Elgin's alcoholism is aggravated by his guilt feelings in connection with the accident that killed the child. In a flashback to the fateful day, Crosby is shown recording a soothing ballad — the one Crowther refers to in his review — while the adoring Georgie and the boy watch.

After the recording session ends, Elgin persuades Georgie to let the boy stay with him while she goes off on some errands. But before Elgin has the chance to take the boy on an outing, the publicity department asks him to pose for some pictures just outside the building. So he takes his son by the hand, the little boy trustingly trudging along beside him, and, still holding the toddler, positions himself next to a giant record hanging on the wall.

When the photographer asks him to turn towards the record so that the famous Crosby/Elgin profile will be displayed to its best advantage, Elgin obliges; in so doing, he momentarily drops his son's hand, the boy dashes into the street and is struck and killed. Elgin naturally blames himself for the boy's accident, and the movie emphasizes those guilt feelings as "The Search is Through," Elgin's signature song — the one he was recording the day his son died — is played at various times throughout the film. Each time Elgin hears it, he is naturally reminded of the death of innocence and of his part in the death. Yet toward the end of the picture, Elgin finally confesses to Bernie that this accident years earlier has been only one of the many excuses he has held onto in order to justify his drinking. Nevertheless, Elgin's memory of that song is used as an evocative motif and contributes to our understanding of Elgin's pain. The memory of the episode, which is custom-made specifically for Bing Crosby's particular talents, is an effective addition to the movie version of *The Country Girl*.

Despite this significant change in the script from stage to screen, the part of Frank Elgin has some similarities in both versions; for instance, it is the character around whom most of the action revolves. Indeed, Crosby is onscreen about eighty-five percent of the time and commands every scene in which he appears, even when he shares the frame with the exquisitely beautiful Grace Kelly as a dependable, downtrodden, loyal, beleaguered wife. Furthermore, the screenplay, like the original stage script, tells the audience from the outset that Crosby's Elgin is an undependable drunk, albeit a talented one.

Before Frank Elgin makes his first appearance on screen, Bernie Dodd (William Holden), a director of Broadway musicals, is facing a crisis: he has a show scheduled to open soon, and he has no leading man. But Bernie has an idea. He tries to convince the show's producer Phil Cook (Anthony Ross) that Elgin would be ideal for the part. Cook is cynical about Bernie's choice, for he knows Elgin's reputation and does not want to sink a fortune into a has-been, drunken crooner. Yet Bernie prevails and summons Elgin onto the empty theater stage. From the outset, Crosby's Elgin looks rumpled, tentative, overly eager to please, unsure about just why he has been invited to try out and about what part he is supposed to play. The number Elgin performs is called "The Pitchman," a patter routine that he supposedly knows by heart because he had performed it many times before in an earlier Broadway musical. Consequently, Elgin's efforts to put across this number are mechanical; moreover, they are as hesitating as his appearance. While his audition is not necessarily bad, it is lackluster and lackadaisical. Crosby expertly demonstrates that Frank Elgin is holding back, as though he is afraid of looking too good, afraid that he might actually get the part.

And Elgin's fears are realized when Bernie tells him that the part is not a minor musical number, as he had at first thought, but that Elgin will be expected to carry the entire show as the leading man. Unable to face the responsibility of having many others dependent on him, Elgin leaves the stage and vanishes from the theater, even as Bernie is finally persuading producer Cook, who is still cynical and skeptical, to take a chance on the down-at-the-heels actor. Not one to give up easily, the determined, hard-edged Bernie goes to Elgin's apartment — a dingy, walk-up, one room flat. It is here that he meets Grace Kelly as Georgie. She is wearing glasses, her hair pulled back from her face, and she is dressed in a conservative skirt, a high-necked blouse, and a sweater. However, no amount of costume design and hair styling can hide her beauty and elegance. This is no ordinary plain country girl; in fact, the only thing plain about Georgie is her manner. She is plain speaking and forthright. This is not a woman to be trifled with, as Bernie soon discovers when he asks her a number of questions about Elgin; he wants to know about their marriage and about Elgin's drinking. Georgie's response is abrupt, flippant, and rude, as she replies that what he asks is none of his business.

After Elgin returns to their apartment to find Georgie and Bernie awaiting him, he tries to explain why he had rushed out of the theater following his audition. He knows that the producer Cook had been hostile, and this opposition had truly frightened him. As he confesses to Bernie: "I can't go to bat unless I feel everybody is rooting for me." Throughout the conversation, it is clear that Georgie runs interference for her husband; furthermore, she sees through the false flattery that Bernie lays upon Elgin. On the other hand, Bernie demonstrates that he has no patience with a man who was fired from his last job because he drank too much. Bernie knows that Elgin can do a good job, but he also has to maintain his reputation as a director and cannot have Elgin falling apart. Bernie appears especially callous and unsympathetic after Elgin pleads that he had broken down and been fired after the death of his son. Bernie abruptly dismisses the incident, saying, in essence, well, so much for that time, but what about the others? Nonetheless, Bernie still wants Elgin for the lead, so he reassures the increasingly nervous actor that there would be no hurry to take the show to Broadway: "The season's still young. We could stay out till you're letter perfect." Finally, both Georgie and Bernie persuade Elgin to try the role — at least through the out-of-town tryouts. Then, after Bernie exits, and Georgie and Elgin are again alone, she turns on her husband, demanding to know why he hadn't told her about the audition, angry that he hadn't consulted her. When Elgin confesses that he had walked along Forty-seventh Street for a long time, unsure whether he could actually enter the theater and go through with the audition, Georgie reassures him that he should nonetheless try, that he has been given a perfect opportunity for a comeback.

So Frank Elgin tries, but he has trouble with his lines and cannot seem to concentrate. Ten days from the opening, he still carries his script and needs prompting during rehearsals. Always eager to blame himself for what has gone wrong, Elgin nonetheless demonstrates the addict's cunning ability to transfer guilt onto another person. When Bernie chastises Elgin for not being prepared, Elgin makes excuses for his shortcomings by telling a slick story, one that even the viewer at this point is led to believe. Elgin's tale is one of attempted suicide and drunkenness on Georgie's part: except that, as we learn later, it is Elgin who is the suicidal drunk, not Georgie. But as Crosby plays him, Frank Elgin is such a smooth liar that Bernie believes Elgin's sad tale of life with Georgie. Elgin claims that he has allowed Georgie to think that she has taken control of his life; this way, explains Elgin to Bernie, Georgie is given a reason to live. But, rationalizes Elgin, Georgie is also the reason that he continues to drink. According to Elgin, Georgie is the weak one, the one who shuns responsibility. By this time, Bernie, who has appeared from the start to resent Georgie's bluntness, is more than ever convinced that Georgie is bad for Elgin, that she must be not be allowed to interfere with Elgin's work.

In point of fact, however, Bernie is attracted to Georgie. Although they address one another as "Mr. Dodd" and "Mrs. Elgin," and although they quarrel bitterly over Elgin's career and over Bernie's interpretation of her intrusive role in it, the attraction is mutual. Their desire for each other is usually masked by their bickering, much of it bitter, about their respective duties to Frank Elgin. "I don't like strong women, Mrs. Elgin," Dodd taunts her at one point. "I'm not here to audition for you, Mr. Dodd," is Georgie's quick comeback. Yet, by the film's end, Bernie has even pleaded with Georgie to leave Frank in order to marry him, though his proposal appears to be based on lust rather than on anything relative to his desire to get married again, his first marriage having apparently been a dreadful experience, his wife a manipulative monster. One feels that, had Georgie left the much older Elgin in order to marry the dynamic, sexy Holden character, she might have again become the fashion model beauty: the stylish, attractive woman as she had appeared in the flashback scene on the day that their son is killed. But she would not have been content with Holden's Bernie Dodd, for Georgie Elgin, as portrayed by Grace Kelly, does indeed require someone to be dependent on her, despite the uncertain agonies she endures as the wife of a talented, but weak and cunning man.

And the agonies are manifest. Just before the Elgins are to leave for the out-of-town tryout, Georgie watches in disgust as two empty liquor bottles roll out from under their sink, hidden there earlier in the day by Frank, but obviously consumed somewhat rapidly. Turning on him with a good deal of bitterness and frustration, she brandishes the bottles over his head, while he sits looking small, helpless, and chastened:

GEORGIE: When did you get these, Frank?

FRANK: Last night, after you fell asleep. I went out and got a paper and... What's the difference? I got a good night's sleep.

GEORGIE: No more, Frank.

Despite her orders, Crosby as Elgin continues his efforts to excuse his weaknesses. Here he protests that he is afraid of messing things up in Boston, just as he had messed up everything else in his life. He alludes to the accident that had killed their son, continuing to blame himself for it. As he reminds Georgie: "He was my responsibility that day. All I had to do was hold onto his hand."

Nor does Elgin become any easier to handle once they get to Boston. He comes down with a cold — or so he claims— which offers an ideal excuse for him to buy some cough syrup, which just happens to contain twenty-two percent alcohol. Even in the matter of the cough remedy, Elgin lies; he tells Bernie that Georgie had bought it for him, that he hadn't even noticed the alcohol content. He also lies to Georgie when he tells her that he had purchased only one bottle of the syrup. And she knows he is lying, as she tries halfheartedly to locate the second one, only to give up, realizing that it doesn't much matter, that her husband will always find ways to deceive her.

The Boston tryouts do not go well; Elgin's reviews are bad. Such discouraging news gives Elgin another excuse to drink, so he goes to a bar; here he smashes the glasses and the mirror behind the bar and finishes the night's frolic in jail. It is right after this debacle that Elgin finally reveals the truth: that he had lied about Georgie, that he had always used his son's accident as a respectable excuse for failure. "I could drink a little more." Then, confesses Elgin, he cut his wrists— his suicide attempt, not Georgie's, as he had earlier claimed. But the cuts were not deep enough for him to die, "just enough to bleed myself back into the center of attention. So everybody felt sorry for me again. They understood." In this scene, Crosby hits just the right note with Elgin. In appearance, he is unkempt; in manner, he is cynical. He is a man who is no longer looking for pity; rather he appears tired, lost, world-weary. Sadly, he admits that he had lied about everything: "I even lied about Georgie."

But Frank Elgin is finally a success when the show goes to New York— in a musical that looks like a bad imitation of *Oklahoma!* So Frank has redeemed himself at last. Additionally, although Georgie and Bernie admit their love for each other, and although Elgin graciously offers to bow out of the scene in order to allow them to be together, Georgie stays with Elgin. In the movie's final scene, we see Bernie watching from an apartment window; then we cut to a long shot, which reveals Georgie running across the street to join Elgin on the corner. While the film ends on a positive note, it still leaves many unanswered questions and many problems unresolved: notably, the dilemma of the recovering alcoholic. Frank Elgin, like Doc Delaney, is always just one drink away from slipping once again into the darkness of the White Logic.

Marriage on the Rocks

Jack Lemmon as Joe Clay in *Days of Wine and Roses* (1962) is the quintessential Company Man: the man who provides complaisant women for clients of his public relations firm; the man who entertains these same clients by trying his best to match them drink for drink. Yet, as a young career man on the rise up the corporate ladder, he feels morally compromised in having to serve as a high-priced pimp, and he consequently doesn't much like himself. When he meets Kirsten Arnesen (Lee Remick), he immediately falls for her clean, open innocence. She is not at all like the hard-drinking, sexually aware women with whom he ordinarily comes in contact in the course of his job. She does not drink; moreover, although she lives by herself in a city apartment, her roots are deep in the country, and she holds traditional moral values. Her father, whom she loves and respects, is tied to the land: he owns a nursery upstate and was, according to Kirsten's account, very much in love with her late mother. In addition, as Joe learns on his first date with Kirsten, she is addicted to chocolate, an ominous sign of things to come.

But Joe Clay is ever eager to please the woman on whom he has developed a crush; despite her protestations on this first outing that she does not like the taste of liquor, he helpfully orders her a Brandy Alexander. Not liking to drink alone, he tries to put her on a more convivial level — one in keeping with his increasing intoxication as their first evening together proceeds. By providing her with a chocolate-flavored drink, Joe Clay initiates the process that will turn his future wife into an alcoholic.

Nevertheless, this process does not occur overnight; it is not the liquor but rather Joe's amiability and basic decency, his ability to make her laugh, that at first appeals to Kirsten. But when he continues to entice her with alcohol, their relationship develops a darker side. Early in their courtship, he brings to her apartment sacks full of groceries and liquor. Included among these goodies are a chocolate cake, the ingredients for a Brandy Alexander, and two other kinds of liquor as well, just in case that brandy will not be enough to last them through the evening. He also brings some bug spray. In a metaphorically charged scene, Joe sprays insecticide around Kirsten's apartment, for earlier she had explained to him that her apartment was a haven for roaches. His cavalier method of insect eradication is obvious, as he appears unconcerned about just where the lethal stuff will land. Both the fumes and the sticky residue itself soon saturate her apartment. For some reason, Kirsten thinks that Joe's efforts are vastly amusing. She becomes even more tickled and begins giggling hysterically when other renters pop out of neighboring apartments and shout angrily at her and Joe because Joe's actions have disturbed the roach equilibrium and obviously moved the roaches out of Kirsten's apartment and into the other residents' various territories instead. Between gasps of laughter, she explains to Joe that he has "undermined the whole basic metabolism of the building" and that he had better move out of town because "word will spread" among the roaches, and these creatures will subsequently drag him down.

The scene comes to have metaphoric significance in light of what will eventually happen to Kirsten and Joe. Kirsten's hysterical laughter at Joe's slightly demented behavior as he tries to eliminate the pests will be echoed later in her laughter as they play in the hay at her father's nursery. This event occurs some time after their marriage and at a point in their lives where both are trying, with the help of Kirsten's father, to stay sober. Yet that same evening, Joe smuggles some liquor into their bedroom and they giggle uncontrollably as they get blissfully, exceedingly drunk. Thus the demons return, even as the roaches had stayed in Kirsten's apartment building, in spite of all of Joe's hard work to eradicate them. The nagging neighbors' voices in the hallways, reminding Kirsten that the roaches are still present, in this later scene become the voices within Joe's and Kirsten's befogged brains, reminding them that the White Logic of alcohol is always with them. Despite their enforced — and by necessity temporary — sobriety as they work at her father's nursery, the temptation to rid themselves once again of the painful ugliness of the world is too powerful to resist. Yet the alcohol is no more effective than the roach killer had been; the fiends are still present and have indeed dragged both of them down.

But before they reach bottom, their downward spirals will take various twists; Joe and Kirsten do not descend at the same speed nor do they reach the same level simultaneously. In fact, for a time, it looks as though Kirsten is going to be the one to rehabilitate herself through the responsibilities of motherhood. She pulls herself together following the birth of their daughter and, for a short while, manages to stay home with their infant and to remain sober. Meanwhile, Joe continues to party with his clients and to nag Kirsten because she is no longer the fun person that she was when she drank with him. No drunk likes to be confronted by a sober spouse. The very sobriety of the partner is in itself an accusation and a reminder of how one person's alcohol addiction can throw a relationship off balance.

The tenuous nature of the Joe/Kirsten marriage shortly after their daughter's birth comes to a head late one night after Joe comes home following an evening of partying, listening to office politics, and drinking; pleasantly plastered, he finds his wife putting their infant back to bed. Joe is angry to see that Kirsten is disgustingly clear-headed and therefore dull. What especially annoys him is the fact that, upon his exit from the taxi bringing him home that evening, he had been drunkenly happy and pleased with himself after he had plucked some flowers from the flowerbed outside their apartment building. Although he had suffered a minor setback when he had hit his head while trying to enter the glass door without opening it, he had planned to deliver the flowers as a love offering to Kirsten, but the blooms had been decapitated by the closing of the elevator door, a fate that he had failed to notice until he gives the remnants to Kirsten. This brief episode with the destruction of the flowers, while somewhat amusing, is a foreshadowing of the later scene where Joe vandalizes every flowerpot in his father-in-law's greenhouse in a drunken rage as he searches for a hidden bottle. Although flowers are traditionally a symbol of love, freshness, and life, in this movie they represent the violent, dark side of a marriage in which two people love each other but tear each other apart little by little. Just like those pesky roaches, the flowers are a continual reminder of the sordidness that underlies their life together. So too, the reflection caused by glass and mirrors will recur as a prominent motif: the glass door that Joe rams his head upon will reappear later as Joe tries to break through a glass entrance and into a closed liquor store following a night of heavy drinking with Kirsten.

But at this point, Mr. and Mrs. Joe Clay have only begun their mutual destruction. Not only is Kirsten unimpressed with the pathetic stalks Joe hands her, but she is also upset by his boisterousness. Having just put the baby back to sleep, she tries to shush him. However, he will not be silenced. He is drunk, she is sober, and he wants her to join him in having fun. When she protests that she cannot drink because she is nursing, he yells at her, demanding that she get the baby a bottle and some formula because he "wants to have a ball." His volume increases as he protests that she is "stone cold sober." His noise finally awakens the baby; when she starts crying, Joe is filled with a blubbery remorse and atones for it by taking another drink.

Holding his head next to her breast, Kirsten capitulates and begins drinking again.

And together they stay drunk for a long time. When we next see Joe, he is hesitantly walking into the office — late as usual — because, as he tells his supervisor, he and Kirsten really tied one on the previous night when they celebrated their daughter's first birthday. (Any excuse will do when an alcoholic needs an occasion to drink.) Moreover, Lemmon's Joe Clay is going to need more excuses from this point on, because he is demoted that same morning and told that he must handle a third-rate drilling account, which means that he will have to travel to Houston. That night, Joe and Kirsten sit in their apartment, nestled at cross angles to each other, shadows falling across their faces, their bodies framed by bottles sitting on shelves surrounding them. They are, of course, drinking; they are also bemoaning Joe's awful fate, all the while making excuses for Joe's demotion. Having decided that jealousy was the boss's motivating drive, they comfort themselves with more booze until they drain the bottles they have nearby. Joe is sure that he has three bottles in reserve, yet when he goes to the cabinet where he keeps his stash, he mutters to himself, "There's only two bottles down there. I thought there was three." Then, opening the penultimate bottle, he muses again, "I could have sworn I had three bottles in there." Clearly, the missing bottle can be attributed to Kirsten's secret drinking while Joe is away at the office. Yet Joe, floating through the hazy mists blurring his vision, is unable to figure out the cause.

Ultimately, however, Joe has no choice but to face Kirsten's increasingly dangerous condition. While Joe is in Houston, trying extra hard to make a good impression on some good ol' boy, oil rig drilling Texans, Kirsten is tending to her domestic duties by spending her days drinking, smoking, watching cartoons on television, and hushing their baby whenever the child calls out for her mother's attention. Finally, during an awkward dinner at a Houston restaurant, Joe learns via phone that Kirsten, drunk as usual, has burned down their apartment. Not only does Joe lose his apartment and most of their belongings, but he also loses his job. They move from an upscale highrise to a seedy, walk-up apartment; no elevator here to trap a bouquet of flowers, even if Joe had had the wherewithal to provide Kirsten with such a romantic token.

Years pass; one day, Joe is walking past a bar, about to go in, when he sees his reflection in the glass. On this occasion, he is sober enough not to ram his head into it; nonetheless, when he looks at himself — disheveled, unshaven, haggard — he has an epiphany of sorts and turns from the bar. He passes up the chance to go in and emerge even more disheveled, unshaven, and haggard, for he has some news to share with Kirsten, a revelation that has come to him as he has glanced at the stranger reflected in the bar's window.

He rushes back to the squalid apartment to announce to Kirsten that they have no choice but to change their lives. He interrupts her drinking long enough to drag her to the mirror. He forces her to look at their images: ugly, worn-out, wasted. Then he lectures her about self-delusion. As Lee Remick's Kirsten looks at Joe in disbelief, Remick somewhat resembles a Tennessee Williams heroine — all passion and pretense and failed dreams. Yet Williams's heroines are deluded by their backgrounds; Amanda Wingfield and Blanche Dubois have created present fantasies out of their past experiences as Southern women who have been taught that preening and posturing represent the only methods of survival in a world gone dark and dreary. Kirsten too sees reality as dark and dreary, but before she met Joe, she had done her best to cope, to live her life cautiously. Once she learns to like what alcohol does for her, however, her fantasies become chemically induced and chemically dependent. In Tennessee Williams, both Amanda and Blanche drink to excess, but drinking is the consequence of their despair, not the cause of it. On the other hand, Kirsten had been a reasonably well-adjusted, content individual until Joe had turned her on to the pleasures of alcohol. So she makes excuses for both of them — rationalizing their failures— not because of the disappointments in her early life but because of the hole in the center of her present one.

Joe tries to drive a nail through this hole and pin her to the wall by propping her up before the mirror and forcing her to look at the distorted creatures staring back at them. "We're bums," he complains. "You know why I've been fired from five jobs in four years, and it's not politics like we always say. It's not office politics or jealousy or any of that stuff. It's *booze*. It's *booze*." Here Kirsten starts to protest, "A couple of drinks..." But Joe tries to intrude upon her self delusion: "We have more than a couple of drinks! We get drunk and we *stay* drunk most of the time." Throughout this part of the dialogue, Joe has moved away from the mirror and circles the room, with Kirsten as the center. The effect of the panning shot as it follows Joe is dizzying and effective, even as he continues to lecture Kirsten, to share his newfound insight: "I'm a drunk and I don't do my job and I get fired and that's it. We should have done this a long time ago and taken a good look at ourselves and realized that we've turned into a couple of *bums*."

And so, with the help of Kirsten's father (Charles Bickford, in a memorable depiction of a stern, loving, desperate father who knows that he has lost his daughter), they go on the wagon. Mr. Arnesen gives them a job tending the plants in his nursery; for a while, their rehabilitation seems to be working. But alcohol is never far from the consciousness of the alcoholic, and one rainy night, Joe sneaks two bottles up to their bedroom. His hiding place is symptomatic of the lengths and pains to which a drunk will go in order to get the liquor past the prying eyes of someone who might interfere: in this instance, his father-in-law. Joe has taped one bottle to each of his legs, just below the knee. His positioning of these goodies is just right; they are hidden by his trousers, but they are not so inaccessible that he has trouble with both the hiding and the removing. Drunks can be both clever and sneaky.

Yet Joe's cleverness on this occasion is his undoing. First, he engages in a bit of self-delusion: the kind of thinking that he earlier criticized Kirsten for engaging in. He adopts his most charming, persuasive manner — the kind that he had used for clients in happier days — and tells her that they have been so very good of late, that they have been almost *too* good. Then he reveals the bottles and their cunning hiding place and insists that they deserve a drink. He further reassures the all-too-willing Kirsten that they absolutely will not get drunk because they have certainly learned their lesson about liquor. Even as he says this, however, it is clear that he is lying to himself and to Kirsten. The fact that he is providing one pint bottle for each of them does not, in fact, suggest that Joe is preparing them for an evening of moderate alcohol consumption. Moreover, he has also thought of keeping on hand an emergency reserve bottle — one that, he assures her, he has ever so astutely hidden in the greenhouse.

The scenes that follow are among the most starkly terrifying ever filmed. It is raining hard, which adds to the horrifying effect of what we are about to see. We begin with a view from the outside, looking in on Joe and Kirsten. Using their bed like a trampoline, they are happily giggling as they bounce. The rain outside, which frames the window through which we see them, emphasizes the contrast between their giddy, childish behavior and the dismal reality that always lurks just beneath the surface. But their games are soon interrupted by Joe's awful realization that they are out of liquor. However, he knows that help is at hand in the form of the bottle that he has so carefully hidden in a pot in the greenhouse. He has even memorized the row number and the location of the pot within that row. Or so he thinks. He staggers out into the rain and frantically heads toward the greenhouse, oblivious to the fact that, by the time he reaches it, he is drenched.

Now he needs to find that life-saving bottle. Jack Lemmon's performance in this scene is haunting, as it gradually builds to a climax where he finally regresses to the stage of a crawling, blubbering infant. At first, Lemmon is confident — or as confident as a thoroughly soused individual can be. He counts the rows until he thinks he spies the pot that has his contraband. But he is wrong; he does not find the expected bottle. Undaunted, he tries again to count the rows and the pots. Once more, after pulling the flowers from the pot, he is disappointed. Now the hunt becomes serious, as Joe stumbles back and forth over the rows, willy-nilly yanking the carefully tended plants. By now, Joe is truly desperate and confounded. How could he have made such a mistake in calculation? He is so frantic that he no longer even tries to poke through the pots but instead just lifts them and smashes them on the ground.

Now unconcerned that he is repaying his father-in-law's generosity by viciously destroying three months of hard work, Joe lies on the greenhouse floor—crying, crawling, screaming, making incomprehensible baby sounds. He has been reduced to the most infantile behavior as, like a thwarted toddler, he gives way to a temper tantrum. Sprawled on his stomach, sobbing, with his head in his arms, Joe is seen in a disturbing close-up. Suddenly, he stops sobbing when he finally spies the long-sought-after bottle, resting next to him in one of the many demolished pots. Having destroyed the Eden he has worked so hard recently to build, Joe completes the job as he grabs the bottle and, without even trying to stand, turns over onto his back and, rain-soaked, sucks on it in great, gasping, grateful gulps. His regression to infancy marks not a return to Edenic innocence but a tragic commentary on the addict's total, helpless dependency. Jack Lemmon's performance in this scene is stunning; he shows us the harrowing picture of man without scruples, without shame, without hope.

Clay's hopelessness is intensified when he awakens in a hospital, straitjacketed, terrified, sweat oozing off, eyes runny. He looks like an institutionalized double of Edward G. Robinson's defeated flophouse gangster in *Little Caesar*. But Robinson's Enrico Bandello lived before the establishment of Alcoholics Anonymous, and so that avenue of hope was not open to him: not that the scofflaw Little Caesar would have taken advantage of such an organization. Lemmon's Joe Clay, however, like Burt Lancaster's Doc Delaney, is not by nature a lawbreaker, and both men are rescued by AA. In both *Come Back, Little Sheba*, and *Days of Wine and Roses*, Alcoholics Anonymous figures prominently in the rehabilitation of the two male protagonists. Both Doc Delaney and Joe Clay are shown attending an AA meeting. But both movies also suggest that Alcoholics Anonymous is not a miracle solution; even with the help of AA, Doc and Joe still learn that they cannot always remain sober. Nor does AA solve their marital problems. In the case of Joe Clay, Kirsten refuses to attend AA meetings with him, claiming that she can stop whenever she wants, that Joe does not belong at those meetings either because neither of them are alcoholics. And Kirsten remains in denial, adamantly refusing to ask for help when, as she insists, she can stop drinking at any time. Nervous, edgy, chain-smoking, she sits at a table in their cramped living area, repeating her belief in her own self-control: "I will just use my will power and not drink and that's the end of it."

But that is not the end of it: one day, Joe comes home to discover Kirsten gone — and she stays gone for days. His AA mentor Jim Hungerford (Jack Klugman) reminds Joe that Kirsten has probably left him in order to find someone who will drink with her, that his sobriety is a continual accusation to her. Now their roles are reversed: it is Kirsten who stays drunk while Joe tries to keep his life together. Listening to Hungerford's suggestion about Kirsten's desire for a new drinking playmate, Joe protests to Hungerford that, despite their arguments and differences, he and Kirsten have always loved one another. In response, Hungerford asks Joe what he did that rainy night after he finally found the bottle amidst the broken flowerpots. Joe answers with some exasperation at the apparently obvious question: "I *drank* it." Hungerford's next question brings Joe up short, however, when he asks if Joe had taken the bottle back to the house in order to share it with Kirsten. Joe is finally learning an awful fact about alcohol addiction: nothing matters anymore to the addict except the location of the next drink.

Joe finally finds Kirsten at a motel some miles away. The work of cinematographer Phil Lathrop, set designer George Hopkins, and art director Joseph Wright contributes to the unsettling, melancholy tone of the scene between Joe and Kirsten in the room where Kirsten has been drinking for many days. As Joe enters, he at first has trouble adjusting to the dim interior. Kirsten is seen in shadows, curled on the bed in a fetal position, watching cartoons. To Kirsten's dismay, Joe turns on the light, so he immediately switches off the light along with the television cartoon characters. Kirsten looks at Joe with a look of bewilderment, tells him that she wants a drink, gulps directly out of a bottle. Then, puzzled, as though she had not realized who her visitor was, as though she had been expecting someone else, she turns on Joe: "Oh, it's you. What do you want?" Irritated at his all-too-sober presence, she sarcastically refers to him as "Sober Joe." Now sitting upright on the bed, clad only in a slip, with shadows slightly obscuring her face, she restlessly, unsteadily, rocks back and forth, unable to stay still. Joe repeatedly offers to take her home, but she just as insistently refuses. Remick looks like a child as she rests on her haunches, head bowed, cradling her bottle, shadows falling across her body in the pattern of prison bars. And, like a child, she is querulous, pleading with him that she is lonely, that she wants him to drink with her. When he refuses, she orders him to go away. As he prepares to leave, he gives her a cigarette. Joe's gesture is photographed

Lee Remick and Jack Lemmon as Kirsten and Joe Clay in *Days of Wine and Roses* (Warner Bros., 1962) are a couple for whom alcohol becomes their only reason for being. In this scene, Joe goes looking for Kirsten, who has been drinking for several days. He finds her in a sleazy motel and, although he has been sober for some time and is trying to stay that way, he finally succumbs to Kirsten's entreaties and drinks with her (Photofest).

from above; the camera angle emphasizes Remick's disheveled hair and makes Kirsten's character look more paradoxically youthful and wasted than ever. Like a recalcitrant child who declares to a parent her decision to run away from home, Kirsten stubbornly reiterates that she is never coming back because Joe is "too good" and "there is no bore in the world like a goody good." Lee Remick's interpretation in this scene of the desperate Kirsten — the "good" girl who cannot seem to reclaim her life — is extremely powerful. She manages to reveal a number of conflicting emotions — appearing remorseful, culpable, but also pathetic as she begs Joe to stay and drink with her.

This time, the roles are reversed. Whereas in two earlier instances, Joe had been the instigator of their binges, in this instance, it is Kirsten who persuades Joe to resume drinking. Undeniably, the marriage of Joe and Kirsten has been built around liquor; when one of them is sober, the balance is so upset that they cannot communicate on the same level. But the level to which they descend when both are drunk persists in its instability. In a scene that parallels the one that culminates in Joe's destruction of the greenhouse, Joe, having finally succumbed to Kirsten's pleas for a drinking companion, stumbles from the motel in search of another bottle. In a scene echoing his earlier collision with the glass front of the building housing the posh apartment later burned down by Kirsten, Joe smashes his face against the glass entrance to a closed liquor store. Whimpering, whining, once more infantile, he forces open the door in order to grab a bottle, lurches outside, and again lands on his stomach. Only this time, Joe has some sadistic help; in a perverse parody of the greenhouse episode where he greedily sucks from his recovered bottle, Joe now looks up from the ground and sees the liquor store proprietor (Ken Lynch) — who, minutes earlier, had turned him away from his closed shop — gleefully teasing him by pouring the contents of a full liquor bottle over his head. A low-angle point of view shot is used here to reinforce Joe's utter helplessness as he watches the liquid splayed over his face. Then we are switched to a shot of Joe's expression; his face — twisted and distorted — is no longer the face of a human. All the while, the proprietor is laughing: a mocking, taunting laugh. As before, Joe awakens in the hospital, strapped to a bed, dressed only in his shorts. Once more he pulls himself together, this time determined to make amends to his father-in-law.

But what he learns from the embittered Mr. Arnesen is hardly comforting. Joe discovers that Kirsten, who is now living with her father, now disappears for days on end, always with a different "bum." Furthermore, Arnesen blames Joe for hooking his daughter on booze, reminding Joe that Kirsten had always been a "good" girl, obeying her parents, and never drinking until she had met Joe. Now, weeps Arnesen, he never knows where she is. Despite the accusations, Joe insists on giving Arnesen a check as the first installment for the damage he had caused when he vandalized the greenhouse. When Arnesen's says that he doesn't need Joe's money, Joe argues that "I need for me to do it." Then he leaves, abandoning Arnesen to his recurring nightmares about his lost child.

Days of Wine and Roses has an uncertain, downbeat ending. The final scene begins with a shot of Kirsten walking up a hill toward the apartment now shared by Joe and their daughter. She is framed on one side by a flashing bar sign. She has been sober for two days. She has pulled herself together, she tells Joe, so that she can at least "deserve" to talk to him, for she wants to come home. However, she also confesses to having other men, whom she refers to as "lots of detours," though she claims she "never looked at them." Looking shaky and sad, holding herself up as though she stood on fragile ground, she is nonetheless determined to finish her statement. And thus she explains to Joe that she thought these men would keep her from feeling lonely, but she wound up "just as lonely because love is the only thing that keeps you from being lonely, and I didn't have that." Yet even love cannot keep Kirsten from drinking. She tries to explain her predicament: "You see, the world looks so dirty to me when I'm not drinking." But Joe now knows that he cannot take her back on her conditions; he knows that she will drag him under with her: "If you'd just say that you'd *try*," he entreats her. Her response exposes her continued refusal to face reality: "If only we had it back like it was." To this, Joe recollects how it *really* was: "You and me and *booze*. A threesome? Remember?" Kirsten's expression reflects longing, horror, and astonishment as she listens to Joe turn her away, telling her that he has no room for her if she continues to drink. As she turns to leave, Joe asks her to look in on their daughter, who is sleeping in an adjacent room. But Kirsten knows that she doesn't have the strength to do that. Their final conversation is brief, stark, and telling:

KIRSTEN: You'd better give up on me.

JOE: Not yet.... Kirs—take care of yourself.

At this, she turns to look at him, her face framed in light with just a hint of a shadow falling on it. After she leaves, Joe goes to the window and watches as she walks down the hill and crosses the street — away from the flashing sign: BAR.

One is tempted to see Kirsten's final movement away from the bar as a positive sign: one that at least suggests the possibility of her regeneration. So too, one might view Joe Clay's subsequent dialogue with his daughter as offering some hope. After looking at Kirsten from the window, Joe goes into his daughter's room. When she asks if her mother will ever recover from her "sickness," Joe replies that Kirsten might very well get better. His last words are fraught with promise: "*I did, didn't I?*"

Yet the movie leaves the viewer with ambivalent feelings. Although Kirsten has briefly managed to get herself into a faintly presentable condition so that she might be worthy of visiting Joe, she is still in the self-annihilating quagmire typical of alcoholics. She is lonely and unhappy when she is drunk, and she is lonely and unhappy when she is not drunk. She stays wedded to alcohol's White Logic, and its hold on her seems absolute.

In his review of *Days of Wine and Roses*, Bosley Crowther briefly criticizes the way the script develops the two protagonists. Although he admires the performances of Remick and Lemmon, he sees them as cardboard characters out of some old melodrama:

As a straight, ruthless visualization of an alcoholic's fate, with the bouts of delirium tremens and "dry-out" and all the rest, it is a commanding picture, and it is extremely well played by Mr. Lemmon and Miss Remick, who spare themselves none of the shameful, painful scenes. But for all their brilliant performing and the taut direction of Blake Edwards, they do not bring two pitiful characters to complete and overpowering life. The couple in this picture, unlike the sot in "The Lost Weekend," seemed to be horrible examples that we face objectively. We shudderingly watch them suffer, we do not really suffer with them. They are impressive performers in a temperance play, and in the background one senses the tinkle of "Father, Dear Father, Come Home to Me Now."[8]

Crowther's assessment of the lack of emotional identification with the characters of Joe and Kirsten is puzzling. It is hard to be objective as we watch Lemmon tearing apart and smashing those flowerpots, then groveling on the ground, gulping from the bottle. Nor can we be objective as we look at Lee Remick's Kirsten in the final scene: her face scrubbed, her hair combed, her appearance neat, her demeanor trembling and uncertain; but for all that, with her pale complexion and her haggard appearance, she looks like an invalid just arisen from the sickbed. Here we recognize a woman who is tiptoeing on fragile glass, who knows that those things we value most are the most easily broken.

Here it is important to note that JP Miller's original television play as well as his later stage adaptation of that teleplay, which was produced live on *Playhouse 90* on September 13, 1958, takes a different approach to the character of Kirsten. Miller's original script for both television and stage introduces Kirsten as a hard drinker before she even meets Joe Clay. In fact, when Kirsten first appears in the stage adaptation, she is at a party for the Traynor Drilling Corporation, and she is drinking. Furthermore, it appears that she has been drinking most of the evening. Her first words are a reference to her empty glass: "All gone."[9] Joe is intrigued by her appearance, for she is conservatively dressed and does not look like the other women there; he approaches her and asks about her work:

JOE. (*Indicating party girls.*) You're not one of them.

KIRSTEN. Them? Who? Oh. Maybe I'd be better off. No. I'm one of these. (*Indicates typewriter, pantomimes typing.*)

JOE. Secretary? (*She nods, drinks.*) Where you storing that stuff?

KIRSTEN: Why?

JOE: You've made more trips to the well tonight than anybody, except maybe me.

KIRSTEN: Hollow leg. (*She has trouble with it, tries it again.*) Hollow leg. Ever try to say that?

JOE: Not lately. At least I put ice in my drinks.

KIRSTEN: Ice hurts my teeth. I don't remember you.[10]

In both the original television presentation and the subsequent stage adaptation, then, Joe does not tempt Kirsten into taking her first drink; she is already a seasoned drinker when Joe first encounters her at a company party. However, the screenplay for the 1962 movie, also credited to JP Miller, puts the responsibility for Kirsten's alcoholism solely on Joe. The author's alteration is a curious one; perhaps Miller's screenplay shows us that it is Joe who introduces Kirsten to the pleasures of alcohol because such a change to the original story makes Kirsten's downfall all the more tragic; she becomes the victim of her trust in and love for Joe. Therefore, the movie version creates an additional tension not present in the teleplay. This tension arises from the discrepancy between Kirsten's situation before she meets Joe—content with her job, capable, dependable, but not particularly happy, and addicted to chocolate—and her situation after she takes that first drink at Joe's urging. Kirsten ultimately metamorphoses into a desperately unhappy woman: intelligent enough to know what she has forsaken, but not strong enough to stop drinking and thereby regain her lost family. Of significance, too, is the fact that in all three versions—teleplay, stage, and movie—Mr. Arnesen blames Joe for Kirsten's dilemma. When Joe goes to the greenhouse to try to make amends for all the damage he has caused to Arnesen, the old man turns on Joe, accusing him: "You started my daughter drinking! When she lived here with me and her momma, she never took a drink! We never even gave her one beer! You started her!"[11] At this point in all three versions, Arnesen starts toward Joe, as though he might choke him.

Likewise, in all three adaptations, Joe Clay's final words to Kirsten are the same and contain a tone of finality to them: "Kirs—Take care of yourself." He speaks these lovingly but with determination as, in all three stories, Kirsten turns to leave Joe's apartment; she knows that she cannot stay with him because she knows that she cannot stay sober.

A comparison is possible between the 1958 *Playhouse 90* live television production of *Days and Wine and Roses* and the movie version completed four years later, thanks to the preservation of the teleplay on video. The original cast included Cliff Robertson as Joe and Piper Laurie as Kirsten. Charles Bickford played Mr. Arnesen, the only one of the players to repeat his role in the movie. Because of the limits imposed on live television by both time and space, the earlier production looks more stagy, the actors less free to move about. As Joe, Robertson is less frenetic, more controlled than Lemmon. Lemmon's Joe always appears to be on the edge of crashing emotionally, even when he is sober. Robertson, on the other hand, is tight-lipped, seemingly able to withstand both the terrors of excessive drinking and the equally horrifying effects of alcohol withdrawal. He lacks Lemmon's quirkiness, his earnest desire to be liked. For instance, even in the greenhouse scene, where Joe destroys almost every flowerpot in search of that elusive bottle, Robertson is more deliberate and systematic in his rampage. As an actor, Robertson never really allowed emotions to rule; unlike Lemmon, he was not prone to wear his heart on his sleeve. Lemmon usually appears as a likeable guy about to crack up; Robertson usually appears as the guy who might make him do it.

As Kirsten, Piper Laurie, with her hair carefully pulled back and her makeup neatly applied, is more glamorous than Lee Remick. She, too, like Robertson, is more controlled, less nervous than her movie counterpart. When she is drunk, Laurie is less overwrought. For instance, in the motel scene when Kirsten calls out for Joe to stay and drink with her, chastising and pleading with him simultaneously, Laurie seems less desperate, although still yearning for a drinking companion. In many respects, then, she is as convincing as Remick, especially in showing the desperation of a woman who knows that she is losing everything but also knows that there is nothing she can do about it.

A comparison between these two versions of the JP Miller play needs also to take into account the fact that, with live television, there is no chance for a retake: no opportunity to smooth over the ragged edges or to repeat a flubbed or a forgotten line. Therefore, it is remarkable that the 1958 *Days of Wine and Roses* contains no obvious mistakes: no missed cues, no awkward silences, no garbled speeches. The play flows effortlessly, with all of the actors giving flawless performances. It would be a mistake to try to judge which is the better version or which actors give the better interpretations. Whereas Lemmon and Remick are more energetic and high-strung and show more genuine feeling for one another, Robertson and Laurie are also compelling in a different way. Through their more understated performances, both reveal the quiet attempts at normality that underlie the daily existence of the alcoholic.

One film historian has made another comparison: this one between *Days of Wine and Roses* and *The Lost Weekend*. Noting that, with the superb *Days of Wine and Roses*, *The Lost Weekend* had "finally met its equal,"[12] Douglas Brode is of the opinion that Ray Milland's writer was not one with whom most viewers could really identify:

> Weekend remains a film about a particular, peculiar kind of man, and his unique problem; it can be interpreted not so much as a warning about alcoholism as about the dangers of writing as an occupation. In Wine and Roses, the focus is on two extremely normal people — an average couple, the alcoholics next door — and the force of the film was increased through audiences' awareness that this was indeed a typical, rather than extreme, experience.[13]

Can These Marriages Survive?

All of the preceding movies demonstrate the destructive mix of alcohol and marriage. All three illustrate the stranglehold that alcohol can have on a couple's relationship; what is more, all three have a nervous quality, for all reveal the disquieting atmosphere that often makes life with an alcoholic hell. In all three marriages, there is a sense that neither partner can ever relax. Throughout each of these pictures, conflict is continually present, even when both husband and wife are sober. Although two of the movies have upbeat endings, with both the Delaneys and the Elgins happily reconciling, the viewer still cannot be certain that these marriages will last. Doc Delaney might possibly run off with the next nubile boarder whom Lola blithely allows to invade their space. Frank Elgin, insecure and unable to believe that he can hold onto such a young, beautiful wife, will doubtless relinquish Georgie to the next aggressive male who pursues her. With Joe and Kirsten Clay, the chance that Kirsten will return — sober — and that she will be able to remain sober is exceedingly remote. As she admits to Joe in their final encounter, the world is too ugly for her when she is not drinking. Perhaps if Kirsten had had the opportunity to use an anti-depressant, she might have been able to make one drug substitute for another, thus enabling her to live with "sober Joe." But perhaps not. What is certain from each of these screenplays—as well as from the original plays from which each was adapted — is that there are no absolute answers to the impasse posed by the alcoholic marriage.

Annotated Filmography

DeWar's—It's Scotch. Edison Manufacturing Company, 1898. Four men dressed in kilts dance happily as they show what fun it is to drink Scotch whiskey. This was probably the first advertising film. Available on DVD with a brief introductory comment in a set called *The Movies Begin.*

Let Me Dream Again. Dir. George Albert Smith. With George Albert Smith and Mrs. Smith. George Albert Smith, 1900. A man and woman sit in a restaurant, flirting and drinking. But the luckless man is magically transported to another place and time, only to wake up in bed with his ugly wife. His awakening is meant to be seen as his worst nightmare. Available on DVD with a brief introductory comment in *The Movies Begin.*

A Chess Dispute. Dir. Robert W. Paul. Brit Acres/R. W. Paul, 1903. Two men seated at a chessboard get into an argument for some unknown reason. After one squirts the other with a cocktail mixer, they pummel each other. Available on DVD in *The Movies Begin.*

Buy Your Own Cherries. Dir. Robert W. Paul. Brit Acres/R. W. Paul, 1904. Two men stand at a bar. When one of the men tries to sample some cherries that are in a plate on the bar, the barmaid decides she doesn't like his looks and gets angry. After taking a drink, the irate customer leaves. He wanted some of those cherries. Available on DVD with a brief introductory comment in *The Movies Begin.*

Rescued by Rover. Dir. Cecil Hepworth. With Cecil Hepworth, Mrs. Hepworth, Baby Hepworth, and Lindsay Gray. Hepworth Production Company, 1905. This is an important, pioneering film that used some advanced cinematic techniques to tell a story. A drunken gypsy kidnaps an infant, but the clever Rover leads his master to the baby and recaptures the toddler. Available on DVD with a brief introductory comment in *The Movies Begin.*

Rêve à la lune. Dir. Gaston Velle and Ferdinand Zecca. With Ferdinand Zecca. Pathé, 1905. Director Zecca specialized in trick photography. In this film, Zecca focuses on a drunk who thinks he is sees champagne bottles that can dance.

The Dream of a Rarebit Fiend. Dir. Edwin S. Porter. With Jack Brawn. Edison Manufacturing Company, 1906. The hero of this clever movie drinks too much at a fancy restaurant and suffers one terrific hangover. Miniature demons hit his head with little pitchforks, and his bed levitates out the window and flies him across the landscape. Available on DVD with a brief introductory comment in *The Movies Begin*.

The Curtain Pole. Dir. D. W. Griffith. With Mack Sennett, Harry Solter, Florence Lawrence, and Linda Arvidson. American Mutoscope & Biograph, 1908. One of D. W. Griffith's few directorial ventures into farce, this movie traces the misadventures of a drunk who tries to carry a curtain pole through the streets and back to the home of a lady he is trying to impress. Sennett is excellent as the drunk. Available on DVD in *Before Hollywood, There was Fort Lee, N.J.*

Max, victime du quinquina. Dir. Max Linder. With Max Linder, Georges Coquet, Maurice Delamare, and Georges Gorby. Pathé, 1911. Max takes his doctor's advice and drinks medicine laced with alcohol. His subsequent, silly antics show that, while he is still ailing, he is nonetheless much happier.

Max et la statue. Dir. Max Linder. With Max Linder. Pathé, 1912. The drunken Max, dressed in a suit of armor, is mistaken for a statue and is put on display at a museum. The real statue has been stolen, but neither Max nor the museum patrons can tell the difference.

Tango Tangles. Dir. Mack Sennett. With Charles Chaplin, Roscoe "Fatty" Arbuckle, Chester Conklin, and Ford Sterling. Keystone, 1914. One of Chaplin's earliest films for Mack Sennett, this one has Chaplin and Arbuckle drinking in a restaurant. Then they fight in a cloakroom over a woman. The movie has a lot of action and almost no plot. The alliterative title is a good one. Available with commentary on DVD in *Chaplin: The Collection, Vol. 2*.

His Favorite Pastime. Dir. George Nichols. With Charles Chaplin, Roscoe "Fatty" Arbuckle, and Viola Barry. Keystone, 1914. This is another of Chaplin's relatively plotless movies for Mack Sennett. The title tells the story. Chaplin's favorite pastime is, of course, drinking. While drunk, he pursues a woman to her house and pesters her and her family.

The Rounders. Dir. Charles Chaplin. With Charles Chaplin, Phyllis Allen, Roscoe "Fatty" Arbuckle, and Minta Durfee. Keystone, 1914. Chaplin is still with Sennett, but this time he is allowed to direct. Chaplin and Arbuckle are drinking buddies who try unsuccessfully to outwit their formidable wives. Available on DVD in *Slapstick Encyclopedia*.

A Night Out. Dir. Charles Chaplin. With Charles Chaplin, Fred Goodwins, Ben Turpin, and Edna Purviance. Essanay, 1915. In order to have more control over his material, Chaplin left Sennett. In this picture, his second for his new studio Essanay, Chaplin and Turpin spend a boozy evening on the town, causing havoc to both people and objects. Available with commentary on DVD in *Chaplin: The Collection, Vol. 3*.

One A.M. Dir. Charles Chaplin. With Charles Chaplin and Albert Austin. Mutual, 1916. After the first minute or so, Chaplin is the only performer in this movie. The carefully constructed, well-balanced, symmetrical set design is the perfect antithesis to Chaplin's unbalanced, inebriated movement. Most of the plot involves Chaplin's drunken efforts to get upstairs to bed. Available with commentary on DVD in *The Chaplin Mutuals, Vol. 3*.

Easy Street. Dir. Charles Chaplin. With Charles Chaplin, Albert Austin, Henry

Bergman, and Eric Campbell. Mutual, 1917. This picture has a serious undertone. Set in the London slums, it portrays alcoholics and drug addicts living in deplorable conditions. Chaplin returned to his childhood roots in this one. Available with commentary on DVD in *The Chaplin Mutuals, Vol. 1.*

The Cure. Dir. Charles Chaplin. With Charles Chaplin, Henry Bergman, Eric Campbell, and Edna Purviance. Mutual, 1917. Chaplin goes to a posh spa in order to use the restorative waters to cure his alcoholism. The hefty Eric Campbell chases Edna Purviance around the spa, wealthy ladies mistakenly drink alcohol-laden water, and Chaplin vows to stay sober. Available with commentary on DVD in *The Chaplin Mutuals, Vol. 1.*

Broken Blossoms. Dir. D. W. Griffith. With Lillian Gish, Donald Crisp, and Richard Barthelmess. United Artists, 1919. There are no happy endings here. Lillian Gish is terrorized and beaten to death by her brutal, alcoholic father, played by Donald Crisp. Gish's vulnerability has never seemed more pitiable. Available on DVD with commentary and the complete text of Thomas Burke's original story.

The Mad Whirl. Dir. William A. Seiter. With May McAvoy, Jack Mulhall, Myrtle Stedman, and Barbara Bedford. Universal, 1925. Wild parties are the focus of a teenager's life in this cautionary film. The story tells the adventures of a hard-drinking young man, played by Jack Mulhall, whose middle-aged parents act foolishly as they try to show that they can be their son's best friend. This is a fairly typical Jazz Age movie, with an excellent cast.

Wings. Dir. William A. Wellman. With Clara Bow, Charles "Buddy" Rogers, Richard Arlen, and Gary Cooper. Paramount, 1927. One of the most memorable scenes in this visually stunning film focuses on aviators of the Great War. Here we see them drinking in a French tavern, trying to forget that they will soon be engaged in treacherous aerial combat. Available on DVD.

After Midnight. Dir. Monta Bell. With Norma Shearer, Lawrence Gray, Gwen Lee, and Eddie Sturgis. MGM, 1927. Norma Shearer and Gwen Lee are sisters living in New York and enjoying cabaret nightlife. Norma is a good-hearted cabaret hostess while Gwen is an evil golddigger. Joan Crawford and Anita Page would reprise these stereotypical roles two years later in *Our Modern Maidens.*

Our Dancing Daughters. Dir. Harry Beaumont. With Joan Crawford, Johnny Mack Brown, Dorothy Sebastian, and Anita Page. MGM, 1928. This was one of the most popular of the Jazz Age flapper movies. Joan Crawford is noble and patient; Anita Page is sly and cunning. Everyone drinks too much, but Page pays the ultimate price when, having spent the night drinking, she is killed in a fall down a flight of stairs.

The Crowd. Dir. King Vidor. With Eleanor Boardman, James Murray, Bert Roach, and Estelle Clark. MGM, 1928. An extraordinary movie, one of the most memorable of the 1920s, *The Crowd* tells the story of an ordinary couple caught in a dehumanizing, indifferent world. James Murray is superb as the Everyman who fails at everything, including his marriage. One evening he leaves his wife and her relatives and spends the evening partying and drinking with some flappers.

The Docks of New York. Dir. Josef von Sternberg. With George Bancroft, Betty Compson, Olga Baclanova, and Clyde Cook. Paramount, 1928. Some film historians have called this movie director Josef von Sternberg's masterpiece. Evocative cinematography contributes to the film's despairing tone. Much of the action takes place in a sleazy waterfront saloon, where George Bancroft rescues the desperate Betty Compson from her life of alcoholic despondency.

Big News. Dir. Gregory La Cava. With Robert Armstrong, Carole Lombard, Wade Botelier, and Charles Sellon. Pathé, 1929. Robert Armstrong is a reporter with a penchant for drink. He finally redeems himself by solving a murder and promising his wife that he will never again drink anything stronger than tea.

Our Modern Maidens. Dir. Jack Conway. With Joan Crawford, Rod La Rocque, Douglas Fairbanks Jr., and Anita Page. MGM, 1929. Another Jazz Age movie in which Anita Page and Douglas Fairbanks Jr. get drunk, then Anita gets pregnant, and Fairbanks marries Joan Crawford. But Fairbanks finally does the right thing by Anita, dumps Joan, marries his pregnant lover, and legitimizes their baby. Joan is not left with much of anything. Fairbanks does a pretty good imitation of a thick-headed, hypocritical prig.

Madame X. Dir. Lionel Barrymore. With Ruth Chatterton, Lewis Stone, Raymond Hackett, and Holmes Herbert. MGM, 1929. Chatterton is the adulterer who is cast out by her unforgiving husband and forbidden to have any contact with their young son. Alone and abandoned, she discovers the pleasures of absinthe and is eventually destroyed.

Men Without Women. Dir. John Ford. With Kenneth MacKenna, Frank Albertson, J. Farrell MacDonald, and Warren Hymer. Fox, 1930. Movies have traditionally shown military personnel drinking in a tavern, even as they anticipate the coming battles and hardships. In this film, superb cinematography highlights the young faces of sailors lined up in a Shanghai bar. They drink for hours in anticipation of their next assignment: an order to go down in a submarine beneath the China Sea.

All Quiet on the Western Front. Dir. Lewis Milestone. With Louis Wolheim, Lew Ayres, John Wray, and Ben Alexander. Universal, 1930. Once again, soldiers are shown drinking in a bar, this one in France: only this time, they have already seen combat and have watched many of their comrades die. There is poignancy in the naïve, winsome quality of Lew Ayres and John Wray as they raise their mugs in a wistful salute to a girl pictured on a poster. Available on DVD.

Doorway to Hell. Dir. Archie Mayo. With Lew Ayres, Dorothy Mathews, Robert Elliott, and James Cagney. Warner Bros., 1930. Lew Ayres is the mob boss in the booze racket and Cagney is his second in command. Clearly, the roles should have been reversed. Ayres is not convincing as the bootlegger. On the other hand, Cagney demonstrates the kinetic ferocity with which he would forever be associated.

Little Caesar. Dir. Mervyn LeRoy. With Edward G. Robinson, Douglas Fairbanks Jr., Glenda Farrell, and William Collier Jr. Warner Bros./First National, 1931. Edward G. Robinson *is* convincing as the mob boss in the booze racket. And, in the best gangster style, he dies well in the end. Available on DVD in a Warners Gangster Collection that also includes *The Public Enemy, White Heat, Angels with Dirty Faces, The Petrified Forest,* and *The Roaring Twenties,* with extra features and commentary.

The Public Enemy. Dir. William Wellman. With James Cagney, Jean Harlow, Edward Woods, and Joan Blondell. Warner Bros./Vitaphone, 1931. This is the one with James Cagney and Edward Woods as childhood chums who take advantage of Prohibition by bursting into speakeasies and using violence to coerce the owners into buying a disproportionate number of gallons of bad liquor. The movie also stars Jean Harlow, Joan Blondell, Mae Clarke, and a grapefruit. Available on DVD in a Warners Gangster Collection that also includes *Little Caesar, White Heat, Angels with Dirty Faces, The Petrified Forest,* and *The Roaring Twenties,* with extra features and commentary.

The Last Flight. Dir. William Dieterle. With Richard Barthelmess, Helen Chandler, David Manners, John Mack Brown. Warner Bros./First National, 1931. The setting is France just after World War I. Richard Barthelmess, David Manners, and John Mack Brown are aviators who try to forget their bitter memories of the Great War by drinking their way across Europe.

The Miracle Woman. Dir. Frank Capra. With Barbara Stanwyck, David Manners, Sam Hardy, and Beryl Mercer. Columbia, 1931. In this film, Sam Hardy plays a blackmailer and murderer par excellence. One scene that specifically illustrates his despicable character features a drunken mob that he invites to his apartment and that seems bent on destroying the place while having a raucously good time.

Platinum Blonde. Dir. Frank Capra. With Robert Williams, Loretta Young, Jean Harlow, and Louise Closser Hale. Columbia, 1931. The young, energetic, charismatic Robert Williams plays a reporter who is perpetually drunk: not so drunk, however, that he cannot see the charms of Jean Harlow, specifically the fact that she wears no undergarments. Nonetheless, by the movie's end, he sobers up enough to realize that their marriage was a mistake. Available on DVD.

The Front Page. Dir. Lewis Milestone. With Pat O'Brien, Adolphe Menjou, Mary Brian, and Edward Everett Horton. United Artists, 1931. Alcohol provides the backdrop to this story of reporters who will do anything for a scoop. No hint of reformed drinkers here. Available on DVD.

Scarface. Dir. Howard Hawks. With Paul Muni, Karen Morley, Ann Dvorak, and George Raft. United Artists, 1932. Paul Muni gives what is possibly his best performance as Tony "Scarface" Camonte, a crude gangland thug who tries to muscle in on the illegal liquor trade of a rival. Also on hand as the crime boss whose beer-running business Tony appropriates for himself is Osgood Perkins, father of Tony. When Perkins tries unsuccessfully to remove Tony from the scene permanently, Tony retaliates by eliminating Perkins instead. Available on DVD with commentary.

What Price Hollywood? Dir. George Cukor. With Constance Bennett, Lowell Sherman, Neil Hamilton, and Gregory Ratoff. RKO, 1932. Lowell Sherman's performance as an alcoholic producer is the major reason that this movie has endured so well over the years. Sherman is excellent as a world-weary cynic, bored with life and afraid of the future. In both looks and manner, Sherman resembles John Barrymore, who was at one time his brother-in-law.

The Big Broadcast. Dir. Frank Tuttle. With Stuart Erwin, Bing Crosby, George Burns, and Gracie Allen. Paramount, 1932. This picture is the original in the series, and possibly the best. Bing Crosby and Stuart Erwin become good pals when they meet in a speakeasy, and, accordingly, they get drunk together. Later at Crosby's penthouse, they make a drunken suicide pact and try unsuccessfully to kill themselves by turning on the gas. Friends off the screen as well, Crosby and Erwin were fun to watch as onscreen buddies.

Okay, America! Dir. Tay Garnett. With Lew Ayres, Maureen O'Sullivan, Louis

Calhern, and Edward Arnold. Universal, 1932. A down-and-out ex reporter gives newspaperman Lew Ayres made-up news stories in exchange for money to buy liquor. Ayres feels sympathy for the alcoholic, for he can see many of his own weaknesses in the fellow. This is a fast-paced, entertaining picture, largely overlooked today.

Horse Feathers. Dir. Norman Z. McLeod. With Groucho, Chico, Harpo, and Zeppo Marx. Paramount, 1932. This one has something to do with college politics and football. Groucho, Chico, and Harpo entertain themselves in a speakeasy. As they try to get into the Prohibition bar, Groucho and Chico do a funny send up of the necessity for passwords and secrecy. Available on DVD in a set that also includes *The Cocoanuts, Animal Crackers, Monkey Business, Duck Soup*, and commentary.

The Fatal Glass of Beer. Dir. Clyde Bruckman. With W. C. Fields, Rosemary Theby, George Chandler, and Richard Cramer. Paramount, 1933. In this absurdly delightful short film, W. C. Fields croons a sad tune to Officer Posthlewhistle of the Canadian Mounted Police. The song relates the tragic tale of an innocent country boy who goes to the big city and is ruined when he drinks that fatal glass of beer. The plot is wonderfully incoherent. Available on DVD in *W. C. Fields: 6 Short Films, The Criterion Collection.* The set also includes *The Dentist, The Barber Shop, The Golf Specialist, Pool Sharks,* and *The Pharmacist.*

International House. Dir. Edward Sutherland. With W. C. Fields, Stuart Erwin, Peggy Hopkins Joyce, George Burns, and Gracie Allen. Paramount, 1933. In this one, W. C. Fields loads his autogyro with cases of booze and flies off to Kansas City, Kansas— or perhaps Kansas City, Missouri. However, his boozy flight takes him somewhat off course, and he lands in Wu Hu, China. Fields has some funny exchanges with Franklin Pangborn. Available on DVD in a set that also includes *The Bank Dick, My Little Chickadee, You Can't Cheat an Honest Man, It's a Gift,* and a documentary on Fields.

Viva Villa! Dir. Jack Conway. With Wallace Beery, Stuart Erwin, Leo Carillo, and Fay Wray. MGM, 1934. Stuart Erwin plays a cynical, alcoholic reporter who writes about the exploits of Wallace Beery as Pancho Villa. Inexplicably, Erwin comes to admire the cutthroat Beery. Both actors try hard, but the script defeats them.

The Thin Man. Dir. W. S. Van Dyke II. With William Powell, Myrna Loy, Maureen O'Sullivan, and Nat Pendleton. MGM, 1934. William Powell and Myrna Loy are the sophisticated super sleuths Nick and Nora Charles. Although both stay pleasantly tipsy most of the time, Nick still manages to solve murders with grace and aplomb, while his wife aids him with tolerant, inebriated good humor. Available on DVD.

You're Telling Me! Dir. Earle Kenton. With W. C. Fields, Joan Marsh, Larry "Buster" Crabbe, and Kathleen Howard. Paramount, 1934. In this comedy, Fields spends much time drinking and trying to hide from his termagant wife. An outcast in society, he finally redeems himself by successfully patenting a puncture-proof tire.

It's a Gift. Dir. Norman McLeod. With W. C. Fields, Kathleen Howard, Jean Rouverol, and Julian Madison. Paramount, 1934. Fields is an unsuccessful store owner who inherits a California orange ranch that resembles something out of *Tobacco Road.* Kathleen Howard plays his commanding, disapproving wife who keeps a constant vigil against Fields's wayward ways. Available on DVD in a set that also includes *The Bank Dick, My Little Chickadee, You Can't Cheat an Honest Man, International House,* and a documentary on Fields.

Man on the Flying Trapeze. Dir. Clyde Bruckman. With W. C. Fields, Mary Brian, Kathleen Howard, and Grady Sutton. Paramount, 1935. Some film historians have called this Fields's best picture. Kathleen Howard is once again the ever-watchful wife. Fields manufactures applejack in his basement, fights with his in-laws, and unwittingly leads his employer to believe that his mother-in-law has died from drinking bad liquor.

After Office Hours. Dir. Robert Z. Leonard. With Clark Gable, Stuart Erwin, Constance Bennett, and Billie Burke. MGM, 1935. A wealthy alcoholic is accused of murdering his cheating wife. The accusation is largely the result of the man's inability to remember anything that happened on the night of her death. Gable is a reporter who finds the real killer.

Poppy. Dir. Edward Sutherland. With W. C. Fields, Rochelle Hudson, Richard Cromwell, and Catherine Doucet. Paramount, 1936. Fields is a carny con man who tries various nefarious ways to make a fortune. He also makes very robust home brew. Lynne Overman is especially funny as attorney E. G. Whiffen, who samples some of Fields's strong stuff.

A Star Is Born. Dir. William Wellman. With Fredric March, Janet Gaynor, Adolphe Menjou, and Andy Devine. United Artists, 1937. Janet Gaynor is the girl from the sticks who has stars in her eyes. Fredric March is the alcoholic actor who catches her eye. March is young, handsome, and convincing as Norman Maine; Gaynor is a bit too simpering and sweet. Available on DVD.

Madame X. Dir. Sam Wood. With Gladys George, Warren William, John Beal, and Reginald Owen. MGM, 1937. Gladys George is excellent as Madame X in the second talking version of this old soap opera. As the high class woman cast out by her hateful husband, George asks for neither pity nor understanding. Her later scenes as the alcoholic prostitute are quite touching.

Topper. Dir. Norman Z. McLeod. With Cary Grant, Constance Bennett, Roland Young, and Billie Burke. MGM, 1937. Cary Grant and Constance Bennett get drunk, crack up their car, reemerge as drunken ghosts, and proceed to torment the staid and inhibited Roland Young. As Topper, Young looks like an oversized rodent. Available on DVD in a set, *Topper/Topper Returns.*

Three Blind Mice. Dir. William A. Seiter. With Loretta Young, Joel McCrea, David Niven, and Binnie Barnes. 20th Century Fox, 1938. This one looks like an early version of *How to Marry a Millionaire,* with three women out to snare three rich husbands. Binnie Barnes is both humorous and touching as David Niven's alcoholic sister. In fact, Barnes takes the picture away from Loretta Young, who does little but who looks glamorous.

Holiday. Dir. George Cukor. With Katharine Hepburn, Cary Grant, Doris Nolan, and Lew Ayres. Columbia, 1938. Ayres is the alcoholic son in a family of pretentious social climbers. Although he ostensibly works for his father, a wealthy businessman, his father gives him nothing to do. We are led to believe that Ayres will never quit drinking, for booze is his only way of coping with a world that, for him, has no purpose. Currently available on DVD only in Region 2, which includes Europe and Japan. Not available in Region 1, North America.

The Roaring Twenties. Dir. Raoul Walsh. With James Cagney, Priscilla Lane,

Humphrey Bogart, and Gladys George. Warner Bros., 1939. Cagney is a bootlegger who goes broke when Prohibition ends. When booze becomes legal, Cagney himself becomes a heavy drinker. He is finally killed by Bogart's gunmen, and dies gracefully on the steps of a church. Available on DVD in a Warners Gangster Collection that also includes *Little Caesar, White Heat, Angels with Dirty Faces, The Petrified Forest,* and *The Public Enemy,* with extra features and commentary.

The Bank Dick. Dir. Edward Cline. With W. C. Fields, Cora Witherspoon, Una Merkel, and Franklin Pangborn. Universal, 1940. Fields has a family from hell from whom he escapes by making frequent trips to the Black Pussy Cat Café, which is less café than bar. His best scenes are with Franklin Pangborn as a fussy bank examiner who becomes the victim of Fieldsian chicanery. In an effort to keep Pangborn away from the bank's accounts, Fields slips Mickey Finns to the increasingly nauseated examiner. Available on DVD in a set that also includes *It's a Gift, My Little Chickadee, You Can't Cheat an Honest Man, International House,* and a documentary on Fields.

The Lost Weekend. Dir. Billy Wilder. With Ray Milland, Jane Wyman, Howard da Silva, and Doris Dowling. Paramount, 1945. This is the quintessential movie about the alcoholic personality, with Ray Milland in a superb, subtle performance as the sly alcoholic. The years have not dimmed its power one bit. Available on DVD.

My Darling Clementine. Dir. John Ford. With Henry Fonda, Linda Darnell, Victor Mature, and Walter Brennan. 20th Century Fox, 1946. John Ford retells the legend of Wyatt Earp and Doc Holliday, with Victor Mature excellent as the alcoholic, consumptive Holliday. Excellent black-and-white cinematography contributes to the brooding, romantic quality of the movie. Available on DVD.

The Razor's Edge. Dir. Edmund Goulding. With Tyrone Power, Gene Tierney, John Payne, and Anne Baxter. 20th Century Fox, 1946. This is the movie that reintroduced Tyrone Power to movie audiences following World War II. It has a long, complex screenplay, with a good deal of melodrama; it was not well received by the critics. However, Anne Baxter gives a memorable portrayal as a doomed alcoholic who tries to stay sober but who is taunted by the sadistic Gene Tierney. Baxter finally dies violently: drunk and alone. Available on DVD with extensive commentary.

Key Largo. Dir. John Huston. With Humphrey Bogart, Edward G. Robinson, Lauren Bacall, and Claire Trevor. Warner Bros., 1948. Claire Trevor is the alcoholic caught up with a gang of thugs who burst into a resort hotel in Florida and terrorize the people inside. The picture has good performances but a melodramatic plot. The movie also includes some spectacular shots of a hurricane. Available on DVD.

Come Fill the Cup. Dir. Gordon Douglas. With James Cagney, Phyllis Thaxter, Gig Young, and Raymond Massey. Warner Bros., 1951. Cagney is outstanding as a recovering alcoholic: a newspaperman who is given the thankless assignment of sobering up fellow alcoholic Gig Young. Both actors give fine performances, with Young holding his own in his scenes with Cagney.

Limelight. Dir. Charles Chaplin. With Charles Chaplin, Claire Bloom, Sydney Chaplin, and Nigel Bruce. United Artists, 1952. The last film that Chaplin made in the United States, *Limelight* recreates Chaplin's beginnings in the London music halls. As the aging clown Calvero, Chaplin gives a memorable — albeit occasionally overwrought — performance. He is at his best in the scenes where he is either drunk or remorseful about his drinking. Available on DVD in a 2 Disc Special Edition with commentary and special features.

Come Back, Little Sheba. Dir. Daniel Mann. With Shirley Booth, Burt Lancaster, Terry Moore, and Richard Jaeckel. Paramount, 1952. Shirley Booth is haunting as the downtrodden wife of alcoholic Burt Lancaster. The climax of the movie is a riveting scene between them in which the drunken Lancaster lashes out at her for everything that has gone wrong with their marriage and even threatens her life. Available on DVD.

The Country Girl. Dir. George Seaton. With Bing Crosby, Grace Kelly, William Holden, and Anthony Ross. Paramount, 1954. Bing Crosby is convincing as the musical star whose career is nearly destroyed by his alcoholism. He has good support from Grace Kelly as his patient but hard-nosed wife and William Holden as the cynical director who is willing to give him another chance. Available on DVD.

A Star Is Born. Dir. George Cukor. With Judy Garland, James Mason, Jack Carson, and Charles Bickford. Warner Bros., 1954. This time it is James Mason in the role of Norman Maine, the alcoholic actor whose career evaporates even as his wife's takes hold. Mason is forced to compete for attention with superstar Garland and does a credible job. Many of his best dramatic scenes were cut, however, in order to give more time to Garland's musical numbers. Mason was not at all pleased by the deletion of what he considered to be some of his best work. Available on DVD in a Limited Edition Deluxe Box Set that contains many photographs, lobby cards, scenes cut from the movie, and extensive commentary.

I'll Cry Tomorrow. Dir. Daniel Mann. With Susan Hayward, Richard Conte, Eddie Albert, and Jo Van Fleet. MGM, 1955. This is a powerful movie about singer Lillian Roth and her battle with alcoholism. Susan Hayward gives an outstanding performance as Roth. She is convincing as a successful singer on the vaudeville circuit and in Hollywood, and she is also believable as an alcoholic who sinks so far that she can no longer control her life. In addition, the movie makes much of the fact that, when picking husbands, she was a poor judge of character.

The Bottom of the Bottle. Dir. Henry Hathaway. With Van Johnson, Joseph Cotten, Ruth Roman, and Jack Carson. 20th Century Fox, 1956. Van Johnson is an alcoholic who is sent to prison for killing a man in a barroom fight. He escapes and goes to his brother's ranch in Arizona. Joseph Cotten is his brother, an attorney who finally agrees to help his fugitive brother.

Written on the Wind. Dir. Douglas Sirk. With Robert Stack, Dorothy Malone, Rock Hudson, and Lauren Bacall. Universal International, 1956. Robert Stack is a wealthy, dissolute, thoroughly unlikable drunk in this saga of rich Texans. Lauren Bacall looks glamorous as the wife of the psychotic Stack. Available on DVD.

Auntie Mame. Dir. Morton DaCosta. With Rosalind Russell, Forrest Tucker, Peggy Cass, and Coral Browne. Warner Bros., 1958. Rosalind Russell is in fine form in this adaptation of her Broadway success. Russell's forte was comedy, and in this one she plays the fun-loving Mame Dennis, who lives only for the moment and always seems to have a cocktail in her hand. Available on DVD.

Days of Wine and Roses. Dir. John Frankenheimer. With Cliff Robertson, Piper Laurie, and Charles Bickford. CBS: Playhouse 90, 1958. This live television performance of *Days of Wine and Roses* follows JP Miller's script for the play that he wrote for the stage. Cliff Robertson and Piper Laurie are less frantic, more controlled than their later movie counterparts.

Days of Wine and Roses. Dir. Blake Edwards. With Jack Lemmon, Lee Remick, Jack Klugman, and Charles Bickford. Warner Bros., 1962. This version alters Miller's original script for the stage, but it remains one of the most realistic depictions of alcohol's effects on a marriage. Lemmon and Remick and excellent, and they are ably supported by Jack Klugman and Charles Bickford. Available on DVD with commentary.

Notes

Introduction

1. Terry Ramsaye, *A Million and One Nights* (New York: Simon and Schuster, 1926), 231–32.
2. John Marshall Barker, *The Saloon Problem and Social Reform* (Boston: The Everett Press, 1905), 49–50.
3. Martin Hintz, *Farewell, John Barleycorn* (Minneapolis: Lerner Publications Company, 1996), 13.
4. Barker, 5–6.
5. Barker, 8.
6. Harry S. Warner, *Social Welfare and the Liquor Problem* (Chicago: The Intercollegiate Prohibition Association, 1913), 100.
7. David Shipman, *The Story of Cinema* (New York: St. Martin's Press, 1982), 23.
8. *John Barleycorn* (New York: The Modern Library, 2001), 194.
9. London, 178–79.

Chapter 1

1. David Ragan, *Who's Who in Hollywood*, Vol. 1 (New York: Facts on File, 1992), 181.
2. David Shipman, *The Story of Cinema* (New York: St. Martin's Press, 1982), 24.
3. Walter Kerr, *The Silent Clowns* (New York: Alfred A. Knopf, 1975), 59.
4. *D. W. Griffith: An American Life* (New York: Proscenium Publishers, Inc., 1984), 117–18.

5. Edward Wagenknecht, *The Movies in the Age of Innocence* (Norman: University of Oklahoma Press, 1971), 57.
6. Don Whittemore and Philip Alan Cecchettini, *Passport to Hollywood: Film Immigrants Anthology* (New York: McGraw-Hill Book Company, 1976), 9.
7. Wagenknecht, 57.
8. Linder was an unsuccessful replacement for Chaplin at Essanay; his pictures did not go over in America. The three movies he made for Essanay were box office failures. Frustrated and exceedingly discouraged, Linder subsequently returned to France. Essanay's efforts to find a Chaplin substitute had cost the studio $87,000. On October 31, 1925, Linder and his young wife of two years committed suicide in a Paris hotel. Max Linder was 42. Terry Ramsaye, *A Million and One Nights* (New York: Simon and Schuster, 1926), 738–39.
9. *The Silent Clowns*, 53.
10. Kerr, 51.
11. *The Comic Mind*, 2nd ed. (Chicago, The University of Chicago Press, 1979), 79.
12. Wagenknecht, 195.
13. *Silent Players* (Lexington: The University Press of Kentucky, 2002), 216.

Chapter 2

1. Roger Ebert, *The Great Movies* (New York: Broadway Books, 2002), 94.
2. *The Movies, Mr. Griffith, and Me*

(Englewood Cliffs, N.J.: Prentice Hall, 1969), 217–18.

3. Richard Schickel, *D. W. Griffith: An American Life* (New York: Proscenium Publishers, Inc., 1984), 389.

4. *D. W. Griffith: An American Life*, 393.

5. Gish, 218–19.

6. *The Parade's Gone By...* (New York: Bonanza Books, 1968), 90.

7. Brownlow, *The Parade's Gone By...*, 90.

8. *The Great Movies*, 96.

9. *The Movies in the Age of Innocence* (Norman: The University of Oklahoma Press, 1971), 123.

10. *Classics of the Silent Screen* (New York: The Citadel Press, 1959), 112–13.

11. Bosley Crowther, *The Great Films* (New York: G. P. Putnam's Sons, 1967), 67.

12. *From Quasimodo to Scarlett O'Hara: A National Board of Review Anthology, 1920–1940* (New York: Frederick Ungar Publishing Co., 1982), 102.

13. Jerry Vermilye, *The Films of the Twenties* (Secaucus, N.J.: The Citadel Press, 1985), 191.

14. Robert Grosvenor, "One's an Extra, Two's a 'Crowd,'" *Cinema Art*, Vol. 6, (September 1927), 22.

15. Hal Hall, "James Murray Wins His Fight to Come Back," *Movie Classics*, Vol. 3 (February 1933), 70.

16. Hall, 71.

17. Franklin, 113.

18. Grosvenor, 44.

19. Grosvenor, 44.

20. "The Shadow Stage: A Review of the New Pictures," *Photoplay*, Vol. 36 (July 1929), 54.

21. Vermilye, *The Films of the Twenties*, 245.

22. Vermilye, *The Films of the Twenties*, 245.

23. *Photoplay*, Vol. 36 (November 1929), 98.

24. *Photoplay*, 98.

25. *Screen Secrets*, Vol. 7 (September 1929), 19.

26. William M. Drew, *At the Center of the Frame: Leading Ladies of the Twenties and Thirties* (Lanham, Md.: Vestal Press, 1999), 149.

27. Drew, 149.

28. Katherine Albert, "Home Rules for Hollywood Flappers," *Photoplay*, Vol. 36 (June 1929), 136.

29. Albert, 136.

30. David Ragan, *Who's Who in Hollywood*, Vol. 2 (New York: Facts on File, 1992), 1285.

31. Marc Eliot, *Cary Grant* (New York: Harmony Books), 2004, 54, 57.

32. Eliot, 54.

33. "The Last Flight," *Photoplay*, Vol. 40 (October 1931), 104.

34. Jerry Vermilye, "The Last Flight," *The Films of the Thirties* (Secaucus, N.J.: The Citadel Press, 1982), 65.

35. "The Last Flight," *Photoplay*, Vol. 40 (October 1931), 104.

Chapter 3

1. Martin Hintz, *Farewell, John Barleycorn* (Minneapolis: Lerner Publications Company: 1996), 32.

2. Hintz, 32–33.

3. "You Ain't Heard Nothin' Yet" (New York: Oxford University Press, 1998), 396.

4. *The Drunken Journalist* (Lanham, Maryland: Scarecrow Press, 2000), 3.

5. Herbert Luft, in his career article about Lew Ayres for *Films in Review*, reports that Cagney made his film debut in *Doorway to Hell*. Actually, *Doorway to Hell* was Cagney's second movie. Cagney's first film was *Sinner's Holiday* (1930). "Lew Ayres," *Films in Review*, Vol. 29 (June-July 1978), 348.

6. To illustrate, watch him with Jean Harlow in the 1931 film *Iron Man* and with Teresa Wright in the much later 1950 film, *The Capture*.

7. George Gordon, "Lonely Lew," *Photoplay*, Vol. 37 (May 1930), 92.

8. One noteworthy exception was *Holiday* (1938), where he played the sensitive but alcoholic son in a family of dim-witted social climbers. Then, in that same year, he received good notices when he began playing the title character in the Dr. Kildare series for MGM, but his stint as the caring physician was halted when he declared himself a conscientious objector at the start of World War II. His decision was not a popular one with the American public. Although he served courageously as a medic in the Philippines, he nonetheless did effectively build a wall around himself, trying to stay aloof from the criticism that continued until after the war. By the late 1940s, he had distinguished himself in such movies as *The Dark Mirror* (1946) *The Unfaithful* (1947) and *Johnny Belinda*

(1948), for which he received a Best Actor Academy Award nomination. He also appeared in many television shows as late as the 1980s. In an interview that he gave shortly before his death, Ayres reminisced about his film roles from the early 1930s, briefly mentioning *Doorway to Hell*, which he recalled as being "pretty successful." Steven Randisi, "A Final Interview with Lew Ayres," *Films of the Golden Age*, (Fall 1997, No. 10), 23.

9. Henry Cohen, "Introduction," *The Public Enemy*, Wisconsin/Warner Bros. Screenplay Series, Tino Balio, General Editor (University of Wisconsin Press, 1981), 11.

10. *Cagney by Cagney* (Garden City, N.Y.: Doubleday and Company, Inc., 1976), 44.

11. Leonard J. Leff and Jerold L. Simmons, *The Dame in the Kimono* (New York: Grove Weidenfeld, 1990), 15–16.

12. Kenneth G. Lawrence, "Homage to James Cagney," *Films in Review*, Vol. 25 (May 1974), 293.

13. Sarris, 72.

14. Hintz, 32.

15. I saw *Public Enemy* at a screening at Southern Illinois University in May 1970, at the height of the Vietnam War and just before the Ohio National Guard shot and killed four antiwar student protestors at Kent State University. Following these shootings, antiwar protests on college campuses throughout the nation became even more numerous and violent. When Cagney delivered these lines, the student audience applauded and cheered.

16. Richard Griffith and Arthur Mayer, *The Movies* (New York: Simon and Schuster, 1957), 271.

17. In this final scene, the original screenplay contains instructions for dramatic action that was not included in the finished film. Specifically, it includes directions suggesting that Mike will take revenge for his brother's death. Whereas the final shot of Mike in the movie simply shows him with a look of horror, staggering away from Tom's fallen corpse, the shooting script reads as follows:

220. POWERS LIVING ROOM CLOSE SHOT on Mike standing by Tom's body. The horror on his face gradually giving way to a look of fury. He comes to a decision, turns, and strides toward the closet.

221. CLOSET CLOSE-UP OF AN OLD SUITCASE lying on the floor. Mike's hands come into the SHOT, open up the suitcase. It is filled with war relics: a German helmet, a doughboy's tin hat, a bayonet, etc., and a couple of hand grenades. Mike's hands seize the two hand grenades.

222. LIVING ROOM Mike comes out of the closet stuffing a hand grenade in each pocket, a look of fierce determination on his face. His brother's fate has turned him into a killer. He jams his hat on his head, PAN with him as he strides across the room. He stops for a moment for a last look at Tom's body, then strides out of the house. Cohen, ed. *The Public Enemy*, 176–77.

Surviving material related to the shooting of *The Public Enemy* does not reveal where such changes occurred — whether before filming began, during the filming process itself, or during the editing. Nonetheless, the filmmakers apparently decided that the movie should not end on such a downbeat note: one implying that violence would continue. There is no sense of finality to such a conclusion, no feeling of the ultimate triumph of justice. The last shot as it appears in the finished film is grim enough; the needle at the end of a phonograph arm tunelessly grinds over and over to signal the finish of a continually spinning record — one that has long ago stopped playing.

18. Bella Finkel Muni was the daughter of Emma Thomashevsky, a beautiful actress who had been known in the nineteenth century as the "Gibson Girl" of the Yiddish Theatre. Emma Thomashevsky married Morris Finkel, by whom she had three children: Lucy, Bella, and Abem. But Morris was much older than his beautiful wife and very jealous of other men's attentions to her. By 1904, when Emma was 29, she had fallen in love with a handsome actor her own age named David Levinson. One afternoon, 54-year-old Morris Finkel discovered David and Emma strolling in the woods outside a country farmhouse. With her three children watching, Emma looked on in horror as Morris fired a pistol, barely missing David. Then the desperate Morris fired again, this time hitting Emma at the base of the spine. When she fell, Morris evidently thought that he had killed her. Next, he turned the pistol on himself and died instantly. Emma's three children watched their mother shot and their father die. Lucy was seven, Bella, six, and Abem, four. Emma lived, but never walked again. Paul Muni was reportedly quite devoted to his wheelchair-bound mother-in-law. Jerome Lawrence, *Actor: The Life and Times of Paul Muni* (New York: Samuel French Inc., 1974), 43–44.

19. Todd McCarthy, *Howard Hawks* (New York: Grove Press, 1997), 134.

20. Jerome Lawrence, *Actor: The Life and*

Times of Paul Muni (New York: Samuel French Inc., 1974), 160.

21. *Romantic Comedy* (New York: Alfred Knopf, 1987), 445–47.

22. Neysa McMein, "What's Going on this Month: Motion Pictures," *McCall's*, Vol. 49 (September 1932), 18.

23. McMein, 18.

24. McMein, 18, 40.

25. *Photoplay*, Vol. 42 (June 1932), 14.

26. "'Scarface'—Paul Muni," 27.

27. David M. Kennedy, *Freedom from Fear: The American People in Depression and War, 1929–1945* (New York: Oxford University Press, 1999), 98.

28. *Cagney by Cagney* (New York: Doubleday & Company, Inc., 1976), 89–90.

29. Jerry Vermilye, *The Films of the Thirties* (Secaucus, N.J.: The Citadel Press, 1982), 245.

30. The husky timbre of Gladys George's voice figures in an anecdote related by Mae Clarke, Cagney's grapefruit victim from *The Public Enemy*. In 1974, Ms. Clarke attended the American Film Institute tribute to Cagney and told the following story to writer Kenneth Lawrence. Clarke was a friend of the late dancer Gilda Gray, who had known Gladys George. The night Ms. George died, she had phoned Gilda and had said the following words: "This is George. I need help." Gilda, thinking that her caller was male and that she was listening to a crank, promptly hung up and went back to sleep. When Ms. Clarke saw the AFI tribute clip from *The Roaring Twenties*, she was apparently reminded of this incident. Kenneth Lawrence, "Homage to James Cagney," *Films in Review*, Vol. 25 (May 1974), 287.

31. In Billy Wilder's Cold War satire *One, Two, Three* (1961), Cagney does a send-up of two early gangster films. The first is *Little Caesar*: at one point, facing a particularly difficult dilemma, Cagney mutters, "Is this the end of Rico?" The allusion might very well have been Cagney's idea. He greatly respected Edward G. Robinson and had appeared with him in one film, *Smart Money* (1931). The second reference is to his own *Public Enemy*. Trying to turn the Russian patriot Horst Buchholz into a fashionable capitalist, Cagney prepares a formal table setting so that Buchholz can practice his manners. On the table is a grapefruit that Cagney grabs and threatens to push into Buchholz's face.

Chapter 4

1. *The Stars* (New York: The Dial Press: 1962), 109.

2. *Man on the Flying Trapeze: The Life and Times of W. C. Fields* (New York: W. W. Norton & Company, Inc., 1997), 283.

3. Louvish, 237.

4. Cited by Donald Deschner, *The Films of W. C. Fields* (New York: The Citadel Press, 1966), 77.

5. Deschner, 77.

6. *Man on the Flying Trapeze: The Life and Times of W. C. Fields*, 304.

7. *"You Ain't Heard Nothin' Yet"* (New York: Oxford University Press, 1998), 437.

8. *The New Yorker* (July 11 and 18, 2005), 26.

9. *Eccentrics of Comedy* (Lanham, Maryland: Scarecrow Press, 1998), 99.

10. William J. Mann, *Wisecracker, The Life and Times of William Haines* (New York: Penguin Putnam Inc., 1998), 241.

11. James Robert Parish, *Hollywood Character Actors* (Carlstadt, N.J.: Rainbow Books, 1979), 474.

12. Mann, 255.

13. *As I Remember Them* (New York: Duell, Sloan, and Pearce, 1963), 32.

Chapter 5

1. David M. Kennedy, *Freedom from Fear: The American People in Depression and War, 1929–1945* (New York: Oxford University Press, 1999), 192.

2. Lawrence J. Quirk, *The Films of Myrna Loy* (Secaucus, N.J.: The Citadel Press, 1980), 170–71. Another source suggests that Van Dyke promised Louis B. Mayer that he would deliver the movie in twelve days but that the actual filming took eighteen. Jon Tuska, *The Detective in Hollywood* (Garden City, New York: Doubleday & Company Inc., 1978), 194.

3. "The Shadow Stage," *Photoplay*, Vol. 47 (April 1935), 117.

4. *"You Ain't Heard Nothin' Yet"* (New York: Oxford University Press, 1998), 99.

5. "Introduction," *The Films of Cary Grant* (Secaucus, N.J.: The Citadel Press, 1973), 3.

6. James Harvey, *Romantic Comedy* (New York: Alfred A. Knopf, 1987), 301.

7. Marc Eliot, *Cary Grant: A Biography* (New York: Harmony Books, 2004), 186.

Chapter 6

1. "Many Stars of the Metro-Goldwyn-Mayer Firmament in the Film Version of 'Dinner at Eight,'" *The New York Times* (August 24, 1933), 18, Col. 1.
2. John Kobler, *Damned in Paradise: The Life of John Barrymore* (New York: Atheneum, 1977), 3.
3. Barrymore's brother Lionel and sister Ethel were, of course, equally famous actors.
4. He did, however, once abstain briefly and inexplicably: from the time he appeared on Broadway in the short run of *Peter Ibbetson* (1917) and for two years thereafter while he toured with the play. But then he resumed his regular drinking habits until alcohol killed him in 1942. Gene Fowler, *Good Night, Sweet Prince* (Philadelphia: The Blakiston Company, 1943), 164.
5. Fowler, 345.
6. Fowler, 160.
7. August 24, 1933.
8. John Barrymore once said of his first marriage — to socialite Katherine Harris in 1910: "This event was the first of my three and one-half marriages — all of them bus accidents." Fowler, 141.
9. In fact, only several months after the release of *Dinner at Eight*, Louis Mayer, head of MGM, fired Tracy for a drunken indiscretion, one that occurred when Tracy was in Mexico filming *Viva Villa!* for the studio. Like Barrymore, Tracy had his own problems with the bottle. On this occasion, Tracy got drunk, leaned over the balcony of his hotel, and, with apparent precision, urinated on some Mexican soldiers who were participating in a patriotic parade just underneath the balcony. The Mexican government did not take kindly to what it considered an insult to Mexican national pride. Tracy was arrested, and Mayer was forced to use some delicate diplomacy to get him out of jail. At that point, Mayer removed Tracy from *Viva Villa!* and from the studio altogether. Mayer's revenge effectively stalled Tracy's career from that time on. Moreover, because *Viva Villa!* was already well over budget, an irate Mayer brought cast and crew back from Mexico in order to finish the movie in California. He replaced Tracy with Stuart Erwin, a much more reliable, stable actor. Todd McCarthy,

Howard Hawks (New York: Grove Press, 1997), 193–94.
10. Kobler, 275.
11. Kobler, 275.
12. Kobler, 274–75.
13. Fowler, 356.
14. Kobler, 321.
15. Fowler, 464.
16. Fowler, 466.
17. Kobler, 364.
18. Kobler, 364.
19. *The Lost Weekend, Screenplay by Charles Brackett, Billy Wilder* (Berkeley: The University of California Press, 2000), 27.
20. Jeffrey Meyers, "Introduction to the Complete Screenplay," *The Lost Weekend, Screenplay by Charles Brackett, Billy Wilder*, ix.
21. Maurice Zolotow, *Billy Wilder in Hollywood* (New York: G. P. Putnam's Sons, 1977), 130.
22. Meyers, x.
23. *John Barleycorn* (New York: The Modern Library, 2001), 176.
24. The original screenplay gives this amount as five dollars, but someone perhaps thought that such a small sum would have been insufficient to purchase the amount of liquor that Birnam manages to buy as a result of his theft of the money. On the other hand, in Jackson's original novel, the amount Birnam appropriates is twenty dollars, quite a considerable sum for the late 1930s, the setting of the novel.
25. Charles Brackett and Billy Wilder, *The Lost Weekend, Screenplay*, 63–64.
26. In the novel, we never know how much money the purse contains, for Don never has an opportunity to examine it before he is nabbed on his way out of the nightclub.
27. *The Lost Weekend, Screenplay*, 76.
28. Zolotow, 131.
29. As Ray Milland recalls in his autobiography, he prepared for this particular scene by spending a night in the psychiatric ward at New York's Bellevue Hospital. However, the horrifying conditions that he saw there among those desperate alcoholics prompted him to take the same action as his movie counterpart and sneak out of the hospital sometime after 3 a.m. Dressed in a hospital robe that had *Bellevue* stamped upon it, he was stopped by a policeman who found it hard to believe that Milland was in reality a movie star temporarily residing at the Waldorf Towers. The cop returned the actor to Bellevue, where one of the nurses corrobo-

rated Milland's story and Milland was allowed to go back to his hotel. Ray Milland, *Wide-Eyed in Babylon* (New York: William Morrow & Company Inc., 1974), 215–16.

30. *John Barleycorn* (New York: The Modern Library, 2001), 189.

31. Charles Jackson, *The Lost Weekend* (New York: Popular Library, 1944), 208.

32. Brackett and Wilder, *The Lost Weekend*, 109–10.

33. Charles J. Maland, *Chaplin and American Culture* (Princeton: Princeton University Press, 1989), 299.

34. Chaplin's mother Hannah had borne three sons, but only one of them, Chaplin himself, was legitimate. Chaplin's older brother Sydney and his younger brother, Wheeler Dryden, were the results of Hannah's liaisons with men to whom she was not married. There is much evidence that Hannah was a pitiable but kind woman, devoted to her children, but so mentally and physically ill that she could not cope with everyday living.

35. *Chaplin* (Boston: Twayne Publishers, 1984), 135.

36. Another link to the past in *Limelight* may be found in Chaplin's inclusion of so many of his family members in the film. In addition to his younger, illegitimate half-brother Wheeler Dryden, Chaplin gave parts to five of his children. His oldest sons—Charles Jr. and Sydney—appear. Sydney gives a warm supporting performance as an old love of Terry's. In addition, in the opening scene, Chaplin's three oldest children by Oona O'Neill—Geraldine, Josephine, and Michael—are playing in the street in front of Calvero's flat. The two girls speak to Calvero as he approaches. Finally, in a long shot, Chaplin's wife Oona briefly stands in for Claire Bloom.

Chapter 7

1. John Barrymore and Lowell Sherman were well acquainted and were, in fact, briefly brothers-in-law. Barrymore was married for a time to Dolores Costello and Sherman was married to Dolores's sister Helene. The two actors got along fairly well until they found themselves in-laws, at which time they discovered that they detested one another. Barrymore offered the following summation of Sherman's personality and of their deteri-

orating relationship: "His manners and his wit were in a class by themselves. We were the best of friends until he became an in-law, then something happened. God knows what." John Kobler, *Damned in Paradise: The Life of John Barrymore* (New York: Atheneum, 1977), 255.

2. *Silent Players* (Lexington: The University Press of Kentucky, 2002), 346.

3. Marc Eliot, *Cary Grant: A Biography* (New York: Harmony Books, 2004), 277.

4. James Shelley Hamilton, "A Star is Born," May 1937, *From Quasimodo to Scarlett O'Hara: A National Board of Review Anthology 1920–1940*, ed. Stanley Hochman (New York: Frederick Ungar Publishing Co., 1982), 244.

5. *Photoplay*, Vol. 53 (October 1939), 35.

6. Thomas G. Aylesworth, *Hollywood Kids* (New York: E. P. Dutton, 1987), 140.

7. Ray Behlmer and Tony Thomas, *Hollywood's Hollywood: The Movies About the Movies* (Secaucus, N.J.: The Citadel Press, 1975), 93.

8. *The Stars* (New York: The Dial Press, 1962), 138.

9. Eliot, 278.

10. *Can't Help Singin'* (Woodstock, New York: The Overlook Press, 1987), 275.

11. Quoted in Behlmer and Thomas, 94.

Chapter 8

1. *The Drunken Journalist* (Lanham, Maryland: Scarecrow Press, 2000), 50.

2. Good, *The Drunken Journalist*, 50.

3. Alex Barris, *Stop the Presses!* (New York: A. S. Barnes and Company, 1976), 14.

4. *Screenplay*, Vol. 14 (February 1933), 17.

5. James Cagney, "How I Got This Way," James Cagney as told to Pete Martin, *The Saturday Evening Post*, Vol. 228 (January 7, 1956), 60.

6. H. Allen Smith, "The Cantankerous Cagneys," *The Saturday Evening Post*, Vol. 216 (October 2, 1943), 10.

7. John McCabe, *Cagney* (New York: Carroll & Graf Publishers, Inc. 1999), 3.

8. Gladys Hall, "James Cagney's True Life Story," *Modern Screen* (October 1937), 52.

9. Hall, 52.

10. *Cagney by Cagney* (Garden City, New York: Doubleday and Company, Inc., 1976), 6.

11. "How I Got This Way," 60.

12. McCabe, 27.

13. Quoted in Hamilton Benz, "The 'Gentle Tough' of Martha's Vineyard," *Coronet*, Vol. 39 (November 1955), 137.

14. George Eels, *Final Gig* (New York: Harcourt, Brace, Jovanovich, 1991), 56.

15. Eels, 84.

16. *Come Fill the Cup* (New York: Random House, 1952), 17.

17. Ware, 14.

18. Quoted in Patrick McGilligan, *Cagney: The Actor as Auteur* (San Diego: A. S. Barnes and Company Inc., 2nd ed., 1982), 212.

19. *Curtains: Selections from the Drama Criticism and Related Writings* (New York: Atheneum, 1961), 359.

20. *James Cagney, A Celebration* (Boston: Little, Brown, and Company, 1985), 155.

Chapter 9

1. James T. Patterson, *Great Expectations: The United States, 1945–1974* (New York: Oxford University Press, 1996), 318.

2. Patterson, 348.

3. Quoted in Jerry Vermilye, *Burt Lancaster: A Pictorial History of His Films* (New York: Crescent Books, 1971), 67.

4. William Inge, *Come Back, Little Sheba* (New York: Samuel French Inc., 1949), 37.

5. The smashing of the bottle is not in the stage version, perhaps because of the danger to the actors with broken glass on the stage.

6. "Screen: Crosby Acts in 'Country Girl,'" *The New York Times* (December 16, 1954), 51, Col. 1.

7. Clifford Odets, *The Country Girl* (New York: Dramatists Play Service, Inc., 1949), 17.

8. "Screen: 'Days of Wine and Roses,'" *The New York Times* (January 18, 1963), 7, Col. 1.

9. JP Miller, *Days of Wine and Roses* (New York: Dramatists Play Service Inc., 1973), 9.

10. Miller, 9.

11. Miller, 43.

12. Douglas Brode, "Days of Wine and Roses," *The Films of the Sixties* (Secaucus, N.J.: The Citadel Press, 1980), 116.

13. Brode, 116.

Bibliography

Albert, Katherine. "Home Rules for Hollywood Flappers," *Photoplay*, Vol. 36 (June 1929), 32–33, 134–36.

Alpert, Hollis. *The Barrymores.* New York: The Dial Press, 1964.

Aylesworth, Thomas G. *Hollywood Kids.* New York: E. P. Dutton, 1987.

Barker, John Marshall. *The Saloon Problem and Social Reform.* Boston: The Everett Press, 1905.

Barris, Alex. *Stop the Presses!* New York: A. S. Barnes and Company, 1976.

Behlmer, Rudy, and Tony Thomas. *Hollywood's Hollywood: The Movies About the Movies.* Secaucus, N.J.: The Citadel Press, 1975.

Benz, Hamilton. "The 'Gentle Tough' of Martha's Vineyard," *Coronet*, Vol. 39 (November 1955), 134–38.

Brode, Douglas. *The Films of the Sixties.* Secaucus, N.J.: The Citadel Press, 1980.

Cagney, James. *Cagney by Cagney.* Garden City, N.Y.: Doubleday and Company, Inc., 1976.

_____. "How I Got This Way," James Cagney as told to Pete Martin, *The Saturday Evening Post*, Vol. 228 (January 7, 1956), 17–18, 59–62.

Cantor, Eddie. *As I Remember Them.* New York: Duell, Sloan, and Pearce, 1963.

Crowther, Bosley. *The Great Films.* New York: G. P. Putnam's Sons, 1967.

_____. "Screen: Crosby Acts in 'The Country Girl,'" *The New York Times* (December 16, 1954), 51, Col. 1.

_____. "Screen: 'Days of Wine and Roses,'" *The New York Times* (January 18, 1963), 7, Col. 1.

Deschner, Donald. *The Films of Cary Grant.* Secaucus, N.J.: The Citadel Press, 1973.

_____. *The Films of W. C. Fields.* New York: The Citadel Press, 1966.

Dickens, Homer. *The Complete Films of James Cagney.* New York: The Citadel Press, 1993.

_____. *The Films of Gary Cooper.* New York: The Citadel Press, 1970.

Drew, William M. *At the Center of the Frame: Leading Ladies of the Twenties and Thirties.* Lanham, Md.: Vestal Press, 1999.

Ebert. Roger. *The Great Movies.* New York: Broadway Books, 2002.

Eames, John Douglas. *The MGM Story.* New York: Crown Publishers Inc., 1975.

Eels, George. *Final Gig*. New York: Harcourt, Brace, Jovanovich, 1991.

Eliot, Marc. *Cary Grant*. New York: Harmony Books, 2004.

Fisher, Irving. *Prohibition at its Worst*. New York: Alcohol Information Center, 1927.

Fowler, Gene. *Good Night, Sweet Prince*. Philadelphia: The Blakiston Company, 1943.

Franklin, Joe. *Classics of the Silent Screen*. New York: The Citadel Press, 1959.

Gish, Lillian. *The Movies, Mr. Griffith, and Me*. Englewood Cliffs, N.J.: Prentice Hall, 1969.

Good, Howard. *The Drunken Journalist*. Lanham, Maryland: Scarecrow Press, 2000.

Gordon, George. "Lonely Lew," *Photoplay*, Vol. 37 (May 1930), 71, 92.

Griffith, Richard, and Arthur Mayer. *The Movies*. New York: Simon and Schuster, 1957.

Grosvenor, Robert. "One's an Extra, Two's a 'Crowd,'" *Cinema Art*, Vol. 6, (September 1927), 22, 44.

Hall, Gladys. "James Cagney's True Life Story," *Modern Screen* (October 1937), 51–66.

Hall, Hal. "James Murray Wins His Fight to Come Back," *Movie Classics*, Vol. 3 (February 1933), 44, 70–71.

Hall, Mordaunt. "Many Stars of the Metro-Goldwyn-Mayer Firmament in the Film Version of 'Dinner at Eight,'" *New York Times* (August 24, 1933), 18, Col. 1.

Harvey, James. *Romantic Comedy*. New York: Alfred Knopf, 1987.

Hintz, Martin. *Farewell, John Barleycorn*. Minneapolis: Lerner Publications Company, 1996.

Hirschhorn, Clive. *The Universal Story*. New York: Crown Publishers Inc., 1983.

_____. *The Warner Bros. Story*. New York: Crown Publishers Inc., 1979.

Hochman, Stanley, ed. *From Quasimodo to Scarlett O'Hara: A National Board of Review Anthology, 1920–1940*. New York: Frederick Ungar Publishing Co., 1982.

Inge, William. *Come Back, Little Sheba*. New York: Samuel French, Inc., 1949.

Jackson, Charles. *The Lost Weekend*. New York: Popular Library, 1944.

Kennedy, David M. *Freedom from Fear: The American People in Depression and War, 1929–1945*. New York: Oxford University Press, 1999.

Kerr, Walter. *The Silent Clowns*. New York: Alfred A. Knopf, 1975.

Kobler, John. *Damned in Paradise: The Life of John Barrymore*. New York: Atheneum, 1977.

"The Last Flight," *Photoplay*, Vol. 40 (October 1931), 104.

Lawrence, Jerome. *Actor: The Life and Times of Paul Muni*. New York: Samuel French, Inc., 1974.

Lawrence, Kenneth G. "Homage to James Cagney," *Films in Review*, Vol. 25 (May 1974), 286–93.

Leff, Leonard J., and Jerold L. Simmons. *The Dame in the Kimono*. New York: Grove Weidenfeld, 1990.

London, Jack. *John Barleycorn*. New York: The Modern Library, 2001.

Louvish, Simon. *Man on the Flying Trapeze: The Life and Times of W. C. Fields*. New York: W. W. Norton & Company, Inc., 1997.

Luft, Herbert. "Lew Ayres," *Films in Review*, Vol. 29 (June-July 1978), 345–55.

Maland, Charles J. *Chaplin and American Culture*. Princeton: Princeton University Press, 1989), 299.

Mann, William J. *Wisecracker, The Life and Times of William Haines*. New York: Penguin Putnam Inc., 1998.

Mast, Gerald. *Can't Help Singin'* Woodstock, New York: The Overlook Press, 1987.
_____. *The Comic Mind*, 2nd ed. Chicago: The University of Chicago Press, 1979.
McBride, Joseph. *Frank Capra: The Catastrophe of Success.* New York: Simon & Schuster, 1992.
McCabe, John. *Cagney.* New York: Carroll & Graf Publishers, Inc. 1999.
McCarthy,Todd. *Howard Hawks.* New York: Grove Press, 1997.
McDonald, Gerald D., Michael Conway, and Mark Ricci. *The Films of Charlie Chaplin.* New York: The Citadel Press, 1965.
McGilligan, Patrick. *Cagney: The Actor as Auteur.* San Diego: A. S. Barnes & Company, Inc., 1975.
McMein, Neysa. "What's Going on this Month: Motion Pictures," *McCall's*, Vol. 49 (September 1932), 18, 40.
Milland, Ray. *Wide-Eyed in Babylon.* New York: William Morrow & Company, Inc., 1974.
Miller, J.P. *Days of Wine and Roses.* New York: Dramatists Play Service, Inc., 1973.
Odets, Clifford. *The Country Girl.* New York: Dramatists Play Service, Inc., 1949.
Parish, James Robert. *Hollywood Character Actors.* Carlstadt, N.J.: Rainbow Books, 1979.
Patterson, James T. *Grand Expectations: The United States: 1945–1974.* New York: Oxford University Press, 1996.
Photoplay, Vol. 36 (November 1929), 98.
Photoplay, Vol. 42 (June 1932), 14.
Photoplay, Vol. 53 (October 1939), 35.
The Public Enemy. Wisconsin/Warner Bros. Screenplay Series, Tino Balio, General Editor. University of Wisconsin Press, 1981.
Quirk, Lawrence J. *The Films of Joan Crawford.* New York: The Citadel Press, 1968.
_____. *The Films of Myrna Loy.* Secaucus, N.J.: The Citadel Press, 1980.
Ragan, David. *Who's Who in Hollywood*, Two Vols. New York: Facts on File, 1992.
Ramsaye, Terry. *A Million and One Nights* New York: Simon and Schuster, 1926.
Randisi, Steven. "A Final Interview with Lew Ayres," *Films of the Golden Age* (Fall 1997), 18–27.
Robinson, David. *Chaplin: His Life and Art.* New York: McGraw Hill, 1985.
Room, Robin. "The Movies and the Wettening of America: the Media as Amplifiers of Cultural Change," *British Journal of Addiction*, Vol. 83 (1988), 11–18.
Sarris, Andrew. *"You Ain't Heard Nothin' Yet."* New York: Oxford University Press, 1998.
"'Scarface,'—Paul Muni," *Photoplay*, Vol. 42 (June 1932), 27.
Schickel, Richard. *D. W. Griffith: An American Life.* New York: Proscenium Publishers, Inc, 1984.
_____. *James Cagney, A Celebration.* Boston: Little, Brown, and Company, 1985.
_____. *The Stars.* New York: The Dial Press: 1962.
Screen Secrets, Vol. 7 (September 1929), 19.
Screenplay, Vol. 14 (February 1933), 17.
"The Shadow Stage: A Review of the New Pictures," *Photoplay*, Vol. 36 (July 1929), 54.
"The Shadow Stage: A Review of the New Pictures," *Photoplay*, Vol. 47 (April 1935), 117.
Shipman, David. *The Story of Cinema.* New York: St. Martin's Press, 1982.
Sklar, Robert. *City Boys: Cagney, Bogart, Garfield.* Princeton, New Jersey: Princeton University Press, 1992.

Slide, Anthony. *Eccentrics of Comedy* Lanham, Maryland: Scarecrow Press, 1998.
_____. *Silent Players*. Lexington: The University Press of Kentucky, 2002.
Smith, H. Allen. "The Cantankerous Cagneys," *The Saturday Evening Post*, Vol. 216 (October 2, 1943), 9–10; 99–101.
Smith, Julian. *Chaplin*. Boston: Twayne Publishers, 1984.
Sragow, Michael. "*International House*," *New Yorker*, July 11 and 18, 2005, 26.
Thomas, Tony. *The Films of the Forties*. Secaucus, N.J.: The Citadel Press, 1975.
_____, and Aubrey Solomon. *The Films of 20th Century Fox*. Secaucus, N.J.: The Citadel Press, 1979.
Tuska, Jon. *The Detective in Hollywood*. Garden City, New York: Doubleday & Company, Inc., 1978.
Tynan, Kenneth. *Curtains: Selections from the Drama Criticism and Related Writings*. New York: Atheneum, 1961.
Vermilye, Jerry. *Burt Lancaster: A Pictorial History of His Films*. New York: Crescent Books, 1971.
_____. *The Films of the Thirties*. Secaucus, N.J.: The Citadel Press, 1982.
_____. *The Films of the Twenties*. Secaucus, N.J.: The Citadel Press, 1985.
Wagenknecht, Edward. *The Movies in the Age of Innocence*. Norman: University of Oklahoma Press, 1971.
Ware, Harlan. *Come Fill the Cup*. New York: Random House, 1952.
Warner, Harry S. *Social Welfare and the Liquor Problem*. Chicago, Illinois: The Intercollegiate Prohibition Association, 1913.
Whittemore, Don, and Philip Alan Cecchettini. *Passport to Hollywood: Film Immigrants Anthology*. New York: McGraw-Hill Book Company, 1976.
Wilder, Billy. *The Lost Weekend, Screenplay by Charles Brackett, Billy Wilder*. Berkeley: The University of California Press, 2000.
Zolotow, Maurice. *Billy Wilder in Hollywood*. New York: G. P. Putnam's Sons, 1977.

Index

Page numbers in **bold italics** refer to photographs.